Sati, the Blessing and the Curse

"Procession of Hindoo Woman to the Funeral Pile of her Husband," by William Hodges. From his *Travels in India During the Years 1780–1783* (London: the author, 1793). Reproduction courtesy of the Department of Rare Books, William R. Perkins Library, Duke University.

Sati, the Blessing and the Curse

THE BURNING OF WIVES
IN INDIA

Edited by

John Stratton Hawley

New York   Oxford
OXFORD UNIVERSITY PRESS
1994

Oxford University Press

Oxford   New York   Toronto
Delhi   Bombay   Calcutta   Madras   Karachi
Kuala Lumpur   Singapore   Hong Kong   Tokyo
Nairobi   Dar es Salaam   Cape Town
Melbourne   Auckland

and associated companies in
Berlin   Ibadan

Copyright © 1994 by Oxford University Press, Inc.

Published by Oxford University Press, Inc.
200 Madison Avenue, New York, New York 10016

Library of Congress Cataloging-in-Publication Data
Sati, the blessing and the curse: the burning of wives in India/
edited by John Stratton Hawley.
p.   cm.   "A project of the Southern Asian Institute,
Columbia University" – P. ii.
Includes bibliographical references.
ISBN 0-19-507771-7.—ISBN 0-19-507774-1 (pbk.)
1. Sati. I. Hawley, John Stratton. II. Columbia University.
Southern Asian Institute.
GT3370.S27   1994
392—dc20   92-23468

−47485
16.00

1 3 5 7 9 8 6 4 2

Printed in the United States of America
on acid-free paper

*A project of
the Southern Asian Institute,
Columbia University*

ACKNOWLEDGMENTS

Bringing an edited volume into existence is rarely an easy task, but difficulties increase when some of the contributors live halfway around the world from the others and when the home team itself is rather given to travel. For their patience and fortitude in such circumstances, I wish especially to thank Ashis Nandy, Veena Oldenburg, and Vidya Dehejia. A debt is also owed to the staff of the American Institute of Indian Studies and to its executive director, Pradeep Mehendiratta, for facilitating quick communication on occasions when it might otherwise have seemed impossible.

Kristie Contardi, formerly the administrative coordinator in the Department of Religion at Barnard College, has been an invaluable help in preparing many sections of the manuscript for print. Of late, she has been cheerfully assisted by her successor at Barnard, Tara Susman, and by Elizabeth Maebius and Sang Lee, staff members of the Southern Asian Institute at Columbia University. The Institute sponsored the conference where this book began, in October 1988. I am grateful to Ainslie Embree, its director at that time, for his enthusiasm about both the conference and the volume, as shown by his willingness to pitch in as a contributor. Robert Cessna, the Institute's administrative assistant, helped greatly in ensuring the conference's success.

Other institutions have been involved in different, but equally critical ways. A sabbatical leave from teaching duties at Barnard College in 1990–1991 gave me time to devote concentrated attention to the project, and a secret office at Union Theological Seminary afforded the place. For my hideaway at Union, I am deeply grateful to Janet Walton, its kind proprietor, and to Holland Hendrix, now the seminary's president. I am also grateful to the National Endowment for the Humanities, whose generous grant in the category of individual fellowships for university teachers helped me make ends meet while I was on leave.

My wife Laura Shapiro, consummate editor, untied knots in the prose at numerous points and has been ready with steady measures of the caustic good faith that is her special patent. Cynthia Read and her staff, especially Peter Ohlin, and the copy editor Steven Gray have made publishing with Oxford University Press—once again—a true pleasure. Julia Leslie offered extremely helpful comments about certain sticking points in the manuscripts; and several of the contributors, especially Paul Courtright, Lindsey Harlan, and Veena Oldenburg, were kind enough to look over my shoulder now and again, as was James Lochtefeld, then my student but already quite an expert on various aspects of Hindu ritual law. Another student, Pamela Morris, devoted many hours to collecting newspaper accounts of events related to the sati of Roop Kanwar. In the same vein, Maxine Weisgrau drew together a general bibliography on sati that has contributed to the one that appears in this book. Finally let me express special thanks to Veena Oldenburg, who stepped in at the last moment, when one of the original essays was withdrawn, and substituted for it an essay (Chapter 4) whose scope and originality have made the book far stronger than it was before.

The list is long and varied, and shows clearly that this volume is a collaborative effort. My sincere thanks to all who have been involved.

New York   J. S. H.
May 1993

CONTENTS

LANGUAGE AND TRANSLITERATION

The issues that surround the transliteration into English of words that originally occur in Indic languages are vexing indeed. No one solution satisfies all needs. Since this book is intended for a wide readership, we have adopted something less than a purist's approach. In the main text, we have elected to transliterate in a manner that conveys the actual sound of Indic words rather than hewing to a system that would enabled readers in all cases to reconstruct the Indic word with flawless accuracy. Furthermore, we have chosen to keep the main text free of diacritical marks, reserving the information they convey for the notes and bibliography.

This means, for example, that the word meaning "great sacrifice" is rendered as *mahayagya* rather than the technically more correct *mahāyajña*. Similarly the two distinct sibilants approximating English *sh* are allowed a single transliteration: Shiva, *shabd*; equally, *vishvavidyalay*, *kshatriya*. A number of Indic words—especially the names of certain gods, groups, and places—are regarded as having attained sufficient currency in English that they do not require italicization, and these are capitalized where appropriate. Often they have a conventional anglicized spelling, which we retain. No such currency is assumed for other words, which are set off in italics. A difficult case for transliteration is presented by the unaspirated palatal stop, which is classically rendered as *c* despite the fact that it sounds more like English *ch*. For reasons stated above, we prefer *ch* (as in *ashaucha* or Bachao), and we transliterate the less common aspirated palatal stop with *chh* (as in *chhatri*).

We have tried to standardize alternate spellings wherever we could, as in the case of the semivowel v/w. The word *Mewar*, for example, always appears with its by now thoroughly conventional *w*, whereas the first word in the name of the Vishva Hindu Parishad is standardized so as to be spelled with a *v* near the end, although the organization itself accepts both that spelling and the one that employs a *w*. Again, the *chunari* rite, which is discussed in many essays here, is always so spelled, despite the fact that its neutral *a* and variant pronunciations have led to a variety of transliterations elsewhere (*chunri, chundri, chundari*). Where it seems helpful, we indicate such variants in parentheses, as in the case of Rajasthani *srap*, which is *shrap* in modern standard Hindi. Occasionally it has also seemed helpful to supplement a Hindi term with its Sanskrit analogue (*vrat, vrata*), especially when the Sanskrit version is preferred elsewhere in the book. Typically such differences merely mean that in Hindi or Rajasthani speech the final *a* is mute. We allow the difference in spelling to persist, even within a single essay, in response to context (*svargalok, svargaloka*). As for nasalization, we use an *n* in both the intermediate and final positions (*sansara, shikhayan*), even though this sometimes means departing from the *m* that is normative in transliterating Sanskrit (*saṁsāra*).

Most technical terms such as these appear in the glossary, where a standard system of transliteration using diacritics is indicated in parentheses, just before the English definition. Readers wishing definitively to reconstruct the spelling of Indic words are referred to those parenthetical entries and to the bibliography, which operates according to the same, more rigorous system of transliteration. In the notes, the more rigorous system, using diacritical marks, is adopted in the case of actual citations to works in Indic languages; otherwise the notes match the main text.

ABBREVIATIONS

Angl.   Anglicization

Bgl.   Bengali

BJP   Bharatiya Janata Party (Indian People's Party)

DMK   Dravida Munnetra Kazhagam (Pre-eminent Party of the Dravidians)

Govt.   Government

MSH   Modern Standard Hindi

Raj.   Rajasthani

RSS   Rashtriya Svayamsevak Sangh (National Volunteers' Society)

Skt.   Sanskrit

Sati, the Blessing
and the Curse

SATI-RELATED SITES IN
RAJASTHAN

Introduction

JOHN STRATTON HAWLEY

The idea of sati has long been a central feature in the Western image of India. *Suttee*, as Westerners have often spelled the word, describes the ritual according to which a Hindu wife follows her husband to his death by ascending his pyre with him or ascending one of her own shortly afterward. Yet words can be deceiving, particularly when they travel from one language to another. For many Hindus, sati is not a woman's deed but the woman herself. More of that in a moment — and throughout this book. For now, let us return to the Western idea of sati: sati the practice.

Modern research confirms what traditional brahmanical treatises imply — that sati has always been very much the exception rather than the rule in Hindu life. Yet from the time of Marco Polo until well into the nineteenth century (sati was officially abolished in Bengal in 1829), Westerners publishing diaries of their travels in India almost always included a chapter on a sati they had witnessed. These men watched their satis in horror but with admiration, too, for the courage and dignity of the women involved. If their books were even sparsely illustrated, a drawing of the sati was sure to appear (see Frontispiece). What were Western readers being asked to see in these verbal and visual portraits? An icon in reverse — something from which the eye should be averted — or in some clandestine way an icon in fact? A condemnation of sati the practice, or a secret adulation of sati the heroine victim?

Ananda Coomaraswamy, who from his position at Boston's Museum of Fine Arts was the foremost historian of Indian art in the early decades of the twentieth century, took European portraits of sati at face value: as "anti-icons." His life with Boston's Brahmins apparently caused him to hear a great deal of the rhetoric that accompanied these images, criticizing Hinduism for its oppression of women. In 1924 he responded by writing a now famous essay in which he defended the "Status of Indian Women" and appealed for an even-handed study of sati:

> [N]ow that nearly a century has passed [since the abolition of sati] it should not be difficult to review the history and significance of Sati more dispassionately than was possible in the hour of controversy and the atmosphere of religious prejudice.[1]

Many years later we find ourselves, in this volume, attempting just such a review, but the years intervening between Coomaraswamy time and our own have done little to simplify the task. Although the law of independent India reaffirmed the criminality of sati by incorporating the body of precedent that developed when sati was outlawed in earlier British legislation, and although independent India is ever more securely a part of a shared international order—economically, socially, even religiously—Coomaraswamy's "hour of controversy" is still upon us. Occasional instances of sati are reported in major Indian newspapers, and at least as significant as the events themselves is the relentless debate surrounding them. Major newspapers react to sati with such horror-stricken headlines as "Barbaric tradition comes alive" and "Festive 'chunri' veils monstrous deed,"[2] while voices raised in the defense of sati are just as strong as they were in the early nineteenth century. In 1830 a Dharma Sabha ("Religion Congress") was organized in Calcutta to defend the Hindu right to sati before the British Privy Council; in 1987 a Sati Dharma Raksha Samiti ("Committee for the Defense of the Religion of Sati") sent 70,000 pro-sati demonstrators into the streets of Jaipur shouting for the same cause. Sati is now a very infrequent occurrence, but the idea of sati seems as powerful now as ever it was.

New temples to the goddess Sati have been constructed in many of India's great cities. This same goddess, depicted as a multi-armed woman sitting on a bed of flames, comprises the logo for an importer of basmati rice with branches all over the United States. The chunari celebration following a sati that occurred in 1987 at Deorala, some 50 miles from Jaipur in the state of Rajasthan, drew 200,000 to 300,000 people. Meanwhile the Indian feminist movement, much more powerful now than it was in Coomaraswamy's time, has united around this issue and mounted a major protest. Whole issues of Indian journals, feminist and otherwise, have been devoted to exploring how the worship of sati can still flourish—and how to stop it. And the government has found it necessary, or at least convenient, to issue new legislation outlawing sati: in 1987 "the glorification of sati," not just its practice, became a legal offense.

Thus the controversy over sati continues, and it necessarily rages through many parts of the present volume. The spirit of calm for which Coomaraswamy hoped is still a long way from descending. We need in new ways to dispel the seemingly monolithic "atmosphere of religious prejudice" that Coomaraswamy felt he confronted, and one of the purposes of this book is to do so. Hence we include essays that try to understand and in some ways to defend proponents of sati.

We also hope to call attention to the element of ambivalence that has characterized many Western responses to sati, and thus to help make it plain that at no stage in history was the debate about sati simply a standoff between Europeans and Indians. There were (and doubtless still are) Westerners who idealized sati as much as Indians did, and there were and are Indians who reviled it. This message emerges strongly from the fact that ours is a binational book, Indian and American, and from the fact that every author has been shaped to some degree by both cultures. The controversy over sati may in some sense be a debate between cultures, but the cultures are not neatly divided along national lines.

Every author in this book attempts to make the controversy intelligible, but our collective purpose is not to settle or even mute disagreements. That is not possible in a situation where people cannot always agree on the most basic issues:

- What actually *is* sati? A person, an event, or both? Some writers deny that there is any such thing, properly speaking. Is there a single "traditional" conception of sati? If so, how long has it been in existence?
- What causes sati? In particular, what caused the celebrated sati of Roop Kanwar in the town of Deorala in 1987? Was this sati voluntary or coerced, and can one even ask such a question sensibly?
- Why did this sati receive such prominent attention? Why did it arouse such passions? Who has argued for what, and why?
- How, does the controversy over Roop Kanwar's and other satis relate to the much wider debate about sati that has been going on for centuries? What stakes have Westerners—and Indians—had in the debate? Clearly a back-and-forth process of interaction between Britishers and Bengalis produced the regulation outlawing sati in 1829. How does the dialogue between India and the West impinge on the debate today?

These are large questions, and no single, systematic answer can be offered in these pages. Instead we hope to present, collectively, a more accurate picture than has usually been given of what is in fact a genuinely complicated landscape. Readers are invited to come to their own conclusions on the basis of a series of essays and comments that approach the central questions from many angles. Some writers may seem less ideologically engaged than others, but the "ideologues" do not hesitate to point out that the "armchair" group are in certain senses no less involved than they are. For sati seems to demand moral response, as Allan Bloom has recognized in the opening pages of his much-read book *The Closing of the American Mind*. Sati is the stock example he employs in trying to confute what he sees as the complacent relativism of American undergraduates: "If you had been a British administrator in India, would you have let the natives under your governance burn the widow at the funeral of a man who had died?"[3] We may disagree with Bloom's implication that there is a proper answer to this question,[4] but it is hard to dispute that the idea of sati presents many people with an ethical imperative. Even those who argue that an outsider should suspend judgment often feel a necessity to frame their argument in moral terms. For better or worse, there is something galvanizing about sati.

In this book's title we hope to reflect something of that urgency. In her essay, Lindsey Harlan describes how a woman who has vowed to become sati is understood by those who surround her to be filled with the galvanizing presence of *sat*, a palpable force of virtue and truth. They come before her expecting that in the final hours of her life this *sat* will burst forth from her mouth in a series of blessings and curses—blessings upon the good and faithful, curses upon those who defy what is right or who stand athwart her path. In a larger sense, too, sati has been experienced as blessing and curse: to its partisans, a noble thing that has the power to ennoble others; to its enemies, an infamy that ought to have been erased long ago. And for some, as for the crowd who gather before the sati herself, it is both blessing and curse. In this volume we hope to uncover many of the nuances this ambivalence suggests. Yet there is no way to escape the conflicts that arise between those who are persuaded that sati has its blessed side, and those who find it an unutterable curse.

The Sati of Roop Kanwar

It is hard to appreciate both the tone and the substance of major sections of this book without knowing something about the sati of Roop Kanwar, which occurred in Deorala, Rajasthan, on September 4, 1987. This sati and the events that followed in its wake prompted a nationwide debate and were covered substantially in the international press. The verbal brouhaha has subsided somewhat, since no other well-publicized satis have occurred. (Some observers feel this reflects the force of new legislation put into effect at the time). Yet the issues raised for feminists by Roop Kanwar's death persist in the maltreatment of women elsewhere in Hindu life, particularly in the numerous "dowry deaths" of young urban women in recent years. Many observers think these deaths are murders committed by in-laws disappointed by the amount of money and goods brought into their families when their new daughters-in-law arrived.

Another aspect of the Roop Kanwar controversy persists as well: the intense debate over whether India ought to be shaped by a secular vision or a Hindu one. This debate, in fact, has greatly deepened since the time of Roop Kanwar's death. The groups that came together to defend her sati are at work in Hindu fundamentalist struggles that have riven the country in other places, particularly at Ayodhya, where the god Rama is believed to have been born.[5] Two governments have fallen in large part because they could not deal with these new challenges. Thus the broader legacy suggests the importance of understanding events surrounding the death of Roop Kanwar, as does the virulence of the immediate controversy it caused.

At the end of summer, 1987, Roop Kanwar, a pretty, well-educated Rajput girl of eighteen, had been married for eight months to a twenty-four-year-old Rajput man by the name of Mal Singh. On September 3, Mal Singh died suddenly from a malady that has been variously diagnosed as acute gastroenteritis, a burst appendix, and suicide by poisoning. The motive for the last might have been supplied—at least partially—by the fact that Mal Singh had recently failed his examinations for admission to medical school the second time.[6] Whatever the cause, its effect was that Roop mounted Mal Singh's funeral pyre with him the next day, and there her body was consumed in the flames along with his.

Despite the fact that this event was witnessed by thousands, people strongly disagree over what actually happened. According to early accounts, Roop Kanwar willed her own death and carried it out with dignity and resolve. In commenting on this fact, sympathetic observers often say that Roop had prepared herself for such an event before she had any inkling that it might become a part of her own life. She is said to have been a visitor to the great sati temple at Jhunjhunu and more than once to have been present at a sati temple in far-off Ranchi, Madhya Pradesh, where she spent a considerable portion of her childhood because her father, a businessman, was employed there.

On the day of her own sati, all this preparation came to fruition. In the traditional fashion, it is said, she took her husband's head in her hands as she seated herself on the pyre and submitted calmly to the flames. The force of her inner truth (*sat*) ignited the pyre, making it plain to profane eyes that she had been transformed from a human being into a goddess, a *satimata*. Icons issued to commemorate the event—primarily tableaus composed from photographs taken independently of Roop Kanwar and Mal Singh while both were alive and healthy—recall it in just this way. For those who buy them, the icons serve not only as mementos but as powerful amulets that carry forward the inner significance of the event, whereby the force of self-sacrifice becomes available to those who present themselves before it.

But this, of course, is a sympathetic view of what happened on September 4, 1987. Opponents of sati worship tell the story quite differently. According to them, villagers' reports indicate that Roop Kanwar was drugged into submission by her in-laws. Even so, she had the strength to try to escape from the pyre once—or as many as three times, some say—but she was pushed back on. (The alternate version of the story says she fell from the pyre and was assisted in the task of mounting it again.) Other reports say that in her last moments she called out to her father for help or uttered cries that could not be understood because they were drowned out by the exuberant roar of the crowd.[7]

As for the other participants in the event, Roop Kanwar's in-laws are said to have acted primarily on economic motives. How else to explain the fact that they arranged for her to be immolated on a plot near their own home rather than on the town cremation grounds, as custom dictated? This bit of evidence leads critics to believe that Mal Singh's family expected large numbers of worshipful spectators to make offerings on the occasion of the sati itself, and to continue their generosity once a shrine (*sati sthal*) was established on the site of Roop Kanwar's death and transfiguration.[8]

Moreover, critics say, there is no question of the pyre having burst into flame spontaneously. It had to be lit, and the person responsible for touching a torch to it was Pushpender Singh, the younger brother of Mal Singh, a lad of fifteen. This role would have fallen to Pushpender in the regular course of traditional Hindu mortuary practice, whether or not his brother's corpse had been joined on its pyre by Roop Kanwar. In any case, for the role he played in the death of Roop Kanwar, this youth was arrested by local police on the day after the event and charged with murder. When the local constabulary came under criticism for not having taken steps to prevent the sati (and thereby uphold the law of the land), further arrests were made: Mal Singh's father and three other male members of his family were imprisoned.[9] Some say the authorities jailed 100 people on suspicion of having conspired in the event, but a number—by now, in fact, all—have since been set free, and none has yet been prosecuted.

Given the values expressed in India's secular constitution, it is to be expected that much of the discussion about Roop Kanwar has focused on the issue of whether this was a voluntary sati, and on the question of what punishment should be meted out to those who share responsibility for its occurrence. But equally significant is the stir it caused. Why did this sati become such a celebrated case when earlier examples of sati, even those that occurred in villages not far away, attracted little notice? Why did such huge crowds gather to observe the event and to participate in the *chunari*[10] ceremony solemnizing it after the fact? And when feminists and others gathered in Jaipur to protest the continued presence of sati in the fabric of Rajasthani life, why did tens of thousands of people march in counter-demonstrations, urging that the government had no right to intrude into the realm of religion by attempting to suppress the practice of sati? Finally, who organized this multitude?

The group most immediately concerned was formed shortly after Roop Kanwar's sati. At first it called itself the Sati Dharma Raksha Samiti ("Committee for the Defense of the Religion of Sati"), but after the Rajasthan High Court seemed to forbid precisely this activity as "the glorification of sati," the group shortened its name and became the Dharma Raksha Samiti, the "Committee for the Defense of Religion."[11] The Dharma Raksha Samiti is based in Jaipur, not Deorala, and is run by educated Rajput men in their twenties and thirties. The convenor was a man named Narendra Singh Rajawat, the proprietor of a lucrative leather export business. When a group of women in Jaipur organized themselves to protest the lionizing of Roop Kanwar, they were able to mount a solemn, silent demonstration involving some 3,000 people, almost all women. But the Dharma Raksha Samiti vastly outdid them. It responded with a demonstration two days later (October 8, 1987) that brought 70,000 people into the streets—mainly Rajputs and often quite young, at least in the case of the men.[12]

Many other groups and figures were involved. The Vishva Hindu Parishad—the most prominent Hindu revivalist organization active in India today, and the main actor in the Ayodhya affair concerning Rama's birthplace—remained officially silent, taking neither side in the debate. Apparently it did not wish to identify itself with a cause that remains controversial even within the Hindu fold, and with a ritual that has never been practiced by the majority of Hindus. Other large Hindu organizations were not so hesitant. The Hindu Mahasabha ("The Great Hindu Assembly") —a venerable national religious organization— weighed in early on the side of pro-sati Rajputs; and the Dharma Vishvavidyalay ("University of Religion") —a significant regional organization headquartered in Churu, Rajasthan—also joined these forces. Its leader, Svami

Shivanand Maharaj, appeared on the dais in the first great Jaipur rally, praising the essential role of sati in true Hindu religion.[13] Finally, the Shankaracharya of Puri, a major Hindu religious leader, lent his support to the cause, although his even more significant counterpart, the Shankaracharya of Kanchipuram, stayed away.

Among political groups that rallied to the cause, the Rajasthan branches of the Janata Party and the Bharatiya Janata Party (BJP) were undoubtedly the most eager. Not surprisingly, their most important leaders are Rajputs. Although one might expect the BJP, of the two parties, to voice the rhetoric of Hindu conservatism, several Janata leaders wanted to portray their party as the ally of the local Hindu majority and to cast the then-ruling Congress Party in the role of an outsider. This was convenient insofar as the central government in Delhi did indeed play a role in attempting to suppress any celebration of Roop Kanwar's sati—if belatedly. (Rajiv Gandhi responded to pressure from anti-sati groups on September 22, more than two weeks after Roop Kanwar's death and long after it had become a major public controversy.) Despite Rajiv's hesitancy, certain prominent Janata members personalized their enemy by placing on him much of the responsibility for what they called "government repression." Bhakti Lal, a former Janata member of parliament from Rajasthan, called the Prime Minister "a Parsi married to a foreign woman, who is insulting the Hindu religion."[14]

The head of the Janata Party in Rajasthan, Kalyan Singh Kalvi, was no less shy about speaking the language of religion as well as of politics. Responding to an interviewer's suggestion that the practice of sati demeans women, he said, "In our culture, we worship the motherland, *dharma,* and *nari"* (motherland, religion, woman).[15] In this trio, an unspoken affinity exists between the two feminine entities, and religion is apparently the glue that keeps them together. By religion, Kalvi meant specifically Hindu religion—the majority religion—which he depicted as having been singled out for victimization by governmental policies. "Jains are known to die by fasting. Buddhists are known to immolate themselves. So why apply this law only to us?"[16]

This feeling that the supposedly secular government only discriminates against the religion of the majority is shared by many who identify themselves with the cause of Hindu revivalism. Even the Rajasthan Congress Party bent before it. The then-Chief Minister of Rajasthan entered into an accord with the Dharma Raksha Samiti that effectively permitted the celebration of the first anniversary of Roop Kanwar's sati by allowing a week-long recitation of the *Bhagavad Gita* to take place in Deorala at that time. Although a ban on written slogans praising sati was observed, sati was certainly glorified at the oral level, which is far more important. The air as filled with chants such as *satimata ki jay, rup kanvar ki jay,* and *deorala dham ki jay* ("Victory to Mother Sati," "Victory to Roop Kanwar," "Victory to holy Deorala.")

Finally, the partisans of Roop Kanwar's sati found a powerful ally in the Marwari community, which constitutes the nation's most important group of merchants and industrialists. During the past century, the Marwaris have fanned out from their caste home in the district surrounding Jhunjhunu and made their presence felt throughout the country. But the focus of their clan devotion, honored on an annual basis in a great gathering not far from Deorala, is the Rani Satimata (Narayani Devi) who rules in Jhunjhunu. Now she is a maternal form of god; but in the seventeenth century she was the bride in an unconsummated marriage—a virgin sati.

This groundswell of support for the manner in which Roop Kanwar died, at least as much as the fact that she did die, caused genuine alarm among those in modern Indian society who oppose the practice of sati. In New Delhi the feminist journal *Manushi* devoted the greater part of a double issue to the matter in late fall 1987, and the elite monthly *Seminar* followed soon after with a symposium on "widow immolation and its social context." The national and regional presses were full of discussions of sati for months, and the issue revived as the date approached for the one-year anniversary celebration of Roop Kanwar's sati at Deorala. Events more dramatic in terms of political cost and loss of life have largely replaced sati in the headlines from 1989 onward, but their relation to the same Hindu fundamentalist sentiment that helped make Roop Kanwar's sati such a volatile issue seems clear. Its opponents—secularists, feminists, Muslims—have often felt feel on the defensive in the changed climate of public life that now prevails in the India.

The Word Sati

The debate over the sati of Roop Kanwar has greatly influenced the discussion that is recorded in this book. Before we launch into that discussion, however, we had best stop to consider just what we mean by the word *sati*, since there is ample room for confusion. This stems from the fact that the term *sati* has a wide semantic range, with marked differences of emphasis depending on what language is being spoken. *Sati* can refer to the action or event whereby a woman is immolated on her husband's pyre, to the woman who is at the center of this spectacle, or to Sati as a goddess.

In English, the first meaning is dominant: sati as an action or ritual. English usage sometimes makes sati the object of the verb "to perform," but the more common habit is to associate it with the verb "to commit," which tends to characterize sati as something in the nature of a crime or a form of suicide. In English, one commits suicide; one commits a crime. But whether one performs sati or commits it, the noun itself describes not a person but a thing—often, implicitly, something that ought to be halted. Specifically, as *Hobson-Jobson*, the great Anglo-Indian dictionary says, sati is "the rite of widow-burning; *i.e.*, the burning of the living widow along with the corpse of her husband, as practised by people of certain castes among the Hindus, and eminently by the Rajputs."[17] The phrase "widow-burning" reinforces the suggestion that a force external to the woman herself is responsible when sati takes place, even though many of the passages quoted in *Hobson-Jobson* to establish the history and range of the term's usage stress the firm intentions of the woman concerned. When sati was outlawed, it was in just these terms. In 1829 the Governor-General of Bengal forbade "the practice of Suttee; or of burning or burying alive the widows of Hindoos . . . ."

One can find traces in European languages of the second major use of the word *sati*—to denote the person who burns rather than the circumstance in which she dies—but this meaning is distinctly secondary, although historically more venerable. In a letter written in 1792, for example, Sir Charles Malet spoke of "the poor suttee," meaning, clearly, the woman who perished.[18] But significantly such instances were usually derived directly from the diction of an Indian language, with little intermediary syntax in English. Malet himself tells us, on another occasion, that suttee was "the name given [by Hindus in Pune] to the person who so devotes herself," and when the orientalist Sir Williams Jones says that a woman "became a sati," he was actually quoting a biographical remark by an Indian acquaintance.[19]

In a language such as Hindi or Marathi this usage is very much the rule rather than the exception: sati is a person, not a practice. In the standard, multivolume dictionary *Hindi Shabd Sagar* all relevant usages are confined to this range, and the first meaning actually has nothing to do with the "widow" implied by English usage. For the *Hindi Shabd Sagar*, *sati* is initially any woman who confines to her husband all thoughts about men, save those that relate to her father. A sati is a good woman (*sadhvi*), a woman devoted to her husband (*pativrata*). Only in a subsidiary sense is the term *sati* used to designate a woman who "is burned on the pyre along with the body of her husband," and even then, conspicuously, no direct mention of widowhood is made.[20]

The contrast with English is telling, and *Hobson-Jobson* concedes that "[t]he application of this substantive to the suicidal act, instead of the person, is European."[21] In its origin, *sati* is a Sanskrit feminine participle derived from the verb "to be." As its various forms show, however, this verb connotes not only what is—the existential realities of life—but what ought to be: life's essentials, the things that make it good. Hence *sati* is a good woman; and because, according to classical Hindu formulations, a good woman is one devoted to her husband, *sati* comes to mean a truly faithful wife. As Paul Courtright and Lindsey Harlan explain in their essays, Hindus often hold that this quality of faithfulness on the part of a wife is largely responsible for her husband's health and welfare. By the same token, if he dies before her, as can often happen with older husbands, something appears to have gone awry. Hence there is something inherently suspect and inauspicious about widowhood—not just in Hindu reckoning, as Ainslie Embree points out in these pages, but in many societies.

From the point of view of its partisans, sati is a means of avoiding widowhood. Since the husband is not considered really to have died until he is cremated (or, occasionally, buried), his wife has the brief time separating his physical death and his ritual one to avoid this undesirable state by joining him on his pyre. To adherents of "the religion of sati," then, *sati* and *widow* are mutually exclusive categories; as one text says, a sati is a "nonwidow woman" (*avidhava nari*).[22] This is utterly different from the European conception, which assumes that the practice of *sati* can only be undertaken by widows.[23]

Educated, urban Hindi-speakers often take the word *sati*, meaning the woman, and set it apart clearly from "the practice of sati," which is identified by just that phrase (*sati pratha*). But it is worth noting that when this is done the practice is spoken of as if it were the derivative element, rather than the other way around. This accords with traditional usage. Every time a genuine sati is enacted, it signifies the flowering of a seed of virtue sown in the woman herself, from childhood on. The true devotion of a wife to her husband, her moral "truth" (*sat, satya*), becomes manifest at the moment she becomes sati, but her virtue has existed long before.

Because this is the moment at which such virtue becomes fully visible, however, there is a sense in which sati as person depends on sati as practice—the actual act of immolation.[24] Indic speech prefers the phrase "being" or "becoming" sati (*sati hona*) and finds it awkward to think of "performing" or "doing" sati, but the connection remains close—perhaps even essential. Hence one occasionally finds even Hindi-speakers referring to the rite, the act, as sati. Sanskrit never yielded to this ambiguity. While vernacular languages made it possible to designate the practice by using some permutation of *sat*, Sanskrit restricted itself to more precise terms such as *sahagamana* ("going together with [one's husband]") or *anumarana* ("following [one's husband] in death").

In addition to sati as person and sati as practice, the word has a third dimension—one that appears both in Indian and in European languages. It can be a proper noun, referring to the goddess Sati.[25] As is noted at several points in this book, particularly in comments by Vidya Dehejia and Veena Oldenburg, there is no tight fit between any prominent version of the myth of the goddess Sati and the practice of female self-immolation. Strictly speaking, Sati does not commit sati—at least not in any major version of her myth. True, she does sacrifice herself for the sake of her husband Shiva, whom she feels has received a grievous insult from her father Daksha, either in words or by being excluded from a sacrifice Daksha was sponsoring. Yet nowhere does Shiva predecease Sati. He is alive and well as he carries her corpse throughout India, even if he is driven almost insane by her death. Interestingly, the motif of self-immolation is entirely absent in several tellings of this story: Sati dies not by burning but by retreating into an irreversible yogic coma.

Despite these qualifications, however, Sati as the wife of Shiva (and an earlier incarnation of Parvati) often figures importantly in discussions of the practice of sati, both when it is defended and when it is opposed. For the Sati legend provides a general paradigm for a woman's boundless devotion to her husband.[26] Sati's defiance of her father is the ultimate test. But while this myth is the one best known throughout India, most people actually involved in the religion of sati today are apt to associate the practice of sati not primarily with Sati but with one of the goddesses known as "sati mother" (*satimata*), as is shown in the essays of Paul Courtright and Lindsey Harlan. The sati goddesses are venerated at numerous spots in Rajasthan and surrounding regions.

From the point of view of English usage, these *satimatas* are "real" satis, in that they are believed to be women who immolated themselves on their husbands' pyres at some point in the past. While many outsiders might conclude that their stories blur the line between myth and history, they are regarded by those who worship them as having lived in historical rather than mythic time, sometime during the last millennium. Nonetheless, they are often thought to be goddesses, too, or at least a somewhat superhuman form of ancestor, and to have extended their powerful maternal protection over people other than their husbands after they gave up their human lives. This power to protect is in fact largely responsible for the recall of their human acts by later generations.

When the word *sati* is used in Rajasthan, the reference is likely to be to one goddess within the general class of "sati mothers," but often one not clearly separated from others in the group. As Lindsey Harlan points out, the word *sati* tends to be used in the singular, as if every human who attains the status of sati is really just an instance or manifestation of one essential being.

The word *sati* remains a matter of major debate among scholars contributing to the present volume. Some, like Ashis Nandy, wish to distinguish sati as person and goddess from sati as action. Thus Nandy is careful to draw a line between an individual incidence of sati (*ghatana*) and the general practice (*pratha*). Others, such as Veena Oldenburg, implicitly question whether one can rightly think of sati in personal, divine, or ideal terms without assuming the notion of sati as action or event.

Such matters, because they concern the relation between religion and other aspects of human society, are bound to be controversial. Coomaraswamy's serene confidence that one could discuss a bygone practice as a dim but noble reflection of a living ideal was misplaced; instances of sati continue to occur. And since both the ideal and the practice are charged with meanings much broader than they themselves connote, one should not be surprised at the vigor of the debate. Undoubtedly, as Lindsey Harlan suggests, some of the acrimony in this debate is generated by the fact that pro-sati and anti-sati forces often talk past one another, each misunderstanding what the other means by the term *sati*. Yet is is hard to believe—and Harlan hardly implies—that imprecise terminology is at the root of the problem. If anything, it seems the other way around: part of the reason the term *sati* is so complex, both within and across linguistic boundaries, is that is touches on areas of experience that are perceived with great ambivalence and are strenuously debated.

Contents of the Volume

The essays presented in this book move from the general to the particular, and from the past toward the present. In the opening essay, Paul Courtright lays the groundwork for much of what follows. Choosing his material from the wide range of sources he has studied in the course of preparing a book on sati, Courtright focuses our attention on two archetypal "iconographies" of sati: that of "traditional" Hindus, and that of the mercantile and colonial British. He uses both narrative and visual material to sketch in the details of these two composite iconographies. Then he briefly points the way forward to what he considers a major departure from either: a contemporary iconography of sati shaped primarily by the concerns and perceptions of modern feminism. He concludes that, while each of these iconographies is distinct, they form an interlocking group. Collectively they are situated on a series of "fault lines" that often make discussions of sati erupt in anger or dissolve in ambivalence.

At the heart of Courtright's essay is his contrast between traditional and colonial understandings of sati. Using myths and icons associated with *satimatas* worshiped at various locales in Rajasthan and Gujarat, Courtright shows how a woman's self-sacrifice for the sake of her husband is believed to unleash powers of generativity that become available not just to her spouse, as he passes into a different form of life, but to any mortals left behind who come before her in worship. Just prior to the woman's death, when her divinity is revealed, and long afterward, the sati dispenses her blessings. Courtright argues that these blessings serve to protect culture (which is primarily defined along agnatic lines) from the vicissitudes of nature. A sati is in a position to offer such protection because she has sacrificed herself to her husband, thereby showing herself to embody the form of nature—the divine Mother—that nourishes human society. The poses most often chosen to depict satis clearly express this perspective. The sati is shown either in a seated position, supporting her husband's reclining body in her lap, or, as in older "sati stones," raising her hand from the pyre in a gesture signifying that there is no reason to fear. Courtright describes a ceremony performed before one such stone in which the *satimata*'s protection is solicited for a young boy whose "spiritual mother" she is believed to be.

In commenting on Courtright's essay, Vidya Dehejia clarifies the point that this iconographic complex, however central it may be to Hindu depictions of sati, has boundaries. Courtright refers, for example, to an icon in which Shiva and Parvati are shown as the divine background against which a particular instance of sati—that of Narayani Satimata—is to be understood. Dehejia turns the coin to its other side, noting the mythological discontinuities between the self-immolation performed on behalf of Shiva by Sati, as an earlier incarnation of Parvati, and the self-immolation that occurs when an "ordinary" sati such as Narayani Satimata's takes place. Dehejia then offers a brief historical sketch expanding on Courtright's introductory observation that, while representations of sati are to be found in many periods and places of Hindu history, they are by no means ubiquitous.

Courtright's second iconography, the colonial one, brings us into the realm discussed by Dorothy Figueira in her essay on eighteenth- and nineteenth-century European depictions of sati in music, drama, and literature. Courtright focuses on British citizens who traveled in India in the decades just before sati was banned. He shows how their images of sati increasingly drew attention to the culpability of Brahmin priests and sometimes made the point even more vivid by contrasting this cruel Brahmin resolve with the horrified, averted gaze of any British spectator who happened to be present. Yet the moral certainty that condemned the "mummeries" responsible for such atrocities was often accompanied by an open admiration of the silent heroism of the woman involved—the "glowing enthusiasm of her mind," as Richard Kennedy put it in describing a sati he witnessed in 1823. Kennedy's gaze was hardly averted; it was riveted.

Dorothy Figueira, by focusing on other literary genres than travel accounts and by surveying German, French, and Italian sources rather than British ones, shows how widespread and powerful this ambivalence was in the European understanding of sati. Works of the imagination tended utterly to dissociate the two aspects of sati — practice and practitioner — by pitting them against each another. The Brahmins held responsible for the practice were invariably condemned, and often served as an indirect avenue by which rationalist Enlightenment thinkers, especially in France, could criticize the failings of Christian clerics without naming them explicitly. For such thinkers, the practice of sati offered dramatic testimony not just to the dangers of Hinduism's illusory belief in metempsychosis (although German writers often saw its wisdom), but to the cruelty and irrationality of religion per se. To the exotic imagination, India was a place where religion held untrammeled sway. Consequently, its excesses could be seen there in pure form.

As for the victim of sati, the woman herself, she was lionized in a way that separated her entirely from the pinched, contorted morality that religion was understood to support. At the hands of continental poets and librettists, the sati typically — and amazingly — became a lover, not a wife; commonly she was depicted as a bayadere (the British "nautch-girl") or prostitute. Her death then demonstrated how the nobility of devoted love could triumph in the most savage circumstances.

The idea of *Liebestod* was clearly the lodestar that led Westerners to conceive of sati in this way, but an added element was provided by attributing to the woman involved a low social status. This made it possible to see her death as redeeming an unworthy life, and she became a new prototype of the noble savage — an "Indian Mary Magdelene," as Figueira at one point says. Peculiarly, as Figueira's phrase suggests, the "husband" for whom the sati died was sometimes actually deified in the Western imagination, as one can see in the title of Goethe's poem "Der Gott und die Bajadere." This apotheosis went considerably beyond the Hindu notion that a husband was to be regarded by his wife as if he were divine. It provided a way for Europeans to imagine how the man could bear the weight of his woman's extreme devotion. Another means of separating the man involved from the corrupt herd of the Brahminical "bourgeoisie" was to make him into a parish priest, as in Bernardin de Saint-Pierre's novel *La Chaumière Indienne*. Now both the husband and his common-law wife could act as spokespersons for the virtuous, common humanity that was believed by many Enlightenment and Romantic thinkers to lie beneath the twisted confines of culture.

Many variations were contrived on this central plot, as Figueira shows, but each reveals how difficult Europeans found it to accept that a woman might submit to death to keep her contract with a "Brahminical" marriage—that is, with something conventional and arranged, and not chosen by the heart. In this the British agreed, as Robin Lewis shows in a comment on Figueira's essay that is designed otherwise to contrast continental attitudes to sati with those held in the European country most directly involved in dealing with its actual practice. This fact made a crucial difference. It created a British sense of personal involvement with sati that was absent on the continent, with the result that in Britain opera and poetry, with their evident appeal to the imagination, were usually not the places where sati was discussed. Nonfictional genres such as memoirs, diaries, and letters were better suited to the task; and when sati entered fiction, as in the case of Mrs. General Mainwaring's huge novel *The Suttee*, it was with a practical purpose. Mainwaring wrote to influence public opinion about the debates then before the Privy Council, as to whether sati should be banned in British domains.

It would be a mistake, however, to believe that nonfiction lacks plot. Lewis finds that the guiding motif in British interpretations of sati was the projection of oneself—either a person or an entire culture—as hero. On a practical level there might be ambivalence: should British officials intervene? But at the moral and literary levels, such doubts disappeared. Lewis quotes two contrasting reports of attempted British intervention—one successful (so to speak), and the other not—to show that in either case the British "self" emerges as a heroic figure in the romantic mode. Whether or not policy questions were at issue, both Lewis and Figueira show that European emplotments of sati tended to have far more to do with Europe than with Asia. And Paul Courtright's review of British "iconographies" of sati leads to the same conclusion.

With Lindsey Harlan's essay, we turn from Western interpretations of sati toward those that operate within India itself. Harlan's discussion of the idea of sati held by contemporary Rajput women living in western Rajasthan introduces us to a particular tradition of exegesis on the "traditional Hindu iconography" of sati set forth by Paul Courtright. Harlan pays special attention to the importance of intention (as distinct from action) in these women's conception of what makes a true sati, and to the continuum of virtue (*sat*) for which the act of self-immolation serves as the seal. When the immolation occurs, the fiery *sat* itself is understood to consume both the woman and her husband; the profane blaze merely serves as a shield. This spontaneous combustion manifested by the woman's virtue demarcates the second and third stages of a true sati's existence, transforming her from a *sativrata,* one who has undertaken a vow to become sati, to a *satimata*, a "sati-mother." It also confirms that she fulfilled her calling in the first stage of her married life, when she was a *pativrata,* a wife devoted to her husband.

The women Harlan interviewed believed such self-sacrificing virtue to be almost entirely the preserve of Rajputs, with their heroic tradition. This view could be expected to confirm Roop Kanwar's sati, but in fact Rajput women are by no means unanimous in concluding that women today can be satis.[27] In the Roop Kanwar case other issues would play a mitigating role: rumors about Roop's marital infidelity and an awareness that, given the nature of modern Indian law on the subject, a woman who became sati might actually bring harm to her family. They looked with even greater caution upon most non-Rajput satis, being suspicious even of the idealization of sati by other caste groups. Such doubts would devalue the majority of satis for which we have historical evidence, as is hinted by references to Brahmin, merchant-caste, and lower-caste satis in the essays contributed by Courtright and Nandy. Of course, it also differs markedly from the standard European conception, in which Brahmins were the principal actors, at least at the ritual level.

In another respect, however, European feelings toward sati are supported to some extent by what these Rajput women said. Harlan examines the curses (*srap, shrap*) and proscriptions (*ok*) a sati is expected to pronounce just before her *sat* consumes her: the curses are directed primarily against men in her in-laws' family, while the proscriptions are expected to be observed by their women. Although Harlan's Rajputs depicted these as vehicles by means of which the sati could protect the agnatic family that would honor her after her death—she corrects their misbehavior for their own good—the element of ambivalence is hard to miss. One can scarcely hear these curses and proscriptions leveled against the sati's in-laws without detecting a strong element of anger and protest.

In her comment on Harlan's essay, Karen McCarthy Brown picks up this point and examines it as evidence of a fundamental ambivalence in the very image of sati. The woman on the pyre who curses, vents her anger, and commands obedience—all the while cradling her husband's head in her lap in what Brown sees as a "breastfeeding posture"—is an archetypal mother, as nurturant as she is potentially devastating. All over the world, Brown points out, a mother is bad by the same token that she is good: what she gives she sometimes takes away. And Indian patterns of childrearing keep children almost exclusively dependent on their mothers until nearly school age. In the ritual of sati, especially in the simultaneous adulation and punishment of womanhood that seems so prominent, Brown discerns an infant's-eye-view of Mother. And for once, she notes, the infant gets the last word.

In the essay that follows, Veena Talwar Oldenburg takes us directly into the debate that has raged around the death of Roop Kanwar. She does so by providing an analytic chronicle of responses to that death by Indian feminists—and to some extent, necessarily, by their opponents.

Oldenburg proposes that the celebrity of Roop Kanwar's sati is owing entirely to the vigor of women's reactions to it; otherwise, it would have gone virtually unnoticed among a series of other satis that until 1987 had occurred at periodic intervals in the Shekhavati region of Rajasthan.

Oldenburg brings a number of interesting patterns to light. She identifies the crucial role that was played early on by one woman living in Jaipur, Dr. Sharada Jain, and describes how feminist groups and publications in Bombay and Delhi later became involved. She emphasizes the overwhelming gender disparity between leaders who argued against sati and those who defended it — women opposed, men in favor — and she shows what pressure women had to exert before local and state officials took action to prevent any further sati celebrations on the site. Yet she suggests that the women stopped their drive against sati too soon. In her own after-the-fact sleuthing, Oldenburg returns to important bits of evidence that lead her to propose a new explanation of what may actually have happened to cause the death of Roop Kanwar. Because Oldenburg reconstructs the events of early September 1987 as a detective might, it would be unfair to reveal her conclusions here. Suffice it to say that, as far as Roop herself was concerned, the verdict is murder.

Oldenburg's analysis would seem to present grounds for concerned persons to reopen the case and pursue criminal charges, and she clearly hopes that this will happen. Indeed, at one point she wonders why feminists have been so slow to follow up on clues that would vastly strengthen the case for prosecuting Roop Kanwar's in-laws. Yet she certainly stops short of providing the sort of answer one might infer from the next chapter, written by Ashis Nandy. Here Nandy sets forth a revised version of an essay that provoked a storm of criticism from Indian feminists when he first published it in Delhi in January 1988. A major reason for the intensity of that response (and Oldenburg continues to register it in her subsequent comment here) was Nandy's suggestion that the horror expressed by India's literate, liberal, opinion-making classes at Roop Kanwar's death was largely symbolic in nature and ultimately self-serving. Nandy tries to show that this horror had primarily to do with internal preoccupations of the urban *haute bourgeoisie* and that those who professed it were unable to grasp the real dynamics of what happened in Deorala. One might extrapolate to the conclusion that they were ultimately also uninterested in doing so; hence, certain critical details in the case have remained uninvestigated to this day.

The crux of Nandy's argument is that a rapidly changing "politics of public consciousness" has put the upper *bourgeoisie* on the defensive. As nonmodern sectors of Indian society express their convictions with increasing success in a democratic electoral system, these erstwhile leaders feel instinctively that they must shore up their position of political and social hegemony by portraying themselves in moral terms. They wish to be perceived as the "bastion of rationality" under furious attack by the forces of irrationality, backwardness, and corruption. Nandy attempts to "reproblematize" four features of the modernist response to Roop Kanwar's sati, items he feels these modern critics would prefer to consider undiscussable: the conviction that Roop Kanwar's death was coerced; the idea that one ought to attack not only the practice of sati but its "glorification"; the assumption that sati degrades women; and the notion that social intervention, through legislation, can stop further satis from occurring.

Two common threads appear at various points in Nandy's analysis. The first is that, despite the modernist depiction of sati as atavistic, instances of sati that have occurred in the last two centuries can only be understood in relation to the "market morality" introduced into India in colonial times. Using a traditional Hindu periodization, Nandy refers to this colonial and postcolonial period as the *kaliyuga*—the final, degraded world-epoch in which values earlier held dear have fallen into disarray. Nandy considers that, by destabilizing traditional values, the British bear some responsibility for the many satis that occurred in Bengal at the beginning of the nineteenth century. He also indicts the principal legatees of the British Raj, the Westernized culture of which he himself is a prominent member. If colonial culture had much to do with introducing the economic and social mechanisms that encouraged profit-based satis, postcolonial culture is directly involved in making a spectacle of the death of Roop Kanwar. The urban middle class produces the newspapers and magazines that made her sati such a celebrated case.

In a second thread that runs through his essay, Nandy insists that, unless one appreciates the values that caused satis to be revered throughout the centuries—an appreciation of self-sacrifice and a celebration of the power of women—one's criticisms will not be heard by those sympathetic to sati. This perspective pits him against many of his fellow Indian intellectuals, who resent being called neocolonial and find no reason to countenance any adulation of sati. According to Nandy, such people find their secular rationality uncomfortably mirrored in the cost-calculating mentality of those who profited from Roop Kanwar's sati. The fact that hundreds of thousands of villagers would gather in Deorala to celebrate it, moreover, remains deeply perplexing to urban moderns; indeed, it arouses such profound anxiety that it must be simply and loudly rejected.

One of the major figures in the history of controversies about sati is Rammohun Roy, the Bengali intellectual whose attempts to reform Hinduism made him one of the most vivid and influential figures in Indian history. For Nandy, Rammohun's great virtue was that, while he opposed the practice of "widow-burning," as the British called it, he appreciated the convictions that undergirded it—the ideal of sati as wifely fidelity. For this reason he doubted that legislation directed against it would succeed; education and persuasion were required. Ainslie Embree, in responding to Nandy's argument, questions this interpretation of Rammohun Roy. He presents evidence that renders dubious both the view that Rammohun sensed the "epidemic" of satis in early nineteenth-century Bengal as "a product of colonialism" (to quote Nandy) and the idea that Roy might have had some sympathy for Hindu conservatives' defense of the practice.

Apart from questions of historical veracity, this disagreement is significant because of the strong parallels Nandy draws between the earlier Bengali situation and the one surrounding the sati of Roop Kanwar. In his view, the class most affected—and deracinated—by the British presence in the early 1800s, the upper middle-class *bhadralok*, comprised those who most frequently resorted to sati; and indeed, the colonial discourse criticizing sati became dominant. Today, in the late 1900s, the *haute bourgeoisie* speak the language of the colonial officials, and the newly deracinated part of society is a different stratum of the middle class—less metropolitan, more traditionalist. Embree suggests that at various points Nandy draws back from the rigor of his own comparison, allowing himself to depict the latter group not as victims and opponents of neocolonialism (though they often depict themselves in just this way) but as "real Indians" in some generic sense: traditionalists who are idealized for the contrast they present to the "brown Englishmen" of Nandy's own class. In so saying, Embree wholeheartedly embraces Nandy's notion that sati must be appreciated for its symbolic force and for the role that it plays in real—in this case, modern—time, but he places greater stress on Rammohun Roy's own sense (also articulated by Nandy in his essay on nineteenth-century Bengal) that sati stands as an unhappy symbol of the way in which a culture can fear its women.

The final contribution to this book comes from Veena Oldenburg, who provides a second comment on Nandy's celebrated views. Oldenburg's major concern is to insist on an aspect of Nandy's own argument that he himself, she believes, abandons: namely, that sati is a tradition continually being invented. Her criticisms are far-reaching. She attempts to show a number of ways in which Nandy falls into the trap of seeing the "self-sacrificing, self-immolating widow" as "a mythological [personage] with social and historical distortions" rather than as what she is—"a social and historical construct with mythological resonances." Oldenburg attacks the notion that India ever had a univocal, uncontested religious ideology of sati, arguing that Nandy's rigorous sociohistorical attention to the colonial and postcolonial periods allows him, as if by an argument from silence, to idealize the rest. She zeroes in on a speech of Parvati (closely affiliated with Sati) to Shiva that Coomaraswamy and Nandy assume to be serious evidence of a traditional conviction among Hindus that women feel a boundless duty to their husbands. Oldenburg reconstructs its tone as ironic rather than worshipful. The lesson is that myths of sati are not always to be taken at face value, even if they do actually seem to sanction the practice of widow-immolation. In any case the sanctioning is rare and, in the case of Sati/Parvati, problematical.

In a similar vein, Oldenburg questions whether sati was ever a formidable, brahmanically sanctioned Hindu institution. She suggests, instead, that it probably had its origins in *jauhar*, women's collective self-immolation in time of war.[28] This was a non-Brahmin practice reserved for royal women and had no religious rationale; its intent was to prevent rape and pillage at the hands of victorious enemies. Through arguments such as these, Oldenburg contributes to preserving the status of sati as, in her words, "the most controversial social issue in Indian historiography."

Of course, historiography is not all that is involved. The modern debate about sati goes well beyond issues of historical accuracy. It brings to the surface questions of ethics and identity that are as difficult to deal with today as they were in Coomaraswamy's time or a hundred years before —perhaps, indeed, more so. It highlights issues of good faith, not just good scholarship. Sudesh Vaid and Kumkum Sangari, feminist scholars writing elsewhere about the sati of Roop Kanwar, implicitly accuse many readers of this book—and some of its contributors—of purveying "the voyeuristic discourse that widow immolations have produced in colonial spectators and their contemporary progeny."[29] And the likes of Vaid and Sangari are in turn accused of having a hidden agenda, by Nandy.

In bringing to focus major features of the contemporary debate on sati, both in India and abroad, and in commenting not just on sati itself but on the controversy that swirls around it, we hope to generate new light—even if it means releasing a certain amount of additional heat, as Veena Oldenburg acknowledges in her essay here. The context is new: the postcolonial period, with all its vast changes in networks of action and interpretation. Yet the motif is old, for apparently sati continues, as a reality of both mind and body. The purpose of this volume is to clarify what that multiple reality has been through the centuries and to assess what it is becoming today.

Notes

1. Ananda K. Coomaraswamy, *The Dance of Shiva* (New York: Noonday Press, 1957), p. 110.

2. *Indian Express*, September 11, 1987, p. 5; *Hindustan Times*, September 17, 1987, p. 1.

3. Allan Bloom, *The Closing of the American Mind* (New York: Simon & Schuster, 1987), p. 26.

4. This point is argued with great force by Richard Shweder in *Thinking Through Cultures: Expeditions in Cultural Psychology* (Cambridge, Mass.: Harvard University Press, 1991), pp. 12–19.

5. Understandable objections have been raised to the use of the term *fundamentalist* in describing non-Christian groups who were not designated by its original usage. A cogent statement of this position as it relates to various Hindu movements and organizations can be found in Robert Frykenberg, "Fundamentalism and Revivalism in South Asia," in James Warner Bjorkman, ed., *Fundamentalism, Revivalists, and Violence in South Asia* (Riverdale, Md.: Riverdale, 1988), pp. 20–26; cf. also Mark Juergensmeyer, *The New Cold War?: Religious Nationalism Confronts the Secular State* (Berkeley: University of California Press, 1993), preface. I retain the word *fundamentalism* here for two reasons. First, over the course of the last five years it has become standard parlance in journalism having to do with conservative or neotraditionalist Hindu groups. Second, I believe the implicitly comparative use of the term *fundamentalism* is not wholly unjustified, at least when set against the standard of other terms that might be employed in its place. To me, *fundamentalism* describes twentieth-century groups that stand for a return to what are perceived as fundamental, old ways (not necessarily fundamental texts). These groups therefore find themselves in conflict with values that they see being expressed in secular modernity, and they share a psychology of beleaguerment that often revolves around a sense that they represent a mistreated and perhaps unrecognized majority.

6. Meena Menon, Geeta Seshu, and Sujata Anandan, *Trial by Fire: A Report on Roop Kanwar's Death* (Bombay: Bombay Union of Journalists, 1987), p. 6. The number of failures is reported as three, not two, in *Link* [New Delhi], September 29, 1987, p. 5.

7. *Hindustan Times*, September 17, 1987, back page. Sakuntala Narasimhan and other critics of the practice of sati believe that the din of the crowd at such a time – or at least the noise raised by the funerary party — is consciously intended to make the woman's own cries inaudible, primarily out of concern that they might carry curses (Narasimhan, *Sati: The Burning of Widows in India* [New York: Anchor Books, 1992], p. 92).

8. E.g., Modhumita Mojumdar, "A Visit to Deorala 'Peeth'," *Mainstream*, December 26, 1987, p. 22. According to Mojumdar, the money that had been gathered by Roop Kanwar's in-laws by December 12, 1987, was said to be in the neighborhood of Rs. 950,000. *Time* (September 28, 1987) reported the considerably larger figure of $160,000.

9. *New York Times*, September 20, 1987. On Pushpender, see *Hindustan Times*, September 17, 1987.

10. The *chunari* rite, practiced among Rajputs, occurs twelve days after a sati's death, and is an analogue to the *shraddh* ceremony performed at that interval after the death of a Rajput man. The feminist magazine *Manushi* criticizes its practice in the case of Roop Kanwar as being a *chunari mahotsav*, "a great *chunari* festival," not the solemn occasion that tradition would dictate. Madhu Kishwar and Ruth Vanita, "The Burning of Roop Kanwar," *Manushi* 42–43 (1987), p. 18. The word *chunari* (i.e., *cunarī*), which is sometimes also transliterated *chunri* or *chundri*, refers to a long piece of cloth that is placed on the ashes of the sati in the course of the *chunarī* celebration.

11. Problems having to do with the translation of *dharma* as "religion" inevitably hang over our discussion. "Duty," "tradition," and even "propriety" are conceivable alternatives in this context, but on the whole, because of the magnitude of the area being designated and the existence of a secular authority whom the Dharma Raksha Samiti saw as its implicit enemy, "religion" seems the most plausible translation. It is also the one conventionally chosen by users of the term *dharma*.

12. This may be judged both by the reporting and the picture printed in *India Today*, October 31, 1987, p. 38.

13. Some of his speechmaking has been preserved on videotape and made accessible by Ranjani Majumdar and her colleagues in "Burning Embers" (Mediastorm, 1987).

14. *India Today*, October 31, 1987, p. 19.

15. *India Today*, October 31, 1987, p. 20.

16. Ibid. On other aspects of Kalvi's views, see Narasimhan, *Sati*, p. 103.

17. Henry Cole and A. C. Burnell, *Hobson-Jobson* [rev. ed. by William Crooke] (New Delhi: Munshiram Manoharlal, 1979 [original ed., 1903], p. 878.

18. *Hobson-Jobson*, p. 882. The citation is to James Forbes, *Oriental Memoirs* (London: White, Cochrane & Co., 1813), vol. 2, p. 394.

19. *Hobson-Jobson*, p. 882. The citation for Malet is Forbes, *Oriental Memoirs*, 2d ed., vol. 1, p. 178; for Jones, it is John Shore Teignmouth, *Memoirs of the Life, Writings, and Correspondence of Sir William Jones*, 2d ed. (London: John Stockdale, 1807), vol. 2, p. 120.

20. Śyāmsundardās et al., eds., *Hindī Śabd Sāgar* (Varanasi: Nāgarīpracāriṇī Sabhā, 1973), vol. 10, p. 4927.

21. *Hobson-Jobson*, p. 878.

22. Tyambakayajvan, *Strīdharmapaddhati* 43r.5–6, in I. Julia Leslie, *The Perfect Wife* (Delhi: Oxford University Press, 1989), p. 295.

23. Of course, what I am calling "the European conception" is not confined to Westerners or even to those who think, speak, and write in European languages. A notable case in point is P. V. Kane, whose multivolume *History of Dharmaśāstra* is the standard work in English on Hindu law. Kane has a master's familiarity with the relevant texts, yet he subtitles his section on sati "Self-immolation of widows" (Kane, *History of Dharmaśāstra*, vol. 2, fasc. 1 [Pune:

Bhandarkar Oriental Research Institute, 1974], p. 624). At one point he goes so far as to conclude that a queen's "consign[ing] herself to fire when the king was dying" cannot be called "a proper case of sati, as she burnt herself even before her husband died" (Kane, *History* 2.1, p. 628). Interestingly, Kane also makes no effort to address the discontinuity between his attention to "the practice of sati," which he calls just that, and the Sanskrit texts he quotes, in which the word *sati* is used to describe not the practice but the woman involved.

24. Not all native interpreters accept the mere fact of an immolation as proof that the woman who performs it possesses virtue sufficient to make her qualify as a true sati. The reader is referred to Lindsey Harlan's essay for further information.

25. As Gayatri C. Spivak reports, this name can be used for human beings, too, although I have rarely encountered it myself (Spivak, "Can the Subaltern Speak?: Speculations on Widow-Sacrifice," *Wedge* 7–8 [1985], p. 128).

26. This is not to say that the story was a part of Hindu lore from time immemorial. D. C. Sircar points to a predecessor myth that concerned Prajapati rather than Daksha, and identifies the earliest form of the Daksha-Sati myth as the one given in the twelfth book of the *Mahābhārata* (12.282–83; cf. *Brahma Purāṇa*, chapter 39), which he dates to sometime before the onset of the Gupta era in the fourth century C.E. (Sircar, *The Sākta Pīṭhas* [Delhi: Motilal Banarsidass, 1973], pp. 5–6, original ed., 1950?). By the same token, one should not assume that the Sati legend is the one that would normally be cited in Hindu legal analyses of the practice of sati. One very important passage, from the *Shankha* and *Angiras Smṛtis*, compares the exemplary character of a woman who becomes sati to that of Arundhati, rather than Sati (Kane, *History* 2.1, p. 631).

27. Lindsey Harlan, personal communication, June 26, 1989.

28. The word, used in Rajasthani, Gujarati, and Hindi, is apparently derived from Sanskrit **jatughara*, which would mean a "house plastered with lac and other combustible materials for burning people alive in" (R. L. Turner, *A Comparative Dictionary of Indo-Aryan Languages* [London: Oxford University Press, 1966], vol. 1, p. 281).

29. Sudesh Vaid and Kumkum Sangari, "Institutions, Beliefs, Ideologies: Widow Immolation in Contemporary Rajasthan," *Economic and Political Weekly* 26:17 (April 27, 1991), p. WS-3.

1

The Iconographies of Sati

Paul B. Courtright

The word *sati* conjures up a mental picture of a Hindu wife meeting her
violent death amidst the flames of her deceased husband's funeral pyre.
This violent image usually expresses the notion that the woman is undergoing her death out of a sense of duty, even love, and in the belief that
her self-sacrifice will bring great reward in a future incarnation. Perhaps,
too, she will for many generations be honored as a goddess by the
community she leaves behind.

This general image, together with the suppositions that surround it,
has filled Hindu and Western imaginations with revulsion and admiration
for many years, but it deserves a closer look.

Seeing Sati

What is it we are observing when we think of sati? What are we looking
for ? What comes into focus? From what vantage points do we see what
we see? In both Indian history and Western history, we have been offered
many representations of sati, and the word has different but related meanings depending on the context in which it is used. Sati is the name of a goddess—the great goddess Parvati in an earlier incarnation. In a compound
construction, with "mother" (*satimata*), *sati* denotes a village mother goddess whose divinity was confirmed by her self-sacrifice on the funeral pyre.
In the cosmo-moral system of brahmanically influenced Hinduism — a
system articulated in the *dharmashastras* and *puranas* and elaborated

in the folk traditions of elite castes and those who aspire to elite status through traditional values — sati is a virtuous woman, a woman ontologically bonded to her husband. Such a woman goes wherever her husband goes, and even death offers no unbreachable obstacle to their union. In its anglicized spelling, *suttee*, the word refers to the ritual immolation itself rather than to the person who is burned. Finally, both as symbol and as concrete event, sati demarcates the deep division in India today between traditional patriarchal views of women and modern views. For the traditionalist, sati epitomizes wifely devotion; while for modernists, especially feminist writers and political leaders, sati serves as a paradigmatic example of the squalid waste of human life that traditional values can countenance. So in the widest sense, sati is about women, patriarchy, violence, religious symbolism, and the fissures between what we are in the habit of calling "tradition" and "modernity."

Although there is much we do know about sati — its myths, rituals, ideologies, politics, and values; its place in its own cultural settings and in Western imaginings — there is also much we do not know. Much continues to elude us. This is true at a conceptual level (otherwise this volume would have no reason for being), but it is also true in concrete terms. For example, we do not have a thick ethnographic study of a sati (here I use the term in the sense of ritual immolation), as we do for other Hindu funeral ceremonies. No anthropologist has studied in her familial, social, economic, and religious context a particular woman who was cremated with her husband's corpse. No one has inquired, before the fact, about her own understanding of her motivations and actions, to determine whether she is acting out of free choice.

The reason for this lacuna is obvious enough: satis are rare, illegal, and take place with little advance notice. Moreover, each observer has much at stake in describing the sati event one way or another. With sati one cannot escape the realization that facts are not neutral; they are laden with value by those who assert them. As a ritual event, sati does not display itself in the open, like a religious festival or a marriage ceremony or even a cremation. As a performance, sati is not something that can be arranged in advance. An ethnographer cannot hire the requisite ritual specialists to display it for posterity in a monograph or on videotape. Indeed, the thought of undertaking such an anthropological inquiry, even if it were possible, is repulsive to both Hindu and Western moral imaginations.

What we do see about sati, therefore, is visible only from traces left behind: from mythological texts; from the accounts of travelers and colonial officials who, by one circumstance or another, witnessed a sati event prior to its abolition in 1829; and from shrines to goddesses whose divinity was conferred on them as a result of their undergoing the ritual of sati. Such shrines contain icons and accommodate ritual practices that articulate religious sensibilities surrounding the sati as goddess. In the process of "reading" these texts, icons, and ritual practices, we can gain some sense of sati's meanings; yet with sati, as with much of religion, we do not have access to the thing-in-itself. We have only its representations, and therefore we remain at least halfway in the dark.

A related problem is the matter of whether with sati we are dealing with a single, unitary phenomenon. Is the sati of myth, folk-epic, and caste-legend—where the human effortlessly displays divinity in a moment of sacrificial devotion and power—the same thing as the demystified sati of colonial and modern India, where the coercion, greed, concealment, and sexual violence of misogynist Hindu culture go on about their grisly business? Has secular modernity, in rendering the mythic sati problematic, closed access to its "sacred" dimension, so that there are no longer (if there ever were) conditions under which the sati of myth might be manifest before our eyes? Unlike much of the Hindu tradition, toward which academic discourse can remain detached and relativistic, sati calls for closure. It compels us to decide what we think is "really" going on, even if we are haunted by the realization that there may be more to it than meets the eye. It stimulates the language of moral conclusion, justification, and authenticity; it calls on relativism to give account of its limits.

If there have been women who entered the fire out of pure devotion and a compelling confidence in the reality of rebirth and the effectiveness of self-sacrifice, these women must indeed be goddesses, worthy to be venerated by the witnessing community. But if such displays of fortitude and devotion are not possible for women on their own (owing to their abject status, to various levels of coercion, or to the fact that no woman in her "right mind" would undertake such an act of self-annihilation), then what they go through is at best suicide. More likely, in fact, it should be construed as murder at the hands of the surrounding mob. The community that venerates the supposed self-immolation of such a sati is engaging in a heinous form of collective self-deception.

Sati interests us, indeed haunts us, because it exposes the rupture between two incommensurate views of reality. On the one side is a religious view in which lives travel from incarnation to incarnation, and self-sacrificial actions have effects that go well beyond the immediate circumstances in which they are produced. On the other side is a modern view according to which individuals "make themselves" in social environments that are more or less hospitable to a person's self-fulfillment. In the former view, sati is the ideal heroic and sacred action; in the latter, it is a paradigm of powerlessness. Either religion is true, in which case satis are real and heroically efficacious; or modernity is true, and satis are sordid rituals of coercion.

Sati is disorienting to us, not simply because of its torturous violence (if that is what we conclude), but because it makes us see how traditional Hindu ideals such as *moksha*, the goal of liberation from rebirth, and sacrifice are incommensurate with the modern world's experience of person, power, and fulfillment. A conversation about sati that seeks to take its religious dimensions seriously has to explore that rift. And indeed, whether a particular sati is judged "authentically" religious or not, freely undertaken or not, cosmically efficacious or not, one cannot easily argue that religion is irrelevant to sati.

Sati has been represented in Hindu and Western conceptions in a number of ways and contexts. Of these, three modes of representation take on a more or less coherent shape. The first is the sati of traditional Hinduism, in which the sati appears as a sacred person and event, whose stories and shrines serve as focal points for religious activity and values among particular communities. The second is the sati of Western travelers and British colonial culture. Here sati is problematic in the extreme— the very measure of Hinduism's irrationality and superstition. A third is the sati of contemporary India, shaped in large measure by the discourse of feminism, in which sati functions as a limiting case that displays the violence and deceit toward women that patriarchal cultures make possible.

This chapter will present glimpses into the first two of these representations. I leave the third to the discussion between Ashis Nandy and Veena Oldenburg that occurs at the end of the volume. Both of the representations of sati that I will discuss are set within one or more worlds of ideas, narratives, moral commitments, communities, and social and political notions and relations; and each has a characteristic iconography. By *iconography*, I refer to visual modes of presenting the sati event, whether through deities or humans, in ways that disclose its particular meanings. These iconographies will be at the center of my discussion. I will present a series of cameo views of sati that constitute representations of incommensurate and conflicting realities.

The Traditional Sati

Within the multivocality that the word *sati* contains is the meaning of sati as goddess. In the mythology found in epic and puranic sources, Sati is the daughter of Daksha and wife of Shiva. When her father insults her husband by refusing to include him in his sacrifice, she enters the fire herself. She displays her ultimate loyalty to her husband, and his wrath and grief at her death provoke him to destroy Daksha's sacrifice. In some versions of the story, Sati is reborn as Parvati and wins Shiva anew in that life through her extraordinary asceticism; in others, Shiva takes Sati's corpse from the fire and, stunned with grief, carries it across the world. In a gesture reminiscent of the sacrifice of Purusha, the gods dismember her body, and pieces of it fall to the earth, each forming a shrine. Collectively these places of power (*saktapitha*) constitute the distributed "body" of the goddess.[1] Devotees ritually reconnect her body (as does Shiva in some versions of the story) with their bodies, hearts, and minds, as they follow the pilgrimage rounds that link the parts of the goddess like a vast nervous system, each part giving access to the whole. Hence, as Diana Eck has said, "The divided body of Sati is the united land of Bharat [India]."[2]

In addition to the stories of the goddess Sati that emerge from Sanskrit sources, one finds in grass-roots Hinduism local goddesses called *satimatas*. These are especially to be seen in northwest India among communities influenced by Rajput culture. They are often patronized by particular castes or clusters of castes and are associated geographically with shrines. For example, the goddess Rani Satimata (also known as Narayani Satimata), a seventeenth-century Rajput woman who became deified through her sati, is associated with a large temple in the city of Jhunjhunu, in northeast Rajasthan. This goddess is worshipped mainly by members of the Agarwal caste of merchants, who have become successful businessmen throughout north India. Their success has spread her fame, and their prosperity is often attributed to her protection. Rani Satimata shrines may now be found in Bombay, Delhi, Varanasi, Calcutta, and many other cities across India.

A lesser-known shrine (and for that reason perhaps somewhat more typical) is the one devoted to another Narayani Satimata, located in a hilly, fairly wild area adjacent to the Seriska National Forest, in Ajmer District, in the state of Rajasthan. The temple itself sits between a large tree and a tank fed by an underground spring. The patronage for this Narayani Satimata is drawn from the Nai or barber caste, although its temple priests (*pujaris*) are members of the Mina or herding caste. Inside the temple is a stone slab, carved in Hindi, telling visitors the story of Narayani Satimata. The story is illustrated by wall paintings inside the shrine itself and by inexpensive lithographs that can be purchased there and elsewhere (Figure 1). In the lithographs, episodes of the myth may be read in cartoon fashion, proceeding counterclockwise from the top center of the plate around the central icon of the goddess.

The temple version of the myth of Narayani Satimata is as follows:

On the ninth day of the waxing fortnight of the month of Vaisakh in the year 1006, *vikram sanvat* [A.D.949], an auspicious day, in the village of Mora, a

Figure 1. Color lithograph framing picture of Narayani Satimata, Alwar District, Rajasthan. (Photograph, Paul Courtright)

daughter was born to Shiromani Shri Vijayarama. She was named Karmavati and endowed with every good quality. From the beginning she was filled with religious [*dharmik*] inclinations. Because of this her parents began to call her "Narayani" [Goddess]. In v.s. 1014 [A.D. 957], in Rajorgarh, she was married to Karansainji, son of Gangeshji, of the barber community. After completing the wedding ceremony, she returned to her parents' home. Then, in v.s. 1016 [A.D. 959], she prepared to depart to take up residence in her husband's home. As they were going by foot from Moragarh to Rajorgarh, during the hot month of Vaisakh, they stopped beneath a banyan tree in the midst of the jungle to rest and get relief from the heat in the cool shade beneath the tree.

As fate had arranged it [*vidhi ka vidhan tha*], Dharmaraja himself [Yama, the Lord of Death] took the form of a snake to make this couple's love eternal [*prem chirasthayi*]. While Karansainji was asleep, the serpent bit him and took him to heaven [*svargalok*]. When the evening came and Narayani saw that her husband did not awaken, she called to the herdsmen nearby. The herdsmen came and, seeing him unconscious, told her that his life had departed. Knowing her duty, she told them to make a funeral pyre for her husband and herself. Joyfully she sat on the funeral pyre and took her husband's dead body in her lap. The herdsmen prayed to her, telling her that in the jungle there was no water for their herds. She gave them a boon that there would be water flowing eternally from that place. She knew she had such power as a result of her chastity [*satitva*], and because of it the fire ignited by itself.

So it happened on the ninth day of the bright half of Vaisakh at five o'clock in the evening in v.s. 1016 that she became sati. . . . It is meritorious to visit this temple each year on the ninth and tenth of the waning fortnight of Vaisakh, and to attend the fair [*mela*] on the eleventh. Because of this sati, even now there is no strife [*hinsa*] or adultery [*dushcharitrata*] in this place. It is because of the power [*prabhav*] of this sati. Even though lions live in the jungle, during the last thousand years no one has been killed.

The story traces the narrative of the pious Karmavati from an auspicious birth and early inclinations of exceptional religious merit through her marriage. During the fateful migration (through an excessively hot and wild jungle) from her natal home to her husband's village, her epiphany as a goddess takes place. The Lord of Death takes her husband's life to set the stage for her own self-sacrifice. At this point in the story, she takes control of events, instructing the surrounding shepherds to assemble the funeral pyre. She gives them a boon and ignites the fire with the heat of her own moral purity. Through her sacrifice, she brings prosperity and peace; and to any devotees who visit her shrine she distributes auspicious power.

The painted version of this story (Figure 1) is simultaneously narrative and iconographic. Here Narayani Satimata is represented at the instant when her body is devoured by fire yet remains unconsumed. Simultaneously she displays her divine form, which is symbolized by her halo and the transcendent expression on her face. It is a coincidence of opposites—at once her death and deification. The corpse of Karansainji lies across her lap, much as an infant would lie in its mother's lap as it sleeps or nurses. The iconography is somewhat reminiscent of the more familiar image of the goddess Kali, or Bhadrakali, shown as the animating power of the universe who sits on or stands astride the corpse of Shiva. In those moments when Shiva remains inert (*shava,* a corpse), she rises above him, taking control and managing the transition of the cosmic seasons from death and destruction to birth and creation. She is the embodiment of transforming power, dancing astride the corpse of Shiva and arousing his phallus (*linga*) to full vitality.

Narayani Satimata, like Kali, brings her husband to life, this time in the divine world (*svargaloka*), as they pass together through the flaming doorway of the sati fire. Her power, a power derived from her self-sacrifice, makes possible his rebirth as well as her own. Together they "live" eternally in their images at the shrine. From the framework and movement of the myth, we see that Narayani Satimata's story is not about a woman's end but about a new beginning, not about death but about birth and generativity, not about annihilation but about empowerment. Indeed, the narrative of her marriage and her pilgrimage-like passage toward her agnatic home is really just a frame for the central event of the story: the moment in which a human being is revealed to be a *mata*, a "mother," a goddess.

Out of the excess of her energy, her fire, comes the eternal and abundant spring that is found at her shrine. It spills forth the cleansing fluid that yields purity and nourishment. Devotees at Narayani Satimata's shrine stress that the temple tank maintains the same level of water in the rainy season as in the dry season. The transformation of the *satimata*'s fire into water expresses the transformation of the woman into goddess; it is the flip side of her annihilation to this world.

In her most familiar icon, the goddess Narayani Satimata sits up, like the *linga*, poised, eternal, the fixed center of both story and shrine, with Shiva and Parvati pouring down light and flowers. She emerges from the corpse at the moment the flame begins to consume it. The iconography captures her in that transformative instant when humanity and divinity are juxtaposed—or to put it another way, when the categorical division between humanity and divinity is shown to be inadequate to the reality of Narayani Satimata. Her action simultaneously reveals utter self-regard and total regard for others: she maintains her marriage even when death itself threatens to deny it, and at the same time she transforms her cremation fire into a source of well-being for others. In both respects her self-sacrificial action makes connection and continuity victorious over separation and privation.

The logic of exchange that animates the sacrificial tradition of India and permeates the values of Hindu culture is evident here. Out of fire comes water; out of absence comes presence. The myth says that the fire was ignited by her *satitva*, her "sati-ness"; the heat of her devotion and single-mindedness sufficed to light the fire. At her initiation and agency, through her power, the water-producing fire came into being—like Purusha sacrificing himself to the sacrifice. Her body is the oblation, and her *satitva* provides the light (*jyoti*) and power (*shakti*). These two are symbolized by the laserlike beam coming from Shiva's hand to the fire — or is it from the fire toward Shiva's hand? From Parvati come the flowers, the symbols of life and renewal.

At the shrine she is *mata*, mother, source of nourishment. Much of the day-to-day temple activity is carried on by women who bring petitions to the *mata* for fertility, for faithful husbands, and for health and success for their families. Petitions are inscribed on the exterior walls of the shrine with *svastika* designs made of cow dung or tied with red strings to the trunk of the tree. Suppliants may hope for these petitions to succeed because they are directed toward a figure whose self-sacrificial action has unleashed the power of generativity. The image and shrine of Narayani Satimata represent a doorway beyond the realm of the merely human, onto the domain of flow or *sansara*, where each generation degenerates and where birth and death keep an even balance. To worship Narayani Satimata is to be anchored amidst this flux, to gain access to the energy that lies at the junction of destruction and regeneration, fire and water. For her action achieves the kind of deathlessness that Krishna, in the *Bhagavad Gita*, attributes to warriors who die with detached self-surrender in battle:

> [T]here is nothing better for a warrior than to fight according to his duty [*dharma*]. Happy are the warriors, Partha, who by chance get such a fight and open the doors to heaven.[3]

So far, we have focused on the mythology of a local sati, considering matters of ritual only as they became relevant to the living out of that mythology. Shortly we will turn matters on their head, concentrating on a ritual observed at a *satimata* shrine elsewhere in Rajasthan. Before doing so, however, let us consider a series of icons whose widespread distribution suggests that such rituals are by no means local anomalies.

Small sati stones and shrines are to be found in many areas of the Indian subcontinent, especially in the rugged frontier zones of the west and northwest (in the contemporary states of Karnataka, Maharashtra, Gujarat, and Rajasthan), where for centuries martial communities contested each other for control of pastureland and trade routes. There one finds icons depicting the hero killed in battle as he defended land and community; and his wife is at his side, having joined him in his cremation fire. Often one also finds this basic icon presented in a minimally narrative fashion, as in the sati stone from near Jejuri, Maharashtra (Figure 2).[4] Let us note its elements.

The lower panel of the stone depicts the ritual cremation, with the husband and wife laid out on the pyre. On the left is the post, perhaps associated with the pillar (*yupa*) used in Vedic sacrifice or with the *linga*. Out of this post comes the sati's arm and hand, palm facing the viewer, with bangles in place. Bangles symbolize the married state, and the ritual moment when a wife breaks her bangles signals her entry into widowhood. That these bangles remain on the sati's wrist bears witness to the continuation of her wifely status; they confute widowhood, deny that she has been separated from her husband. The gesture in which the hand is raised suggests something more, for it resembles the fear-dispelling gesture (*abhayamudra*) often displayed in icons of deities as a testimony to their power to dispel the terrors of separation and death. The top panel depicts *svargaloka*, the other world where gods and ancestors dwell, with the husband and wife now standing together before the Vedic fire (perhaps their

Figure 2. Sati stone (probably eighteenth century), Pune District, Maharashtra. (Photograph, Paul Courtright)

wedding fire) as two heavenly attendants sing their praises. At the very top is what appears to be a *stupa*, framing the stone as a whole.

The stone at Jejuri marks the spot, at the edge of the village, where a sati took place. As it happens, this particular stone no longer serves as a cultic locus; but many still do, especially in Rajasthan, where such stones are decorated and venerated annually by the sati's descendants. Other ceremonies also occur, such as the rather typical one I witnessed in front of a sati stone at Mandariya, in Bhilwara district, Rajasthan (Figure 3).[5]

The position of the stone and its iconography are familiar. The stone is near the edge of the village, resting upright on top of a raised platform. It is known simply as *satimata*, and this "sati-mother" is construed as a local deity who primarily protects members of the family lineages of a subcaste of Brahmins in the area. On the stone are carved the familiar symbols of the sun and moon—representing the husband and his faithfully attendant wife—aside the upraised, forward-facing, bangled arm and hand.

Figure 3. Haircutting ceremony in front of a satimata shrine, southwestern Rajasthan. (Photograph, Bhojuram Gujar).

The stone marks off the place of habitation of the *satimata*, where a familiar and (at least to high-caste Hindus) obligatory social and religious drama took place.

The devotees arrived at dawn, having walked all night, singing songs of devotion to the *satimata* and other deities. There were about thirty in the group, from the village of Kartunda about 8 miles away. The center of attention was a young boy named Nathu, who was brought to the *satimata*'s shrine to undergo the ancient rite of *chudakarana*, or tonsure. The rite is one of the life-cycle rituals (*sanskaras*) observed by Brahmins throughout much of India, and it is usually performed in the home or at a temple. Nathu's parents brought him to the *satimata*, however, to fulfill a vow made six years before, when they had visited her shrine and asked her for help in conceiving a son. At that time they had vowed that, if they got a son, they would bring him here for this ceremony. Their return expressed their gratitude to the *satimata* for her intervention on their behalf. Their visit and the ritual performance it included also constituted a plea for the continued well-being of the boy and an affirmation of the continuity of family and caste identity. Nathu's parents, uncles, and cousins, as well as others of his caste, accompanied him on the pilgrimage and formed the audience for this auspicious occasion.

After they arrived, Nathu was bathed and his hair was treated lavishly with coconut oil. Preparations for the rite were begun on the platform before the *satimata*'s image. A yellow *udni* (a woman's upper garment) with a silver border was placed around the stone image. In this subcaste of Brahmins, the yellow and silver *udni* is a garment that only married women with living children are privileged to wear. Hence the *satimata* is regarded as Nathu's spiritual mother, a role she also plays for all gathered to worship her. As the members of Nathu's family took their places on the platform, two local persons arrived to join in the festivities.

One of the local residents was a man known at Tolaram, a Brahmin of the same subcaste. The other was a woman named Barji, a member of the potter caste. These two people were important participants in the ritual drama, not because they played any particular role in the performance of the tonsure ceremony itself, but because they both had histories of possession by the two *satimatas* of this village. Tolaram had often been possessed by the Brahmin *satimata* where Nathu's family gathered, and Barji was frequently possessed by a local *satimata* of her own potter caste. Tolaram explained that he had resisted the visitations of the *satimata* for a long time. He did not believe that such possessions could occur; they were merely superstitions. But then he suffered from "craziness" (*pagalpan*) and was treated by various doctors, who could not help him. Finally the *satimata* appeared to his father in a dream and told him to explain to his son that what he was experiencing was not madness, but the presence of the *satimata*, who wanted him to serve her as her medium. Thenceforth, Tolaram put his faith in the *satimata*, and his "craziness" went away. Tolaram's direct access to the sacredness of the *satimata* gave him an informal, charismatic status in the community. His presence at this ceremony lent immediacy to its celebration. Here is the sequence of actions.

* * *

Tolaram washes his hands and rinses his mouth before sitting on the platform with Nathu and his parents, an uncle, and other family members. Nathu's father, who sits facing the *satimata*, asks Tolaram if any obstacles threaten to hinder the success of the ritual: Is this the right and auspicious time? Are any quarrels to be settled before approaching the *satimata*? Have any mistakes or omissions been made in the preparations that should now be corrected? Tolaram moves into a trance state and, as the voice of the *satimata*, assures them that all is well. From this point on, the *satimata* remains with Nathu and his family as they move through the ritual experience. People ask questions of her:

> When will the rains come? Will my son pass his examinations? My son is away; when will he come back? How is he? My friend had some pain in her

stomach and rubbed *bhibhut* (ashes left over from the fire kindled in front of the *satimata*'s image) onto it. Will she get better?

As the group presses its questions on the *satimata*, Tolaram replies.

Nathu's *chudakarana* constitutes a special occasion, but on every day auspicious to this *satimata*—Tuesdays, Wednesdays, and the tenth day of every fortnight—Brahmins in the area come to Tolaram with such questions. Yet they come to the *satimata* not only for help in crisis situations, but for calendrical and life-cycle rituals. She belongs to them; they belong to her. They remember her with worship; she protects their health and welfare. The *satimata* functions in some respects like a village goddess (*gramadevata*), in that she possesses, cures, and afflicts; she predicts; and she manipulates nature. In other respects she resembles a lineage goddess, *kuladevi*, whose work it is to protect those joined by common seed and marriage. Yet she is not restricted by the bonds of place and blood, for she responds to the entreaties of all who approach her with the conviction that her powers will help them. Some *satimatas* have reputations for power over particular afflictions, arising from the testimony of devotees who have been cured, and Tolaram and Barji are called upon by their castefellows to activate this power. The rite involving Nathu, of course, is of a different sort—a life-cycle rite—although its celebration in this instance also attests to the *satimata*'s powers.

The family priest now kindles a small fire in front of the *satimata*'s image. Before the image he places coconuts, various kinds of grain, flowers, sacred *kusha* grass, rice grains rubbed with red powder (*akshata*), and new cloth tied in a bundle.

At this point the potter-caste woman Barji arrives. She seats herself on the edge of the platform, keeping a slight distance from the others, her head and face carefully covered by her yellow sari. Nathu sits on his mother's lap, his long hair flowing about his shoulders. A square piece of red cloth is spread out before him, on which the barber will place the haircuttings. The priest sits behind the *satimata* image and supervises the ritual: the actual offerings and ritual gestures will be made not by him but by Nathu's father and uncle. About sixty people from the local village, nearly all of them Brahmins, gather to watch the ceremony. The father makes a ceremonial cutting of the hair along with sprigs of *kusha* grass. He says, "I cut this hair for long life, well-digested food, welfare, prosperity, progeny, and valor." Then he gives the razor to the barber for the remainder of the haircutting.

The barber mixes ashes from the kindled fire (*bhibhut*—that is, *vibhuti*) with a liquid made from various auspicious substances (water, *ghi*, and curd) and rubs them in Nathu's hair. These substances will purify

Nathu and help him resist the natural pollution that attends the haircuttings on account of their being remnants of Nathu's body that are now dissociated from him. The barber carefully confines these haircuttings to the red cloth. Later he will wrap up the cloth, hold it before the *satimata*'s image in gesture of sacrificial offering, and then submerge it in the nearby river, thus removing the hairs' polluting potential from Nathu and the *satimata*. Before Tolaram can begin this sequence, however, a man who had been standing in the crowd, a distant relative, presses forward, breaks into the ritual circle, and reaches out to touch the haircuttings. He seems to be in a state of possession. Nathu's father, Tolaram, and the others pull him away. They say he may have become possessed by a dangerous spirit (*bhut*) and should be kept at a distance from the *satimata*.

Nathu's head is now totally shaved, except for a small tuft that remains at the crown of the head. This is called the *adhipati* ("overlord") because it marks the place through which the soul passes when it departs from the body during cremation. An ancient medical text says that any injury to this spot will cause sudden death.[6] It is a sacred and vulnerable place, and must be protected by unshaven hair.

Nathu is then dressed in fresh white clothes. His father takes a white Nehru cap and touches it to the *satimata* image before fitting it on Nathu's head. Members of the family bow at the boy's feet. Nathu's father gives Barji a new *udni* with a yellow and silver border, similar to the one used to dress the *satimata*. She then makes an offering of food and uncooked grains to the Brahmins' *satimata*. Then Nathu's father gives Barji a second *udni* to be placed on the barber-caste *satimata*. This brief series of gifts reaffirms the bond between the two *satimatas* and their respective devotees.

* * *

Although the villagers retain no trace of a specific memory regarding details of the immolations that gave rise to these shrines—no names or dates—a fragment of a myth associated with the barber-caste *satimata* shrine does survive, and it says a great deal about the meaning these satis possess. According to Barji, her *satimata* was once a barber-caste woman who passed through the jungle with her husband on their way to his home after being married. Her brother ran after them and tried to take his sister back home. A fight between her brother and husband ensued, and her brother murdered her husband. It was at that point that she committed sati.

As is obvious, this myth fragment highlights the tension between blood relations (brother and sister) and agnate relations (husband and wife). The young bride's self-sacrifice displays her loyalty to her husband as against her loyalty to her brother. In this way the story narrates the dominance of culture, represented by marriage, over nature, symbolized by the bonds of sibling relations.

In the case of Nathu and his *satimata*, too, the dominance of culture over nature is declared. The highly stylized ritual of haircutting is designed to assert that a boy must at some point be released from his natal bond to his mother so that he can assume an identity that is aligned with his father instead. The cutting of the hair, like the cutting of the umbilical cord five years before, is an act of separation from the mother. To bring this action before the *satimata* is to place it within the domain of a figure who serves as a protectress of culture. Not only that, but the *satimata*'s own nurturing energies, which enabled Nathu to be conceived in the first place, are thereby restored to their original frame and made to serve the needs of culture.

Sati shows that a woman's powers are best and most powerfully expressed when they reinforce the culturally defined structures created by marriage. A *satimata* comes into possession of her motherhood, her *mata-ness*, because she sustains the framework of a culture (*dharma*) whose language, rules, and procedures are firmly patriarchal. For that reason the archetypal sati does not have children. For that reason, also, her possessed devotees are men and women. As for the sati herself, she stands on the boundary between male and female: she is female in form but male in function.

The Colonial Sati

Now we must make the substantial journey from representations of sati as a goddess conceived within the Hindu framework to those made by Western travelers and civil servants. Many of these individuals actually saw (or claimed to have seen) the immolations performed, and the immolation itself was what they meant by sati ("suttee"). It was almost a convention for travel books written from the period of early contact between India and the West until the early nineteenth century, when the colonial period began in earnest, to include an eyewitness account of a sati. Most of the contributors to this genre were Westerners who identified themselves as standing outside the assumptions and values of the tradition that produced sati. Usually they were vociferously hostile toward it, although one often finds a strange ambivalence lying beneath the language of condemnation. Both the existence of the genre and the morality that produced it undoubtedly exercised a distorting effect on the veracity of these eyewitness accounts; yet (as we shall shortly see) they, like the testimony given by survivors of severe trauma, can be interrogated in such a way as to move one closer to the reality of sati.

With the establishment of the colonial enterprise in India during the late eighteenth and early nineteenth centuries, British authorities assumed juridical powers that enabled them to contemplate intervening in the prac-

tice of sati. We sense this shift of potential in the engravings that emerge
from this period, for increasingly the agency was displaced from the sati
herself to the attendant priest. Increasingly, too, eyewitnesses claimed that
the woman was a victim of priestly manipulations stimulated by hateful
relatives greedy for the inheritance that Bengali tradition would have ac-
corded to the widow. In Bengal, unlike in most of the rest of North India, widows were entitled to their husbands' share of family lands and
wealth. If unjust enrichment was the ultimate purpose of sati, it clearly
ought to be stopped.

Visual representations of sati that survive from the early nineteenth
century reveal a scene that contrasts starkly with the iconography of
Narayani Satimata. Here the woman hardly sits in divine detachment
amidst the flames. Rather, as in an engraving originally published in the
third edition of James Peggs's influential missionary tract, *India's Cries to
British Humanity* (1832), colonial observers avert their faces in horror
while the sati, with arm upraised in a gesture similar to that of the Hindu
iconography, succumbs to the savagery of her community (Figure 4). This
icon—like the colonial, Hindu reformist, and Christian missionary rhetoric
of the period— begs the East India Company to bring civilizing rationality
to the rescue of this powerless and abject victim so that she may be saved
from her own people. Coercion in the service of reason was required.

One of the most complex and interesting eyewitness accounts of sati
to emerge from this period is one written by Dr. Richard Hartley
Kennedy. Kennedy served as a surgeon in the Bombay Medical Service

Figure 4. Etching depicting a sati, from James Peggs, *India's Cries to British
Humanity* (London, 1832), frontispiece.

and then in the Native Infantry; in 1819 he became surgeon to the Residency at Baroda. He lived in Baroda for about a decade, until his appointment as staff surgeon at Belgaum, and later served with the army in the Afghan war of 1839–1840. He concluded his Indian career as Inspector General for Hospitals in the Bombay Presidency before retiring to London in 1843.

In addition to his medical gifts, Kennedy was an excellent writer. He published poetry, a treatise on cholera, a tragic drama, and a narrative of the Afghan campaign. He also produced a thickly descriptive account of a sati he witnessed while in Baroda on November 29, 1825. Not until some twenty years after the event did Kennedy publish this account in a respected London literary magazine,[7] but the content and style of the testimony suggest that the descriptive material was probably written down shortly after the experience itself.

Like most of his contemporaries in the East India Company, Kennedy believed that Hinduism, for all its superstition and irrationality, exerted enormous and incomprehensible authority over its adherents, and therefore deserved a certain measure of respect. Publishing his account in 1843, he thought that the company had run a "fearful risk" in abolishing the practice in 1829 and had been lucky that Hindu religious passions were not more seriously aroused. "Under Hindooism," he wrote,

> the passive docility of the natural character, and the mental subjection of its votaries, seemed to admit of no other impulse sufficient to kindle resentments, and drive on the sense of injury to any outrage of popular commotion, than some fancied sacrilegious violation of its observances.[8]

The tone of this passage suggests that Kennedy had every reason to be skeptical of what he might see in an actual sati and to resist any impulse to accord it religious meaning. And indeed Kennedy is explicit on the point. He tells us that his goal in writing a testimony to what he saw was to give "a minute history of the details of the mummeries by which a sanguinary and revolting superstition besots the understandings, and hardens the hearts of its victims."[9] For him, sati was the paradigm of all that lurked on the other side of reason and humanity.

On November 29, 1825, word arrived that a Brahmin named Moro Kasinath Abunka, a respected businessman and veteran of many dealings with the Residency, had died after two weeks of fever. Efforts by the British Resident of Baroda to dissuade his wife, Amba Bhaie (Ambabai), from carrying out her intention to perform sati were unavailing; and since Kennedy was powerless to prevent it, he took the opportunity to witness the event. He notes, "The idea occurred to me of preparing this history, and in order to be able to do so, to put myself in the way of having my feelings harrowed, as it were, from choice."[10]

The funeral procession he describes accords in great detail with Brahmin practice, as prescribed in the ritual manuals, with some episodes reflecting elements of Rajput practice embedded within it. The son of the deceased led the mourners from the house, and brought the sacred fire his father had maintained during his life in an earthen pot suspended from a bamboo pole. From the house, the procession moved rather rapidly to the point at which the river was joined by a tributary; to Hindus, such confluences are intrinsically sacred. Ambabai, the wife, as Kennedy describes her,

> walked steadily and unassisted to the scene of her sufferings, and seemed in no way shaken from her steadfastness of purpose, though of necessity she had fasted the whole day, and must have been severely tired by previous vigils, in attendance on the dying man, so that she had everything against her, and nothing but an iron superstition to support her.[11]

To Kennedy she appeared to be "a ghastly-looking figure, her hair dishevelled and defiled, as well as her whole person, with the funeral-powders." She was a woman of about thirty years, with "a round, pleasing face, with features apparently formed to convey a jocund expression of habitual mirthful feelings."[12]

As it happened, Kennedy had known the deceased, having had some unspecified contact with him at an earlier time. This circumstance afforded him the opportunity to speak directly with the woman as she approached her death. "Her manner," he notes, "was wonderfully collected, and even graceful." He made one last try to prevent her from becoming a sati, saying to her that

> if she felt any misgiving, my presence would prevent it from being too late, even at the supposed last moment.... But her look of reply was quite sufficient; she had not come without counting the cost. Her belief in the Pythagorean doctrine of transmigration was firm and fixed; and she looked forward, without a doubt, to secure for herself and her husband, by this sacrifice, a new life of happier existence, and more refined enjoyments than the sordid realities which the world now offered; and her nearest relations about her were evidently of the same opinion, and as perfectly satisfied on the subject as herself.[13]

Kennedy then remarks, with great poignancy, on the demeanor of the participants, calling attention to the generally carnivalesque atmosphere that surrounded the horror that was to take place. This, he felt, was in weird contrast to the crowd's zombielike indifference—the excessively detached or otherworldly meeting with the excessively excited and this-worldly:

> I was struck at once with what I could never have perfectly understood from mere description, however sufficiently intimate I might have thought myself

with the native character, and however well I had heard it described, via the apparent *sang froid* and apathy of all concerned. . . . All the rest were not only indifferent to the horror of the scene, but seemed rather excited—I might almost say, if the European reader could understand and believe it, exhilarated—talking with each other triflingly, and unawed; whilst on one occasion, even the victim herself spoke to me in a tone of absolute jest, on the marked curiosity with which I noted and examined every step of their proceedings.[14]

Kennedy dwells on how the widow appeared to him, her "loftiness of manner . . . gracefulness of speech and attitude, approaching to my conception of the sublime." He compares her to the Pythoness of the Greek oracle. He is fascinated with the woman's peculiar, mythlike appearance:

Perhaps the idea was purely fancied, and the reflection of past imaginings, brought up by the excitement of the moment; but her situation was sufficiently peculiar to believe that my impression might have been a correct observation, formed on the view of a demeanor called forth by carelessness to earth and earthly things, to which she had mentally said her last farewell, and arising out of heavenly aspirations and glowing enthusiasm of her mind.[15]

Baskets of coconut, sugar, and dates were brought before the widow, which she distributed to those who "came to pay her customary devotions." Here Kennedy describes the distribution of *prasad*, food sanctified by its contact with a deity or sacred person, and comments on the manner of the worshippers:

The worship was performed with real or affected extravagance of humility, and ardor in language and manner, indicating the fixed or feigned belief that she stood before them a representation of Divinity, or rather as an incarnation of Divinity, herself a present goddess, capable of conferring blessings, and warding off future evils.[16]

Kennedy describes in detail the transaction between the widow, Ambabai, and her devotees who came for blessing. She appeared to act out of the commonly shared notion that she was a divinity, conveying a presence that transformed the occasion from one of annihilation to one of deification. They fell to their knees in front of her, touching their foreheads to her feet. With her finger she pressed red powder on their brows. They received it as

the sign of a solemn and important benediction, her countenance all the time indicating rather the smiling joyousness of a festival, or elation of a triumph, than the gloom and sorrow of her husband's funeral, or the horror and alarm natural to the thrilling moment antecedent to her own death by fiery torture. . . . [She] exhibited not a sign of reluctance, but conducted herself as one who met her fate with as much inward feeling of alacrity and readiness, as she undoubtedly did with all outward show of superhuman fortitude.[17]

As Ambabai prepared herself to enter the pyre, the priest gave her a mirror to gaze into, just as mirrors are offered to images of deities in other ritual situations. This prompted her to speak, according to Kennedy:

> [S]he declared that she had seen a phantasmagorical representation of the history of her soul gliding over it [the mirror]; it had been thrice before on earth; it had thrice been liberated from earth by similar sacrifices: the present was her fourth cremation; and her destiny reserved her for a fifth, which was to befall her at Kasi [Benares]; Life to animate her, and be her, would return into the bosom and substance of the Creator.[18]

What Ambabai saw in the mirror was not herself in the ordinary sense, but her "not-self" —all the selves she was and would be, selves that enclosed this present self in parentheses. She saw the self that provides the thread of continuity connecting past, present, and future. The mirror reflected the absence of her present life and the presence of her absent lives. It thus served as a portal to the past and to the future. In seeing it, she demonstrated powers associated with renouncers, who are said to be able to remember former lives and to know the circumstances of their deaths and future births. For her, *karma* was not a notion or belief but an actual perception of how things appear when one's eyes are truly open. In this moment, the reality that the ritual constructed seems to have fully displaced the ordinary world.

Finally, as the fire engulfed the pyre, the marriage bed, Kennedy was driven back by the heat:

> [Y]et I retired as slowly as I could, and I think I should have heard any unrestrainable shriek of the extreme agony had it been uttered; and observed any convulsive moment, or desperate attempt to break forth, had it been made. I do not think that either took place.[19]

Kennedy's contempt for Hindu religious practice could not contain his awe at the presence and behavior of Ambabai. Her sacrifice, while certainly manifesting how deeply she felt her religious "superstitions," nevertheless marked her as someone who was, as he says, "superhuman." He returns again and again to the uncanny character of her presence: the strength of her resolve, yet her warmth and good humor; her knowledge of the horror of her action, yet her playful disregard for her own welfare. It was as though she had been there but not there. Like Narayani Satimata, she dwelt in an intermediate zone, surrounded by taboo, contamination, and fear of death, yet filled with power and possessed of the seed of regeneration.

At the conclusion of his essay, Kennedy expresses relief at being back in his own culture and anticipates the salutary (and civilizing influence) of

the young Queen Victoria in relieving her Hindu subjects of such victim-
izing superstition:

> Let us hope that a new day has dawned on India, and that these wretched
> sacrifices may be spoken of by future generations as things there were, before
> British dominion enlightened India.[20]

After nearly three decades of debate within the East India Company
—decades that saw the shift from a hands-off entrepreneurialism to the
embracing of a *mission civilitrice*—sati was criminalized in 1829. Thenceforth, sati disappeared from view in most colonial literature, only being
resurrected for discussion at times when it was strategic to remind Hindus of their allegedly barbaric past, as in the late 1920s when Gandhi's
movement was gaining momentum and Katherine Mayo published
Mother India and Edward Thompson wrote *Suttee*, a "historical" account
of the practice and its abolition under the benevolent leadership of the Raj.

Conclusion: The Contemporary Sati

After India became an independent nation in 1947, occasional stories appeared in the newspapers about a sati in some remote village in Madhya
Pradesh or Rajasthan. Through the 1970s and 1980s, however, either incidents of sati increased or greater scrutiny was brought to bear on the issue, primarily by women's organizations. In its contemporary form, the
phenomenon of sati is framed by an understanding—on both sides—of the
differences between traditional values (represented by wifely obedience and
chastity) and modern notions of personal autonomy that, for the most
part, are guaranteed by the constitution of the republic. In accord with
this, the Roop Kanwar incident has triggered two iconographies of sati.
The one is aggressively traditionalist, with the sati cradling the dead husband in her lap as she faces the flames. The other is diametrically opposed
to this; it articulates the political meaning that sati has for contemporary
Indian feminists, who have argued strenuously against its having any religious meaning.

An example of the latter iconography is provided by a cartoon from
a publication of a women's organization in Bombay (Figure 5). In the top
panel, Roop Kanwar appears in her more or less iconic representation as
a goddess. Immediately below are Rajput men and women raising their
hands, palms pressed together in adoration. Worship, then, is part of the
icon, but not without comment; for just below these worshippers stands
a brick wall, and below that a demonstration of women, with their arms
raised not in surrender but in fist-clenched protest. For modern India, and
especially for feminists, Roop Kanwar has emerged as an icon of what
they stand against, a goddess of negation.

Figure 5. Cover illustration designed by Shakuntala Kulkarni for *Trial by Fire*, a publication of the Women and Media Committee of the Bombay Union of Journalists (Bombay, 1987).

In the beginning of this essay the question was raised as to whether sati is a single reality. I would conclude that it is, for these icons interlock; but it is nonetheless a highly volatile one. Within the unity of sati is a deep fissure, a profound and irreducible cultural ambivalence, shared by Hindus and Westerners alike, whether traditional, colonial, or modern in mentality. In all the representations we have considered, the sati takes her place—and sati takes its place—on a fault line. The conviction of redemptive sacrifice jars against the experience of social and gender coercion; the appreciation of exotic otherness coexists uneasily with a morality of sexual rage; and the nostalgia for the heroic past comes up against the terror of regression into barbarism.

In our explorations, we need to see sati as a whole. To reduce it romantically to the religious is to obscure the violence and manipulation that inevitably seem to be involved; yet to disregard the religious element is to fail to grasp sati's appeal, power, and persistence.

Notes

1. *Mahābhārata* 12.283–85 (Bombay Edition); *Kūrma Purāṇa* 1.13; *Śiva Purāṇa*, Rudrasaṁhitā, 2; *Linga Purāṇa* 1.99–100; *Bhāgavata Purāṇa* 4.2–7; *Skanda Purāṇa* 1.1.1–5; *Padma Purāṇa* 1.5–11; *Vāmana Purāṇa* 1–6; *Devībhāgavata Purāṇa* 30; *Kālikā Purāṇa*. Wendy Doniger O'Flaherty, *Hindu Myths* (Harmondsworth: Penguin Books, 1980), pp. 249–51; Stella Kramrisch, *The Presence of Śiva* (Princeton: Princeton University Press, 1981), pp. 301–321.

2. Diana L. Eck, "The Sacrifice of Dakṣa and the Śākta Pīṭhas." Paper presented at the American Academy of Religion annual meeting, Atlanta, November 1986, p. 13.

3. *Bhagavad Gītā* 2.30–32; my translation.

4. I am grateful to Günther Sontheimer for bringing this stone to my attention.

5. I am grateful to Bhojuram Gujar for his assistance in interpreting this ritual.

6. *Śarīrasthāna* of Suśruta, 6.83. Cited in Raj Bali Pandey, *Hindu Saṁskāras: A Socio-Religious Study of the Hindu Sacraments* (Varanasi: Motilal Banarsidass, 1969), p. 101.

7. R. Hartley Kennedy, "The Suttee: The Narrative of an Eye-Witness," *Bentley's Miscellany*, 13:75 (March 1843), pp. 241–56. I am grateful to Robert Patton for bringing this text to my attention.

8. Kennedy, "Suttee," p. 241.

9. Ibid.

10. Kennedy, "Suttee," p. 242.

11. Ibid.

12. Ibid.

13. Kennedy, "Suttee," pp. 242–43.

14. Kennedy, "Suttee," pp. 243–44.

15. Kennedy, "Suttee," p. 244.

16. Kennedy, "Suttee," p. 245.

17. Ibid.

18. Kennedy, "Suttee," p. 252.

19. Ibid.

20. Kennedy, "Suttee," p. 256.

Comment:
A Broader Landscape

VIDYA DEHEJIA

Paul Courtright's broad-ranging consideration of "the iconographies of sati" plunges us into the heart of the subject; it helps us focus immediately on the main perceptions and debates with which anyone trying to understand sati must contend. At the outset of a book intended to shed new light on the subject, however, it may also be appropriate to consider briefly an even broader picture, especially from a historical point of view. For sati is by no means an eternal aspect of Indian culture; it has its limits, its points of historical genesis and decline. Even its mythological range is not quite what we might suppose it to be after reading Courtright's essay. Let me, then, give a brief description of the landscape surrounding the commanding conceptions of sati that Courtright has put forth.

Courtright embarks on his subject with Sati, who is an earlier incarnation of Parvati—Sati the daughter of Daksha. One wonders, however, whether things really did begin there, even in a mythological sense, for it is curious that the term *sati* came to be used to denote a practice of self-immolation that is quite dissimilar to that embarked upon by the Sati of the Daksha/Shiva legend. One of the earliest versions of the story in which Sati self-destructs (she does not die in the *Mahabharata* version) is contained in the *Vayu Purana* (30.38–47), the bulk of which was composed sometime during the fourth and fifth centuries A.D. The *Purana* leaves vague the exact manner of Sati's self-destruction (broken heart? yoga?), but the poet Kalidasa specifies in his *Kumarasambhava* that she threw herself into fire. The cause of Sati's self-destruction had nothing to do with any belief in rejoining a dead husband in heaven, since her husband Shiva was very much alive at the time. At a much later date (tenth/eleventh centuries A.D.), the *Kalika Purana* introduced the episode in which the distraught Shiva wandered the earth with Sati's corpse on his shoulder; her body had certainly not been consumed by fire, but was totally intact (Figure 6).

One may therefore question whether the mythological Sati of the Daksha/Shiva legend had any real connections with the use of the term *sati* for the practice of widow burning. It seems equally plausible that the name for the practice was derived from the basic meaning of sati as a chaste woman, a virtuous wife. How could a woman whose husband died retain the appellation of chaste wife or sati? Perhaps her only way to maintain such a status (as against the ignominious position of widow) was to join her husband on the funeral pyre and in a world beyond. Perhaps, then, the term *sati* for a virtuous woman was, by extension, applied to the act that enabled a woman to remain a *pativrata*—a true, loyal wife. In this context one may note the ancient custom, persisting to this day, of blessing any woman with the words *sumangali bhava*: "may you be fortunate." Since a *sumangali* ("fortunate one") is a woman whose husband is alive, the blessing really hopes to confer long life on the husband; it expresses the hope that he may outlive his wife. "May you be long-lived" is never the blessing given to a woman.

Sati was introduced into the Indian cultural scene relatively late; only after A.D. 500 did the practice begin to appear with any regularity. A single early reference appears in the *Atharvaveda* (18.2.1), in which a widow who

Figure 6. Shiva carrying the dead Sati. 17th/18th-century bronze, Gwalior Museum. Photograph courtesy of the Archaeological Survey of India.

lies down beside her dead husband is asked to come away, and a prayer is offered for her happy life with children and wealth. The suggestion of widow remarriage is clear. Does the passage indicate the discontinuation of an earlier practice? Or is this single isolated reference perhaps a later interpolation into the text? Whatever the case may be, literary references to sati begin to emerge only around the beginning of the Christian era. It is a custom unknown to Buddhist literature; and if it had existed during the Buddha's time, he would certainly have condemned it. Megasthenes, the Greek ambassador to the court of Chandragupta Maurya (circa 324–300 B.C.), wrote extensively on Indian customs; his silence on sati indicates its nonexistence. Kautilya's contemporary work on polity, which contains much information of cultural significance, likewise says nothing about sati. *The Laws of Manu* (circa A.D. 100/200) laid down detailed rules regarding the duties of women and of widows; clearly sati did not exist at the time it was written.

In the latest parts of the *Mahabharata* (composed between 400 B.C. and A.D. 400), the practice of sati is first mentioned, but even here it is the exception rather than the rule. When Krishna dies, one of his two chief wives, Rukmini, commits sati, while the other, Satyabhama, retires to the forest for penance. When Madri, wife of Pandu, decides on the former course, the assembled sages all try to dissuade her. As against these instances, scores of wives of the epic's numerous fallen heroes do not immolate themselves; instead they perform the last rites and offer funeral oblations.

After A.D. 700, sati began to be extolled. It was suggested that a wife could purify her husband from the deadliest of sins if she burned herself on his funeral pyre; her reward would be to dwell happily with him in heaven for eons:

> As a snake-charmer
> draws a snake from its hole by force,
> so too a sati
> draws her husband from gaping hell;
> together with him she enjoys heaven
> for three score years and a half.[1]

Around this same time, sati stones began to be carved. In South India, in the area around Madras known as Tondaimandalam, stones were carved to depict a row of deities on either side of a lotus pedestal supporting a pair of bangle-laden arms. Indicative of wifely as opposed to widowed status, the adorned arms represent the woman who has burned herself on her husband's funeral pyre. The deities to the left of the sati are generally Brahma, a Shiva *linga*, Uma, Subrahmanya, Narasimha, and the *shrivatsa* emblem of Vishnu, while to the right are Durga, Jyeshtha, and occasionally Ganesha. These *ma-sati-kal* (great sati stones) of the eighth and ninth centuries, which place the woman who has performed sati side by side with major deities, are indicative of the power believed to reside in such souls. Stones were erected to house such spirits, who were then further propitiated.

The practice of sati does indeed seem to have been, in origin, a *kshatriya* custom. A late chapter of the *Padma Purana*, written around A.D. 1000, extols the practice but prohibits it for Brahmin women, and actually declares that a person who helps a Brahmin widow to the pyre is guilty of murder (*brahmahatya*). It is intriguing that, in the Rajput tradition of later times, too (as Veena Oldenburg shows near the end of this volume), the practice was largely confined to the warrior clans. The Mughal emperor Akbar found the practice in vogue in the sixteenth century; without interfering with a Hindu custom, he appointed inspectors to ensure that no force was used.

As will become evident in later portions of this book, the history of British involvement in the practice of sati is turf well plowed but still much disputed. Suffice it to say that the British—and after them, the government of independent India—took a more vigorous role than Akbar did in preventing sati. Yet sati survives in certain places, touching even the lives of scholars. In this connection, let me draw attention to the words of A. S. Altekar in his book on the status of women in Indian civilization. Informing us that he is prepared to believe the reports of British witnesses of sati who spoke of the willingness of the "victims," he quietly mentions his own sister's insistence on performing sati, in the year 1946, despite her having a nursing child.[2] Had history moved forward or backward, or had it stood still? It had all been said, around A.D. 625, by the Sanskrit poet Bana:

> This following another to death is most vain! It is a path followed by the ignorant! It is a mere freak of madness, a path of ignorance, an enterprise of recklessness, a view of baseness, a sign of utter thoughtlessness, and blunder of folly. . . . To the dead man it brings no good whatever. For it is no means of bringing him back to life, or heaping up merit, or gaining heaven for him, or saving him from hell, or seeing him again, or being reunited with him.[3]

Notes

1. *Parāsara-smṛti*, 4.31–32.

2. A. S. Altekar, *The Position of Women in Hindu Civilisation*, 2d rev. ed. (Delhi: Motilal Banarsidass, 1959), p. 137.

3. C. M. Ridding, *The Kadambari of Bana* (London: Royal Asiatic Society, 1896), pp. 136–37.

2

Die Flambierte Frau: Sati in European Culture

Dorothy M. Figueira

Elle espère arriver au nirvana . . . elle croit aux transformations . . .
se fait chrétienne et elle demande naïvement à être brûlée . . . elle fait
dresser un bûcher par les esclaves brunes et se brûle.

Alfred de Vigny, Daphné (1857)

The German Romantic poet Karoline von Günderrode was a woman unlucky in matters of love. She lost Carl von Savigny to Cunegonde Brentano. Her affection for Clemens Brentano could not withstand his extravagant tastes. She then met Frederick Creuzer, a man noteworthy to historians of religion as the author of the light classic, *Das Symbolik*. He influenced Karoline intellectually, enlarging her knowledge and introducing her to Indian thought. Under Creuzer's tutelege, Günderrode's work was inspired by various themes from Indian mythology and philosophy. Works such as *Die Erscheinung, Ein apokaliptisches Fragment*, and the *Geschichte eines Brahminen* all express a vague longing for the Absolute, a belief in perfection of the soul through earthly denial, and the vision of death as a surrender to an Elemental Spirit. Not surprisingly, Karoline's stimulating relationship with Creuzer developed into romance. Unfortunately, the Heidelberg philologist was already married to an older woman, whose wealth enabled him to pursue the life of a scholar.

Creuzer was not a kind man. For years, he tormented Karoline with his jealousy, while encouraging her with promises of his future divorce. He eventually broke with her through intermediaries. On the following day, Karoline committed suicide in a rather dramatic fashion: at sunset, on the banks of the Rhine, she tied a scarf filled with rocks around her neck and stabbed herself in the heart. She left behind a Sanskrit poem.

The melodramatic aspect of this suicide was excessive, even in light of the hypertrophied emotionalism endemic to German Romanticism. In the early nineteenth century, when Günderrode was writing, Indian religious rites and concepts were known to many Germans, even if only superficially. However, they were not so widespread that a German poet would leave a Sanskrit suicide note. Apparently, curious exotic influences contributed to this macabre episode.

Sati in European Letters

Shortly before she took her life, Günderrode composed "Die Malabarischen Witwen," in which she depicted a sati's sacrifice as the pinnacle of eroticism:

> Zum Flammentode gehen an Indusstranden
> Mit dem Gemahl, in Jugendlichkeit,
> Die Frauen, ohne Zagen, ohne Lied
> Geschmücket festlich, wie in Brautgewanden.
>
> Die Sitte hat der Liebe Sinn verstanden,
> Sie von der Trennung harter Schmach befreit,
> Zu ihrem Priester selbst den Tod geweiht,
> Unsterblichkeit gegeben ihren Banden.
>
> Nicht Trennung ferner solchem Bunde droht,
> Denn die vorhin entzweiten Liebesflammen
> In einer schlagen brünstig sie zusammen.
>
> Zur süssen Liebesfeyer wird der Tod,
> Vereinet die getrennten Elemente,
> Zum Lebensgipfel wird des Daseins Ende.[1]

I have always found "Die Malabarischen Witwen" to be a particularly poignant poem. Considering the ritualistic contours of Günderrode's suicide, it might even be suggested that this German poet, driven by the vicissitudes of life to an early death (at twenty-six years of age), masqueraded as a sati. What precisely brought Günderrode to her end is less consequential than the fact that, with this poem, she sought to ennoble her suicidal despair by giving it devotional meaning. On a larger scale, Günderrode's poetic testimony and her death are emblematic of the forces involved in Exoticism, and they exemplify the fruits born of the literary meeting between East and West.

It is clear that Günderrode had no orthodox understanding of the sati's act. She incorporated the widow's sacrifice as part of a personal distortion of Indian religious belief. The sati functioned as a symbol of transcendence, self-immolation being only one path among many. Death on the Rhine was equally symbolic. What was important was that, for Günderrode, the sati's act consolidated honor after rejection, brought about an eternal union with the beloved in death, fulfilled a vague religious longing for integration, and, most significantly, provided the erotic pinnacle of earthly existence. This distortion of the ritual's meaning did not, however, arise solely from Günderrode's despairing mind; it developed from the emplotment of this ritual in European literature. In fact, for many Europeans before and after Günderrode, the ritual burning of widows, more than anything else native to India, attracted interest.

While outraging Western sensibilities and exploiting Western curiosity about the grotesque and barbarian, the sati's existence satisfied European nostalgia for lost innocence. One of the earliest comments on sati was made by the Italian traveler Hieronimo di Santo Stefano (1499), who presents the sati's sacrifice as being a common practice among Indian wives.[2] Another Italian voyager, Ludovico di Varthema (1510), relates in greater detail the celebration surrounding the sati—her ritual clothing, the feast, the music, the dancing, and the act of immolation itself. Varthema comments that the women are often drugged into submission by priests who are "clothed like devils" and have coerced them to kill themselves.[3] In disgust, Varthema notes that the fire is accelerated by adding balls of pitch. If the sati does not die quickly, he says, she is recognized by her family to be a whore. The Genovese traveler Pietro della Valle (1626) shifts emphasis from coercion to devotion. His sati wishes to burn herself out of love for her husband and the desire to join him in death. Della Valle and Varthema do not sentimentalize the sati or her self-sacrifice; but another Italian observer, Nicolo de' Conti (1492), refers to self-immolation as a means by which wives gain honor and make themselves acceptable to their husbands. De' Conti also places blame on the Brahmin priests, who exhort the women to hold life in contempt. These same priests, he reports, are even capable of throwing a woman into the flames if her courage fails.[4] De' Conti romanticizes the sati's martyrdom by describing it as a burning (in the sense of passionate) embrace that the sati bestows on her husband. Although imbuing the sati's act with sexual overtones, de' Conti, like his compatriots, condemns it as cruel torture.

Unlike the Italians, Portuguese travelers ignored the erotic potential and the barbarism of the sati's act. They tended to focus solely on the issue of honor. Tomé Pires (1512–1513) notes that only honorable wives became satis.[5] Although the Brahmin officiants are known to coerce the women,[6] he says, some wives do manage to escape, recoiling before the flames. Their refusal to become satis has dire consequences: they are forced to live the remainder of their lives as temple prostitutes.[7] Duarte Barbosa

(1514) also points to the close association between sati and honor, and adds that this sacrifice allows women of lesser "value" and social standing to upgrade themselves.[8] While alive, husbands owe respect to their wives, since they are potentially capable of such devotion. Women, likewise, should learn from the sati's act, respecting their husbands with a devotion commensurate to that shown by a sati.

Pierre Sonnerat's *Voyage aux Indes orientales* (1782)[9] contributed significantly to the dissemination of information concerning widow-burning. His widely read and richly illustrated travel account relates an instance of self-immolation as a trial of love. Sonnerat's rendition of the tale was particularly titillating because his sati was not a devoted wife but a *fille de joie* whose feelings had overcome her professionalism. This surprising devotion did not go unrewarded. The man for whom she voluntarily sacrificed herself was, in fact, a god who then bestowed on her the gift of immortality.

This particular myth captured European readers' fancy. Similar renditions of the tale were recounted in Rogerius's *Offene Thür zu dem verborgenen Heydentum* (1663)[10] and Dorville's *Histoire des différens peuples du monde* (1770).[11] These historical accounts emphasized that true love and devotion could be found in any woman, no matter how low she had sunk. In fact, with typically irreverent Gallic wit, Sonnerat commented that Indian society could not be all bad, if it had such a high estimation of whores that it immortalized them. (The use of the term *whore* is intentional; other historical accounts used euphemisms, but Sonnerat consistently used the word *putain.*)

These travel accounts differ from earlier treatments of the custom in that they use a myth to rationalize an act that was too strange for Westerners to comprehend. By framing the ritual in a mythological context, Rogerius, Dorville, and Sonnerat displace disgust from the act itself and exploit its comic and romantic potentialities, in much the same manner as did Voltaire in *Zadig* (1747).

In the chapter entitled "Le Bûcher," Voltaire has Zadig convince Almona not to throw herself into the flames. She admits that she seeks self-immolation only to gratify her vanity and in deference to religious prejudice. Zadig then asks the chiefs to abolish the custom or to enact a law forcing widows to spend an hour with a young man before they decide to sacrifice themselves. Although, in this instance, Voltaire seems to make light of the practice, he was actually quite incensed about the sati's fate; he discussed it elsewhere (most notably in the *Questions sur l'Encyclopédie*, under the rubric "Bracmanes, Brames"). Voltaire sympathized with the sati less out of concern for her suffering than out of rationalistic outrage: she represented the ideal victim of religious superstition.

Johann Gottfried von Herder, a vociferous critic of Indian social customs, deplored the practice of widow-burning. In the *Ideen* (1784),[12] he echoed Voltaire's contention that it existed as one evil consequence of the Hindu belief in metempsychosis. Herder noted that the sati, by her act, gains entrance both for herself and for her husband into heaven. He attributed the origin of the practice to the lack of compassion endemic to Hinduism and Indian social organization. Herder strongly criticized the sati's motives: either she was aping some false conception of holiness or submitting to death as punishment. He blamed the Brahmin priests for having ennobled such an unnatural practice and for willfully deceiving the sati with the promise of rewards in a future life. In fact, he saw the institution of widow-burning as a cheap trick to make men's lives (and consequently, men themselves) more valuable to women. This cynical view raised for Herder á larger ethical question. Was love, even in its most intense manifestation, worth possessing if it was elicited by deceit? Voltaire's anticlerical diatribes and Herder's moral critique reverberated in subsequent emplotments of the sati figure. Poetically, she evoked pity, displayed moral courage, or expressed the need for social change and the end of religious tyranny, as in Goethe's poem "Der Gott und die Bajadere" (1797).

Goethe presents a Christlike Indian god who descends to earth in order to test the quality of human love. A young bayadera, with the allure of a prostitute,[13] offers him hospitality. The god's fatigue is soothed and his heart stirred. The bayadera falls in love, and what had previously been commerce becomes devotion.[14] Goethe's poem then relates a simple tale of redemption. The bayadera awakes the next day to find her lover dead beside her. Ignoring the priests' protests, she enters the flames of the funeral pyre. This act of selfless love redeems her otherwise unworthy existence; in thanks, her divine lover rises up out of the flames, and together they ascend to heaven. In a journal entry dating from June 6–9, 1797, Goethe acknowledges that "Der Gott und die Bajadere" was inspired by a German translation of Sonnerat's *Voyage*,[15] which he read in 1785. However, Goethe altered his source material considerably, as can be seen by comparing his poem with the original tale.[16]

The strength of Sonnerat's tale resides in its ironic use of a sexually licentious woman as exemplar of fidelity. Goethe's poem inverts Sonnerat's message by shifting the emphasis from the issue of a whore's faithfulness to that of absolute, self-sacrificing love bordering on religious devotion—a love that is realizable in all women, no matter what their station. Goethe's unchaste sati represents the Eternal Feminine (*das ewig Weibliche*) recast as an Indian Mary Magdalene. There is even some speculation among Goethe scholars that the figure of the sati, presumably

seen by the poet as a sexually loose, low-class woman, symbolized Goethe's
common-law wife Christiane Vulpius. According to this view, Christiane's
rejection by Weimar culture is symbolically represented by the sati's rejection at the hands of authoritarian Brahmin priests. It is noteworthy that
Goethe (and subsequent writers) chose to maintain the tension between the
sexually active female and the male authority figure once it had been
embedded in the sati narrative.[17]

Sati in Drama and Opera

On the dramatic level, the European representation of the sati, borrowing
its style from pseudo-classical tragedy, was both picturesque and sentimental, as in Metastasio's opera *Alessandro nell' Indie* (1730). The sati's love
for her dead husband, which was so intense that it could only be subli-
mated in death, dramatically succeeded when it became a manifestation of
unbridled sexual passion. Thus the perversion of the sati into a "prostitute
with a heart of gold," which occurred in the historical literature and in
Goethe's poem, was retained in subsequent dramatic and operatic presen-
tations. As "noble savage," the sati gave her life for love. Her very
sauvagerie explains and justifies her translation into the European imagination as a *putain*.

In 1801, the then-valued composer Charles Simon Catel wrote the
music for an opera entitled *Les Bayadères* from a text by Joseph Etienne,
dit de Jouy. Here, too, the sati is a fallen woman who evinces absolute love
for a superior male. A king has to choose a wife from among the three best
women in his realm. He loves the bayadera Lamea, inaccessible to him on
account of her consecration to a god. The plot develops through intrigues,
the betrayal of a leader, and the imprisonment of the king. Having promised the enemy that she will kill the king, Lamea rescues him and spirits
him home to victory and celebration. Only after he is believed moribund,
and no woman except Lamea agrees to enter his funeral pyre, does her
selfless love become apparent to all. A religious procession leads her to the
pyre, where she finds the king alive and they wed.

Another sati opera, *Dieu et la Bayadère ou la Courtisane Amoureuse*,
composed in 1833 by Auber with a libretto by Scribe, further exploited
the ironic theme of the sati as prostitute.[18] The god Brama (sic), dramatically portrayed as the *mysterieux étranger*, elicits the love of a
bayadera. He has descended to earth in order to regain his divine
status through the experience of faithful love. Condemned to the flames
for having protected the disguised god, the sati is miraculously saved and

ascends to heaven wrapped in Brama's arms. These satis are always saved by love—either divine love in the form of grace or mortal affection that results in marriage. Their unselfish love purifies them of wanton desires. When a literary or operatic sati escapes death with the aid of a man, he is either a pariah who has nothing to lose or a European empowered by Reason, as in *La Veuve du Malabar ou l'Empire des Coutumes.*

This popular *tragédie-manifeste* was written by Lemierre and opened in 1770. In it, the Enlightenment battle against the absolute power of religious superstitions and customs is set against the backdrop of European imperial designs of hegemony. The French, led by the handsome General Montalban, besiege Malabar in hopes of liberating it from the tyranny of Brahmin priests and their murderous laws. Concerned with civilian conditions, the general sends scouts into the city and discovers that the priests are preparing for a sati's sacrifice. Horrified, he invades Malabar and saves the would-be sati, only to learn that she is an Indian whom he loved in his youth.[19] Here, as in other emplotments of this figure, is society responsible for creating the institution of sati is viewed as culpable. Yet the unquestionably noble outrage against the custom is depicted in this literature not as the reflex of a contrasting culture but as solely an individual conviction. This suggests either that European playwrights and librettists lacked cultural self-consciousness or that social satire was but one issue for them among several thematic concerns.

When not serving as a political or religious satire, the sati drama easily degenerated into a sexual farce. In Hervé's parody of *La Veuve du Malabar,*[20] a Parisian merchant seeks his fortune in India. He succeeds to such an extent that he can marry the Indian princess of Lahore. However, the parvenu bourgeois discovers that she is none other than his Parisian mistress who has been exiled to India. When the merchant is believed to have been killed, there is a çlamor for the false princess to burn herself on the pyre. Then, in a scene reminiscent of Aristophanes, the Indian women rebel against the ritual and prevent it. Another operatic parody of *La Veuve du Malabar*[21] presents a Frenchman in India who has become trapped in marriage by an indigenous *cocotte*. The wife desires to rid herself of her husband and move to Paris. She feigns drowning in the hope that her husband will throw *himself* on *her* funeral pyre. While the authors of these parodies were primarily interested in depicting the sati of the café-concert, they contributed to the literature by bringing to the forefront of their narratives the feminist militancy that always underlay the self-sacrificing courage of the sati.

Religion and Reincarnation

We can isolate two major themes of the eighteenth- and nineteenth-century emplotments of the sati figure: the battle between reason and religion, and the concern to expose (or on occasion, defend) ramifications of the idea of metempsychosis. As to the first, even when the narrative plot appears most absurd, the sati literature expresses the conflict between Voltairean Enlightened Reason and the fanaticism of religious customs, usually personified by the Brahmin priest. In vilifying those responsible for such a practice, writers were often attempting to discredit the Christian clergy. On a more general level, the expression of the conflict between reason and faith exhibited by these fictional satis articulated the artists' desire to challenge the complacency of the bourgeoisie in believing it had arrived at a truly rational practice of life. Thus, in this literature, the sati functions both as an exemplar of bourgeois conjugal virtues and as a courageous rebel against social rigidity. This use of the Exotic for self-definition and intracultural polemic finds perhaps its most cogent articulation in Jacques Henri Bernardin de Saint-Pierre's *La Chaumière indienne* (1790).

In this short novel, the sati resembles the self-sacrificing heroine of the author's masterpiece *Paul et Virginie*, and thereby suggests how well this figure suited the Romantic image of the noble savage. *La Chaumière indienne* tells the story of an Englishman who, having traveled the world over in search of truth and happiness, finds himself in Bengal. There, he is thwarted in his quest by the ignorant pride of the Brahmin priests. Upon leaving them, the Englishman is caught in a storm and is graciously received by a pariah and his would-be sati wife, who relate the story of their romance. The pariah first met his wife mourning the death of her sati mother. Together they wept over this victim of religious prejudice, recognizing that a sati is even more unfortunate than a pariah. Subsequently, the pariah learned that the young woman herself was destined to suffer the ignominious fate of her mother on the pyre of her own aged and unloved husband. At the pariah's entreaty, she broke the bonds of superstition that tied her to society. As a supreme act of rebellion, she ran off to live with the pariah and bear his children.

These outcastes then proceed to answer all of the Englishman's questions about the nature of existence. They possess their intelligence from Nature, which has been their temple, book, and refuge. Through them, the Englishman understands that truth does not reside in a mind troubled by desire and hunger for power, but in a simple heart devoid of selfishness and purified by its contact with nature. For Bernardin de Saint-Pierre, the pariah and his would-be sati wife have become evangelicals: they love their enemies and practice poverty. Most importantly, they offer living proof that a man cannot attain happiness without a good wife—in this case, the sati who has renounced social prejudice and chosen life over a senseless death. Bernardin de Saint-Pierre explicitly identifies the sati's fate with that of the pariah, an idea that was only implied by other European authors. Here, both are clearly disenfranchised victims of religious prejudice, displaying a sense of social protest reminiscent of the hypothetical legislators of Rousseau's social contract.

In 1792, Gaveau adapted *La Chaumière indienne*[22] into an opera with a peculiarly apologetic bent and a plot that differs considerably from the novel's. The wife, rather than accepting her husband's pariah status, is horrified and flees. In despair, the pariah kills himself, only to be resuscitated by St. Francis Xavier. Upon witnessing this miracle, the Indian savages convert *en masse*. The Hindu priests, however, are not pleased. They try to immolate the pariah, his wife, and St. Francis, only to have the funeral pyre, which had been erected on a beach, wash away in a sudden tempest. Fortunately, the pyre serves as a raft and the Indian couple and the saint are eventually saved by a Portuguese ship. I cannot help thinking that the success of this Jesuitical sati opera made poor Voltaire turn in his grave.

Viewed as a whole, these European representations of widow-burning ideally illustrate the function of the Exotic. The fact that authors added scenes of widow-burning even when these were not integral to the plot line suggests that the sati did not function solely as a vehicle for sensuality and local color; rather, it served to exercise a larger European intellectual concern with the moral ramifications of transmigration. By stressing an evident social evil such as the practice of widow-burning, Europeans expressed their moral abhorrence of the belief in transmigration that created the custom.

To the Hindu, transmigration, signified by rebirth, acts out the expiation of sins and moral failings. Once reborn, the soul receives another opportunity to atone by good works, recognize its true identity, and break the cycle of *sansara*. The Indian doctrine that one is reborn in a form commensurate with one's actions in a previous existence was not unknown to nineteenth-century Europeans; they were familiar with it through their reading of Classical[23] and travel literature.[24] Moreover, a collective interest in death and the afterlife was particularly prevalent in Germany during the Enlightenment and post-Enlightenment. Speculations about a continued life in a future state can also be attributed to conventional conceptions of immortality. The writings of Klopstock and Wieland, and the poetry of Young, Gray, and Ossian fed this fixation on death. Eighteenth-century works dealing with death—even when they did not specifically suggest reincarnation—expressed an optimistic expectation of reunions in the afterlife.[25] Why, then, did the sati's act, which aimed at nothing more

than the reunion of husband and wife in a future life, warrant the condemnation that it elicited in the West? Clearly, Europeans could not view the
sati's death as a matter of romantic wish-fulfillment. Its determined self-
affliction and disrespect for life were seen as symptomatic of a dangerously
fatalistic Indian world view. The majority opinion clearly understood
metempsychosis as the genuine evil, although a minority view (which held
sway particularly in Germany) saw the wisdom of the belief in
metempsychosis.

Novalis asked, apropos of metempsychosis, whether earthly birth
might not be the result of death in the beyond.[26] Schopenhauer specu-
lated on the positive effects of metempsychosis, seeing it as a transcenden-
tal truth that was accessible to ordinary people through mythical
representation. He chided his fellow Europeans for sending English
clergymen and Moravian linen weavers to India to teach the Brahmins a
better doctrine and to convince them that they were formed out of nothing.[27] By an odd twist of fate, however, Schopenhauer inspired the most
famous of all operatic satis, that of Brünnhilde at the end of the
Götterdämmerung.

In the grand tradition of European operatic satis, Brünnhilde uses the
occasion of her martyrdom to expound on the intensity of her love for
Siegfried. Ecstatically enjoining her horse Grane to accompany her, she
explains how love has overwhelmed and enslaved her:

> Greetings Grane, my horse.
> Do you know, friend,
> Where I am leading you?
> In the blazing fire
> Lies your master,
> Siegfried, my late hero.
> Do you neigh happily
> To follow our friend?
> Do the laughing flames
> Lure you to him?
> Feel how my breast also burns;
> Bright fire
> Seizes my heart:
> To embrace him,
> To be enclosed by him,
> To be wed
> In the most powerful Love!—
> Hi-ho! Grane!
> Greet our friend!
> Siegfried! Siegfried!
> Let my greeting bless you.[28]

These final lines of the opera were most probably written while Wagner was occupied with *Tristan und Isolde*, and they address the theme central to both operas: the loss of self through the experience of love. In an earlier manuscript of the *Götterdämmerung* (dating from the summer of 1856), however, Wagner has his heroine sing a different tune. In this version, when Brünnhilde lights the pyre, she is no longer a pawn in Wotan's plot for world conquest; rather, she is answering Schopenhauer's call:

> If I journey no more
> To Walhalla's feasting,
> Do you know where I go?
> I leave the Land of Desire,
> I flee the Land of Illusion forever;
> I close behind me
> The open door
> Of eternal Becoming:
> Now she who is wise journeys
> To the desireless and delusionless
> Holiest chosen land,
> The goal of world-wandering,
> Freed from rebirth,
> Everything eternal,
> Blessed end,
> Do you know how I have won it?
> The deepest suffering
> Of sorrowful love,
> My eyes opened:
> I saw the world end.[29]

When Brünnhilde seeks to break the bonds of rebirth and thereby escape the domain of *Kama* and the snares of *maya*, she leaves behind the world of vain cravings and illusion, and her wandering through countless existences ends. In a variant of this version, the Indian elements are equally strong:

> Sorrowful love!
> Deepest pity
> Opened the gates to me
> Who, above all things, respects life.
> Turn your eyes from me,
> Who, out of pity,
> Looks after the departing one.
> To him redemption dawns from afar—
> Redemption which I have attained
> With this greeting. I part from you, O world.[30]

In these versions of the final scene, which were ultimately discarded, Brünnhilde equates the world of the living with the dwelling of the rest-

less. The wise one, recognizing this world to be infested with deceptive il-
lusions and realizing its worthlessness, leaves it gladly. By closing the doors
of eternal Becoming, the initiate escapes future rebirths and attains an eternal End. Brünnhilde here does not refer to an individual cessa-
tion of existence. These lines, written at the height of Wagner's
Schopenhauerwendung, express the heroine's longing for nirvana as
Wagner understood it via Schopenhauer. Ultimately, however, Wagner
was not ready for a sati motivated by a negation of the will (he would not
write *Parsifal* for another thirty years). Love, and love alone, possessed
the power necessary for redemption.[31] Therefore, the Schoperhauerian versions were stricken and Brünnhilde's sati became much more a *Liebestod*.

With the exception of Schopenhauer and Wagner, most Europeans
considered the belief in metempsychosis too deterministic. Herder is an
example. In *Zerstreute Blätter* (1785), he presented his thoughts on
metempsychosis in Christian terms, depicting it as a primitive expression
of penance.[32] By the time he wrote *Palingenesis*, some twelve years later,
he had changed his earlier conception of metempsychosis, but he still rejected it as a concept. Now he saw it as a delusion of the senses[33] and
blamed it[34] for a plethora of India's social ills, including the pariah's and
the sati's status.[35] He noted, however, that a great lesson could be learned
from this delusion: humanity should be ruled by reason.[36]

Was not this rationalist imperative at work in the use of the Exotic
in general, and the sati cliché in particular? Just as Herder's comments on
metempsychosis sounded the clarion call of the Enlightenment, so did the
European sati literature echo a condemnation of religious prejudice and
social rigidity. From Voltaire on, the motif of sati allowed authors to
articulate their hatred of the Church as hypocritical and brutal, without
having to name the Church as French or Catholic. Its prejudiced clerics
could pose as Brahmins, not Jesuits. Indian characters, such as the sati,
the pariah, and the bayadera, became true children of the Enlightenment
when they sympathized with this critical moral stance. In *La Chaumière
indienne*, the sati *manquée*, although initially shocked by the revelation of
her husband's pariah status, quickly renounced prejudice.

Obviously, it was not the intention of these European authors to depict Indian life realistically. In their works, a male India peopled by fanatics and despots incarnating superstitious fatalism and arbitrary power
confronts a female India split between sexual license and matrimonial
rigor. Yet the sati represented in this literature draws these two extremes
of behavior together. She transforms her erotic desire into an oblation.
Günderrode's "Die Malabarischen Witwen" and her own suicide reflect
the morbidity of passionate fidelity that this literature so often espoused.
And in general these consistently drawn and idealized satis epitomized the

positive traits that were felt to be sorely lacking in European society. As such, they suggest a function for the Exotic that went beyond the mere enrichment of poetic vocabularies with tableaux of hypertrophied landscapes. As in Goethe's "Der Gott und die Bajadere" the Exotic was used in a sophisticated way to produce a displacement in time and space and thereby to enable the author to draw universal conclusions about humanity.

The rich intertextuality of the sati literature shows that the Exotic was fashioned in neither a hasty nor a negligent manner. Indian exoticism served the double purpose of introducing the strange and unknown, while genuinely challenging bourgeois values and sensibilities. As an ideal ploy for satire, the Indian Exotic both controverted familiar social structures and challenged the moral implications of rigidly imposed gender roles. Thus "la veuve du Malabar," like all the European satis, is forced to redefine her moral stance and allegiance to duty in order to gain redemption. And some artists climbed to still higher ground. They rose above the urge to blame any given society—or, indeed, all societies—and focused on the figure of the sati because, although superficially sentimental, she seemed to illustrate so well the universal human tension between desire and morality. A twentieth-century sati opera, Roussel's *Padmāvati*, exhibits this tension in a way that is cogently different from its nineteenth-century predecessors. Here the heroine, in her lust for an incendiary coupling, achieves her personal redemption at the cost of condemning her people to subjugation, torture, and death.

We see, then, how these various poems, dramas, and operas addressing the fate of the sati follow a consistent but paradoxical pattern. In them, the sati's strength comes from her absolute and selfless love for the man/god. Yet her status as an exemplar of bourgeois virtue—a good wife—becomes the more salient by arising from ironic character traits: the sati, though righteous in her love and abnegation, comes to that righteousness as an incarnation of unbridled passion. Thus the sati moves from a position of transgression (as an actively sexual unmarried woman—a whore) to a spiritual transcendence that is achieved through absolute love. She conforms to a higher law. When the sati draws back from the fire, another set of complexities ensues. She typically begins, in these dramas and operas, by enacting a radical ideal of disobedience: as a prostitute or pariah she functions outside the standards of conduct approved by religion and state. By contrast, in her initial impulse to become a sati, she becomes an exemplar of virtue; but then, if she decides not to go through with it, she shows herself to be quite a different child of the Enlightenment—a rationalist and free thinker. The sati's virtue is thus embedded in various acts vacillating between transgression and conformity. In this manner, the European representation of the sati demonstrates just how the Exotic elucidates the paradox of the human condition and offers to a custom-bound audience alternative modes of behavior.

Travel literature and primitivism had long since conditioned the European reading public to question some of the more vaunted advantages of rationalistic culture. Kant had proclaimed that the modern state resulted from the progressive development of humanity, but how was one to reconcile such theories with the perception that many primitive peoples were happier and better off than inhabitants of the civilized world? One way, according to popular Enlightenment propaganda, was to question the superior rationality of European culture; one could question that, but not rationality itself. Thus, one might render these noble savages more sophisticated than modern European men and women, and one might recognize their wisdom as directly expressing their feelings. As Herder maintained in the *Ideen*, humanity, even without the benefits of Western culture, has the potential of ascending to the ideal of infinite perfection.

And the French *philosophes*, believing in the unity of humanity, held that all human beings subsisted under the same natural law of right and reason. They supposed that all would participate alike in humanity's progress, and thus history would ultimately produce a uniform civilization, in which all peoples and races shared equally. European writers of the eighteenth and nineteenth centuries used the Exotic to make this point. Their satis attacked the complacency of an age and culture that came too close to believing that, in it, all socio-sexual progress was complete.

The ghost of Günderrode, a casualty of this age, hovers over the pages and stages of these sati narratives. Women do kill themselves for love. But while Günderrode incorporated the sati's sacrifice directly into her own life, her male contemporaries and successors appropriated the sati's act in their own way—to voice their concern for progress. In her death Günderrode lived out a personal mystique of participation; others sought in the sati a metaphor for injustice. Yet all utilized Indian Exoticism as an alibi, in the true Latin sense of the term: an "elsewhere." Thus sati served to satisfy a specific bourgeois intellectual desire: to emphasize, by means of a metaphorical spatial displacement, the need for a new social geography.

Fiction is no stranger than truth. As the rest of this volume will show, the ghost of Roop Kanwar also inspires men—and now women—to debate the relative merits of progress.

Notes

1. My reading of the poem is as follows:

> Women go the banks of the Indus
> For a death by fire,

They go with their husbands, in their youth,
Without hesitation and without song,
Adorned in finery,
As in bridal costumes.
The custom understood the meaning of love,
Released them from the harsh humiliation of separation;
They consecrated death itself as their priest
And gave immortality to their marriage bonds.
Even separation did not threaten such a union,
Since the previously disunited flames of love
Fall together ardently into one.
Death becomes a sweet festival of love;
It unites the separated elements.
The end of existence becomes the pinnacle of life.

2. R. H. Major, ed., *India in the Fifteenth Century* (New York: Burt Franklin, 1857), part 4, pp. 4–6.

3. Ludovico di Varthema, *The Travels of Ludovico di Varthema*, trans. J. W. Jones (New York: Burt Franklin, 1963), p. 207.

4. Poggio Bracciolini and Ludovico de Varthema, *Travelers in Disguise: Narratives of Eastern Travel*, trans. J. W. Jones (Cambridge, Mass.: Harvard University Press, 1963), p. 28.

5. Tomé Pires, *The Suma Oriental* (Liechtenstein: Kraus, 1967), p. 39.

6. Pires, *Suma*, p. 52.

7. Pires, *Suma*, p. 59.

8. Duarte Barbosa, *A Description of the Coasts of East Africa and Malabar*, trans. Henry E. J. Stanley (New York: Johnson, 1970), p. 92.

9. Pierre Sonnerat, *Voyage aux Indes orientales et la Chine*, 2 vols. (Paris: n.p., 1782), 1.17–73.

10. Abraham Rogerius, *Le Théâtre de l'idolatrie ou la porte ouverte*, trans. Thomas la Grue (Amsterdam: J. Schipper, 1670), pp. 220–21. Rogerius relates the following account of the tale. Dewendre comes to earth as a man and visits a whore. He wishes to test whether she can be faithful. He pays her well, and they make love the entire night. In the morning, Dewendre pretends to be dead. The whore wants to be burned with him. In vain, her parents try to dissuade her by saying that she was not his legitimate wife. When the pyre is ready, Dewendre awakens and admits the ruse. As a reward, he takes her to *Dewendre-locan*. In his commentary, Rogerius suggests that, if a society has such a high opinion of whores, it is no wonder that it allows them to serve gods. With this comment, he might very well have inspired Sonnerat.

11. André Guillaume Dontant Dorville, *Histoire des différens peuples du monde, contenant les cérémonies religieuses, l'origine des religions, leurs sectes, leur superstitions, et les moeurs et usages de chaque nation,* 6 vols. (Paris, n.p., 1770).

12. J. G. Herder, *Sämtliche Werke*, ed. B. Suphan, 33 vols. (Berlin: Weidmannsche Buchhandlung, 1877–1913), 14.31.

13. J. W. Goethe, "Der Gott und die Bajadere":

> Schmeichelnd zieht sie ihn zur Schwelle
> Lebhaft ihn ins Haus hinein.

14. J. W. Goethe, "Der Gott und die Bajadere":

> Und er kusst die bunten Wangen,
> Und sie fühlt der Liebe Qual,
> Und das Mädchen steht gefangen,
> Und sie weint zum ersten mal,
> Sinkt zum seinen Füssen nieder,
> Nicht um Wollust noch Gewinst,
> Ach! und die gelenken Glieder,
> Sie versagen allen Dienst.

15. P. Sonnerat, *Reise nach Ostindien und China* (Frankfurt: A. G. Schneider, 1784).

16. Elements in the poem suggest that Goethe was also familiar with Rogerius's *Offene Thür* and Dopper's *Asia oder ausführliche Beschreibung des Reiches des grossen Mogols und eines grossen Teils von Indien* (1681). See A. Leitzmann, "Quellen zu Schillers und Goethes Balladen," *Kleine Texte für theologische und philologische Vorlesungen und Übungen*, ed. Hans Leitzmann, 73 (1911).

17. See also Michael Beer's *Der Paria* (1821).

18. This opera enjoyed tremendous success, with 148 performances.

19. *La Veuve du Malabar* was so popular that it inspired several parodies and several operatic adaptations, the most famous of these being that of Baron Gebler (1779). Other musical scores under the title *Lanassa* were composed by André (Berlin, 1782), B. A. Weber (Berlin, 1797), Ebell (Breslau, 1802) Lindpainter (Munich, 1816), and Lachner (Vienna, 1832). Operas with that title were composed by Kalkbrenner (Rheinsberg, 1792), Tuczek (Pest, 1813), and Spohr (Kassel, 1823).

20. The libretto was written by Delacour and Cremieux.

21. It was composed by Doche, and its librettists were E. R. Basset and Sirandin.

22. This opera appeared under the title *Le Paria ou la Chaumière Indienne.* The librettist was Dumoustier.

23. Orphism, secret religious rites growing out of Dionysian mysteries in the sixth century B.C., included belief in transmigration, reincarnation in animal or plant form, and a wheel of birth. Europeans were also familiar with Pythagoras (c. 582–c. 507 B.C.), who taught palingenesis and consequent kinship with all living creatures, and Empedocles (c. 495–c. 435 B.C.), whose teaching was similar.

24. The teleological aspects of metempsychosis were mentioned by Rogerius (*Offene Thür zu dem verborgenen Heydentum*, p. 447). Mandelslo notes how metempsychosis was connected with works of a person; see Adam Olearus, *The Voyages and Travels of the Ambassadors,* trans. John Davies, 3 vols. (London: Thomas Dring and John Starkey, 1662), 3.68. Mandelslo draws the conclusion that Indians do not kill not out of humanity or sympathy but from religious conviction (Olearus, *Travels*, 3.33–35, 3.43).

25. Liselotte E. Kurth-Voigt, "Existence after Death in Eighteenth Century Literature, "*South Atlantic Review*, 52.2 (1987): 3–11. This author cites Goethe's *Die Braut von Korinth* (1798), Lessing's *Erziehung des Menschengeschlechts* (1780), Wieland's *Sympathien*, and Schiller's "Das Geheimnis des Reminiszenz–An Laura" (1782).

26. Novalis [Friedrich Freiherr von Hardenberg], *Schriften*, ed. Paul Kluckhohn, 4 vols. (Leipzig: Bibliographisches Institut, 1929), 3.33: "Wer hier nicht zur Vollendung gelangt, gelangt vielleicht drüben—oder muss eine abermalige irdische Laufbahn beginnen. Sollte es nicht auch drüben einen Tod geben, dessen Resultat irdische Geburt wäre." See also Heinrich von Ofterdingen, *Schriften* (1.101–2), where Heinrich dreams of metempsychosis. In the cavern of the hermit, he looks through a book with illustrations seemingly depicting him in former existences (1.168–9).

27. Arthur Schopenhauer, *The World as Will and Representation*, trans. E. F. Payne, 2 vols. (New York: Dover, 1969), 1.356.

28. R. Wagner, *Gesammelte Schriften und Dichtung*, ed. W. Golther, 10 vols. (Berlin-Vienna-Stuttgart: Deutsches Verlagshaus Bong und Co., 1913), 6.255–56. The translations of Wagner's poetry are my own.

29. R. Wagner, *Gesammelte Schriften und Dichtung*, 6.255–56.

30. R. Wagner, *Gesammelte Schriften und Dichtung*, 6.210–11. For a discussion of these variants, see Carl Suneson, *Richard Wagner und die indische Geisteswelt* (Leiden: E. J. Brill, 1989), pp. 63–69.

31. From a musical point of view, it is interesting to note that the curse in F# at the end of Brünnhilde's encounter with Waltraute in the First Act is musically recalled in the sati monologue. What is expressed in the First Act as a hope, is fulfilled at the end of the opera: the gods and the world are indeed redeemed.

32. In three dialogues, the characters Charikles and Theages debate the value of metempsychosis. Theages speculates that incarnation as an animal would never result in spiritual or moral improvement, because in animals the very attribute that could improve the soul has been taken away (Herder, *Werke*, 15.299). Moreover, God would not ordain that human beings be given an opportunity to recover the dignity and perfection of the soul, once they lost these through neglect. Theages prefers other beliefs in the afterlife, such as Elysium and Valhalla—they are more attractive than the idea of a cow waiting for the soul of a moribund human (*Werke*, 15.299–300). Charikles offers an adaptation of the theory of metempsychosis, elevating it to a metaphysical idea with a more sublime, though unknown goal.

33. Herder, *Werke*, 16.363; see also 16.349: "Hinweg . . . mit der Seelenwanderung, als einer Büssungshypothese."

34. Most notable is "Über die Seelenwanderung," Herder, *Werke*, 16.341–59. See also *Journal meiner Reise* (1769) and "Palingenesie: vom Wiederkommen menschlicher Seelen" (1797).

35. Herder, *Werke*, 14:30. Herder notes that this doctrine has other unpleasant consequences. It arouses false sympathy for all living beings (16.345–46)

while lessening true empathy for humans, since unfortunates are believed to have
been sinners in a past life (14.30–31).
    36. Herder, *Werke*, 16.367.

Comment:
Sati and the Nineteenth-century
British Self

ROBIN JARED LEWIS

The image of the sati has occupied a central and problematic role in Western perceptions of India since the first European travelers related, often
with lurid emphasis, their eyewitness accounts of satis in the late sixteenth
century. Voyagers like Sonnerat, Varthema, and della Valle struck a chord
in the European consciousness with their tales of this spectacular and (to
Western eyes) puzzling ritual of self-sacrifice. When the great European
trading enterprises began establishing outposts in India as a prelude to
imperial expansion, they too encountered the practice of sati. Probably the
earliest official British response to sati came in 1680, when the Governor
of Madras prohibited the burning of a Hindu widow,[1] while Job
Charnock, the East India Company operative credited with the founding
of Calcutta ten years later, was said to have rescued a Brahmin widow
from the flames of her husband's funeral pyre and taken her as his common-law wife.[2] Clearly, sati was already part of the cultural landscape, yet
the enormous symbolic and political resonance it was to attain among
Europeans in the next century and a quarter was out of all proportion to its
significance within Indian society. What was it, then, about sati that spoke
so powerfully to such a wide range of Enlightenment thinkers and writers?
    Dorothy Figueira provides an answer in her chapter in the current
volume. She suggests that the French and German poets and philosophers
who wrote about sati saw it as a potent symbol of India's exoticism, its
"otherness"; but more importantly, they found it a wry conceit, a symbol
at once sufficiently vivid and malleable to serve as an effective vehicle for
sharp satire of their own societies. Thus, Voltaire's "satiric trivialization"[3]
of sati in *Zadig*, as Figueira rightly points out, dwells less on moral outrage on behalf of the sati than on her perfect instrumentality as "the ideal
victim of religious superstition." By encoding his fervent anti-clericalism
in an Indian setting, Voltaire could indulge in savage criticism of European
values that he would not have dared to represent in a more straightforward fashion.
    Figueira tells us that late eighteenth- and early nineteenth-century
"knowledge" of sati was largely second-hand, derived from earlier Euro-

pean travelers such as Sonnerat and Bernier, whose accounts were based on fleeting encounters with the practice and often reflected the moral or sentimental predilections of the author. This superficial familiarity with the Indian cultural context produced images of the sati that were often idiosyncratic and highly personalized distortions, as exemplified by the poet Karoline von Günderrode's appropriation of sati in her ritual suicide on the banks of the Rhine. Günderrode "understood" sati as a multidimensional symbol, Figueira says, embodying "honor after rejection, . . . an eternal union with the beloved in death, . . . a vague religious longing for integration, and, most significantly, . . . the erotic pinnacle of earthly existence." This last image, of the act of sati as an erotic climax consummated in the "lustful flames" of the funeral pyre, is very remote—almost blithely so—from sati's meaning in the Indian context: nothing better illustrates the essential self-absorption of Western representations of India than this transformation of the chaste sati into the author of an act of radically individualistic erotic self-indulgence.[4] This wholesale appropriation of Indian cultural symbols suggests parallels with the material appropriation of India's wealth and labor that was taking place at the same time.

Thus, as Figueira vividly illustrates, the French *philosophes* and the German romantics utilized sati in various ways: as a symbol of absolute, passionate love; as a grounds for metaphysical speculation, particularly about metempsychosis; and most importantly as a powerful weapon in the ideological arsenal of those whose aim was to demolish the claims of religion in their own societies. The writers Figueira discusses resemble later European commentators on sati in that India serves as the source of a rich array of images to be used as tools of European self-examination and self-definition. In this sense, much of Western writing that is purportedly "about India" is not really about India at all: few Western eyewitnesses of India have displayed the relentless honesty of T. E. Lawrence when, in a different geographical context, he said of his epic account of Arabia, *Seven Pillars of Wisdom*, "In these pages the history is not of the Arab movement, but of me in it."[5]

In the early decades of the nineteenth century, the expansion of British rule in India engendered a fierce debate in England on the role of religion in Indian society, with sati playing a central part in the controversy. While all the concerned parties expressed unreserved moral abhorrence of the practice, they sharply disagreed over whether or not the abolition of sati by the British authorities would be viewed by Hindus as an act of gross interference in their religion. It thus comes as no surprise that British renderings of sati appear primarily in texts such as newspapers, parliamentary debates, and various first-hand accounts, rather than in imaginative genres.

Indeed, in English poetry and novels of this period, sati is encountered only rarely. There are few poems on the subject, mostly by minor poets such as Thomas Skinner, whose poem "The Suttee" (published in 1832) is typical in its portrayal of the sati as a noble figure victimized by the callous males of her family:

> Yes! she rejects this world without one thought
> Of all the bliss but yesterday had brought;
> Sees unconcerned an aged father stand,
> And scarcely owns the pressure of his hand;
> Hears a loved brother urge her on to die
> With cold indifference: not a rebel sigh
> Bursts to declare that yet one pulse remains,
> Against her will to throb at human pains.[6]

Skinner's angle of vision on sati reflects the debate going on in England at the time concerning women's rights: many reformers tended to emphasize that sati was an example of the degraded condition of women in traditional Hindu society. This point of view was instrumental in persuading the Governor General, Lord William Bentinck, to take decisive action, resulting in the promulgation in 1829 of Regulation 17, which banned the practice of sati in the Bengal Presidency.

One element missing in Skinner's poem, however, is the malevolent presence of the officiating Brahmin, a commonplace in novels of the same period. Sati is a subsidiary theme, little more than part of the cultural backdrop, in a very few fancy-dress historical romances of medieval Rajput heroism, but it is the focus in a small number of reform-minded novels, most of them crude and polemical, that appeared in the 1820s and 1830s. Most of these were written from a pious Christian perspective and were designed to illustrate the innate moral depravity of Hinduism and its social practices, of which sati was held up as a representative example.

The most widely read and influential production within this subgenre was a novel that appeared in 1830 entitled *The Suttee, or the Hindoo Converts*, authored by a woman whom we know only as Mrs. General Mainwaring. This earnest writer clearly intended her gigantic three-volume tome, which she began writing in the midst of the debate on sati, to sway public opinion, a point she makes abundantly clear in her dedication:

It is painful to reflect that while Britain has made vast exertions to establish a mighty empire in the East, little has been done to emancipate the Hindoos from the bondage of superstition, under which they have been so long kept by the sanguinary priesthood. At length the call of philanthropy is raised, and the abominations which defile British India must be exterminated. When that desirable work is accomplished, then may it be expected, that the mild quiescent morality of the Hindoo character will bring forth fruits of righteousness, by the influence of the Gospel.[7]

Mainwaring's novel is set in South India in the time of Tipu Sultan, who by 1830 had become demonized as the essential oriental despot, and its titular heroine is the virtuous, loving wife of a Hindu prince who dies in battle. She is propelled onto her husband's funeral pyre by the wicked Brahmin Benrudda, but is rescued at the last possible moment by a troop of British soldiers whose officer castigates those in attendance as "barbarians" and orders them to "cease your impious rites, or go exercise them with devils like yourselves."[8] The officer then shoots Benrudda, who falls into the very flames intended for the heroine Temora. The book ends with the intended sati's conversion to Christianity, a supreme example of evangelical wish-fulfillment. Mainwaring's work is paradigmatic of early nineteenth-century British constructions of sati, wherein, as Lata Mani has pointed out, "the widow is always a victim and the pundit always corrupt."[9]

This crude melodrama, replete with ludicrously stereotypical characters, is in marked contrast to the high seriousness with which sati is portrayed in most of the works Figueira discusses. This is no doubt owing to the fact that French and German thinkers of the Enlightenment and post-Enlightenment were, with the possible exception of Herder, fundamentally concerned with moral philosophy and metaphysics, rather than with the reform of Indian society. On the other hand, nearly all British treatments of sati in this period are marked by a strong sense of personal emotional involvement, and nowhere is this more evident than in the voluminous literature of first-hand accounts of sati that appeared in British diaries, journals, memoirs, and letters.

Relatively few scholars have delved into this rich source of information which, unlike the French and German models Figueira characterizes as "picturesque and sentimental," is documentary rather than imaginative art and therefore particularly valuable in analyzing the European encounter with sati. These texts emerge as testimonies of ambivalence not on a moral plane but on a practical one: the dilemma tends to center on the person of the observer—nearly always male—and what role he is to play in the highly charged social drama to be enacted.

British travelers and officials who encountered sati in the years before its prohibition in 1829 were all imbued with a code of chivalric behavior that compelled them to take the role of a kind of secularized romantic hero, defending womanhood in peril and scourging her tormentors. Northrop Frye's classic definition of romance in *Anatomy of Criticism* serves to remind us that romance is by its very nature a highly partisan

form of imaginative expression that glorifies the values of the dominant
elites:

> In every age the ruling social or intellectual class tends to project its ideals
> in some form of romance, where the virtuous heroes and beautiful heroines
> represent the ideals and the villains the threats to their ascendancy. This is
> the general character of chivalric romance in the Middle Ages, aristo-
> cratic romance in the Renaissance, bourgeois romance since the eighteenth
> century. . . .[10]

British eyewitnesses to sati in the early nineteenth century thus cast themselves as heroes in a social drama that enabled them to define themselves
and their role in sati in the paternalistic terms of imperialist discourse,
which Gayatri Chakravorty Spivak has schematized as "white men sav-
ing brown women from brown men."[11]

The results of chivalric intervention in the drama of sati varied widely.
One of the most remarkable such accounts—and it is richly illustrative of
Spivak's formulation—is given in W. H. Sleeman's celebrated *Rambles and
Recollections of an Indian Official*. Sleeman recounts the story of Charles
Harding, a member of the Bengal Civil Service who was in 1806 the Chief
Magistrate of Benares, where he was called on to decide the fate of an
obviously coerced sati who had leapt from her husband's pyre into the
Ganges and floated downstream, out of the immediate reach of her
captors. She was brought to Harding, who soon found himself under
siege:

> Thousands surrounded his house, and his court was filled with the princi-
> pal men of the city, imploring him to surrender the woman; and among the
> rest was the poor woman's father, who declared that he could not support
> his daughter; and that she had, therefore, better be burned, as her husband's
> family would no longer receive her. The uproar was quite alarming to a
> young man, who felt all the responsibility upon himself in such a city as
> Benares, with a population of three hundred thousand people, so prone to
> popular insurrections, or risings en masse very like them.[12]

Harding was unable to convince the crowd that the sati should live, until
he devised an argument couched in a distinctively Hindu cultural idiom:

> [He] said that "The sacrifice was manifestly unacceptable to their God—that
> the sacred river, as such, had rejected her; she had, without being able to
> swim, floated down two miles upon its bosom, in the face of an immense
> multitude; and it was clear that she had been rejected. Had she been an ac-
> ceptable sacrifice, after the fire had touched her, the river would have received
> her." This satisfied the whole crowd. The father said that, after this unanswer-
> able argument, he would receive his daughter; and the whole crowd dispersed
> satisfied.[13]

This dramatic denouement presents the imperial official as the infinitely adaptable hero of classical romance, who often outwits his enemies rather than overpowering them.

More common, however, in these encounters with sati was the image of failed intervention, as typified by the experience of the British merchant Thomas Twining, who came across preparations for the ceremony in 1792 in rural Bengal. Twining made several approaches to the widow, but was thwarted each time by the presiding Brahmins:

> I expressed my grief at her intention, and entreated her to relinquish it for the sake of her children, for whom as well as for herself I promised provision and protection. Although she said nothing, I thought her look seemed to express thankfulness for the proposition she had heard. I had not time to say more, the pressure of the Bramins, watchful lest their victim should escape, obliging her to move on.[14]

Surrounded as he was by overwhelming numbers of Indian participants, Twining was forced to retreat and observe in silence the "last scene of this shocking tragedy."[15]

Both Harding the Twining (and other British observers whom they typify) responded to the challenge of the sati drama by reaffirming their own culture's expectations of them as heroes. In a sense, they participated in the sati event in order to define themselves and their destiny in India. Through their actions, they sought to control India, to make it bend to their will, and their intense absorption in the process of social change regarding sati prefigured the more broadly hegemonistic enterprises of their successors at the height of the Raj. While the French and German representations of sati in Figueira's essay bespeak a special fascination with it as a symbol, they lack the fiercely personal quality of the accounts of the British, for whom sati was hopelessly entangled with self.

Notes

1. Philip Woodruff, *The Men Who Ruled India*, vol. 1 (New York: Schocken, 1964; orig. 1954), p. 66.

2. Woodruff, *The Men Who Ruled India*, p. 74.

3. From Figueira's essay in this volume, as are all subsequent quotations given without footnotes.

4. A similar point could also be made regarding the prevalence in nineteenth-century European poetry and opera of the figure of the sati as a fallen woman, often a prostitute.

5. T. E. Lawrence, *Seven Pillars of Wisdom: A Triumph* (New York: Penguin Books, 1976; orig. 1926), p. 22.

6. Thomas Skinner, "The Suttee," in Kevin Crossley-Holland, ed., *The Ox-*

ford Book of Travel Verse (Oxford: Oxford University Press, 1986), p. 301.

7. Mrs. General Mainwaring, *The Suttee, or the Hindoo Converts*, vol. 1 (London: A. K. Newman, 1830), p. ii.

8. Mainwaring, *The Suttee*, vol. 3, p. 60.

9. Lata Mani, "The Production of an Official Discourse on Sati in Early Nineteenth-Century Bengal," in Francis Barker et al., eds., *Europe and Its Others* [Proceedings of the Essex Conference on the Sociology of Literature, July 1984], vol. 1 (Colchester: University of Essex, 1985), p. 114.

10. Northrop Frye, *Anatomy of Criticism* (Princeton: Princeton University Press, 1968, orig. 1957), p. 186.

11. Gayatri Chakravorty Spivak, "Can the Subaltern Speak?," in Cary Nelson and Lawrence Grossberg, eds., *Marxism and the Interpretation of Culture* (Urbana: University of Illinois Press, 1988), p. 297.

12. William Henry Sleeman, *Rambles and Recollections of an Indian Official* (Oxford: Oxford University Press, 1915; orig. 1844), p. 25.

13. Ibid.

14. Thomas Twining, "A Hindoo widow" (1792), in H. K. Kaul, ed., *Travellers' India* (Delhi: Oxford University Press, 1979), p. 94.

15. Ibid.

3

Perfection and Devotion: Sati Tradition in Rajasthan

LINDSEY HARLAN

Although English defines the term *suttee* as an act, the self-immolation of a widow on her husband's funeral pyre, the Sanskrit and Hindi term *sati* literally means "a good woman," a woman who has become capable of self-immolation. This distinction reveals a crucial presupposition: whereas suttee as an act is something one commits at a particular moment, *sati* as a person is something one becomes gradually through good behavior. This chapter examines the personal ideal of sati espoused by certain Rajput women—those belonging to the erstwhile aristocracy of Rajasthan. It then articulates two often interrelated ways in which those Rajput women practice good behavior by keeping in mind (that is to say, by remembering) those who have died as satis.[1]

My observations are based on fieldwork concentrated in the southwest portion of Rajasthan, particularly around the Udaipur area, where I lived for a year and a half in 1984–1985. When I arrived in Rajasthan, I had not expected to find sati veneration a thriving tradition. I had supposed that, because there was only passing mention of contemporary sati worship in the scant secondary literature available on religious tradition in Rajasthan and because self-immolation had been made illegal by the Indian government, the tradition of veneration would have largely disintegrated. My supposition turned out to be false: although very few women end their lives as satis these days in Rajasthan, sati veneration is a major aspect of the religious lives of Rajput women. It shows no sign of diminishing.[2] To fulfill the terms of my proposal to study the religious traditions of Rajput women, I had to find out what this was all about.

One of the first things I learned is that, from the traditional Rajasthani Rajput perspective, a woman becomes a sati through the acquisition of virtue or goodness—that is, *sat*. Acquiring *sat* is thought to be the consequence of a personal transformation that comprises three conceptual stages, recognized in Rajput tradition as *pativrata*, *sativrata*, and *satimata*. The first is the *pativrata* stage. Rajput women assume that a sati who immolates herself has been a *pativrata*, a devoted wife. In fact, dying as a sati is said to prove that a Rajput woman has been a good wife. It demonstrates to all concerned, including the woman herself, that she has developed appropriate and admirable character.

The notion of *pativrata* is not the exclusive property of Rajput women. The Rajput women I came to know in Rajasthan, however, tend to understand their Rajput constitution as enabling them to be particularly good *pativratas*. Often in conversation Rajput women point out that the ethos of sacrifice with which Rajputs, soldiers by tradition, have been inculcated has enabled wives to sacrifice personal or selfish desires in order to serve their husbands better. This is why, the logic continues, the Hindu tradition of dying as a sati has been primarily practiced by (and so associated with) Rajput women. Self-sacrifice throughout life has predisposed Rajput women to sacrifice themselves at the time of their husbands' deaths.

The term *pativrata* has often been used to refer to any married woman. Even in this basic sense, however, it bears an ideological nuance, for it literally means someone who has made a vow (*vrat*) to her husband (*pati*). The substance of this vow is protection. If a wife is devoted to her husband and therefore protects him, he will prosper. If not, he will suffer and perhaps die.

A *pativrata* protects her husband in two basic ways. First, she serves him: she attends to his personal needs and encourages him to perform his duties. In other words, she both attends him as he is and helps him to become what he ought to be. This is clear not only from women's testimony, but also from the many Rajput stories that celebrate women who have driven their husbands from cowardly retreat into heroic battle. Second, she performs ritual vows (*vrats*), most of which involve fasting. By fasting she pleases various deities, who compensate her by protecting her husband and by helping her to be a better *pativrata*, thus increasing her personal capacity to protect her husband.

According to the traditional point of view, if the *pativrata*'s husband predeceases her, she is culpable. She may be suspected of insufficient or insincere devotion. She can escape suspicion, however, if she takes yet another vow—a *vrat* to die as a sati. If she does so, she enters the second sati stage. She goes from being a *pativrata* (one who has taken a *vrat* to protect her husband) to a *sativrata* (one who has taken a *vrat* to join her husband in the afterlife).

When a woman utters her sati vow, she places herself in the context of a vivid temporal fiction. Time is condensed, so that she becomes a *sahagamini*, "one who goes (*gamini*) together (*saha*) with one's husband." Hence, even though technically her husband has died before she has, she is absolved from blame if she burns herself during his cremation ceremony. Indeed, she is even absolved if she burns herself after his cremation, if his cremation occurs before she learns of his death.

The Rajput *sativrata*'s death is thought to be a manifestation of her goodness, her *sat*. The sacrifices she undertook as a *pativrata* built up in her stores of *sat*, which is a moral heat not unlike *tapas* (ascetic heat). It is said that when the *pativrata* learns of her husband's death, this heat begins to consume her body. So the woman who has taken a sincere *vrat* of *sati* quite literally becomes too hot to touch. Therefore, anyone who tries to restrain her will be burned in the process. When the *sativrata* mounts her husband's pyre, her body explodes into flames, and these cremate her own body and the body of her husband. In the process, the ashes of the two bodies become intermingled, which symbolically affirms the unity of husband and wife that was established at their wedding fire.

During the period between the *sati vrat* and the sati's death, a woman is considered extremely powerful. Because she has renounced life, she has in a sense progressed beyond life. She possesses special powers, among them the power to curse and the power to establish prohibitions, the nature of which will be explored shortly.

In the process of dying, the *sativrata* becomes transformed once again, this time into a *satimata*. The term *mata* (mother), often used as an epithet denoting female divinity, indicates the understanding that a *satimata* cares for the family amidst which she lived quite as a mother cares for children. As a *satimata*, the wife shares her husband's fate while continuing to protect her earthly household.[3]

As a transcendent being, the *satimata* personifies *saubhagya* (good fortune), for she remains married to her husband eternally. As wives live their lives day in and day out, and try to realize the *pativrata* ideal, they look to the *satimata* as a moral exemplar and they pray to her to help them acquire the fortitude essential to achieving the virtue she represents, the virtue that will make them better *pativratas*.

The notion of the *satimata* as a moral ideal and model is so prominent in the minds of her *pativrata* devotees that, however many satis might have taken their lives in a particular family, these satis are almost invariably referred to in the singular. What is important is not the individual woman who dies on a pyre but the transformative reality that her death symbolizes. Thus, generally speaking, in the context of each Rajput family, all satis eventually become *hamari satimata*, as it is said: our *satimata*.[4] Particular features associated with individual satis come to be associated with the amalgamated, condensed, singular sati personality. Instead of many satis with many stories, there is one sati who possesses many aspects.

While reflecting *pativrata* morality, the *satimata* functions as a powerful, transcendent being. She protects by warding off or curing family sickness and financial misfortune. Often, however, she intervenes in family life by issuing warnings to women that, unless they faithfully and sincerely perform domestic and religious rituals—rituals she knows they have been slighting—they and their families will suffer great misfortune. To put women on notice, the *satimata* appears in their dreams, gives them visions, or sends them bad omens.

Rajputs understand the sati tradition I have described as being overwhelmingly *their* tradition: they believe Rajput women to be uniquely capable of possessing the motivation required for a woman to become a valid sati. Of course, non-Rajput women have immolated themselves on their husbands' funeral pyres. Consequently, although all non-Rajputs understand the Hindu sati tradition to have originated with the Rajputs, and although they concede that most satis have in fact been Rajput, they claim that non-Rajput women have also become satis.

On the whole, Rajput women dismiss these supposed non-Rajput satis as insincere and pretentious women. Many imply that most non-Rajput women who have died on their husbands' pyres were only emulating Rajput satis in hopes of gaining status, prestige, and upward mobility for themselves, their families, and their *jatis* (castes).

Rajputs often point out that members of various lower castes have adopted other Rajput customs, including wearing Rajput dress, using Rajput names, and even eating meat and drinking wine, activities that Rajasthani custom specifically designates as Rajput privileges. Given the prevalence of these multiple forms of emulation, Rajput women find it unsurprising that non-Rajput women have also taken to immolating themselves, hoping to elevate their caste position and perhaps eventually allow their caste members to infiltrate Rajput ranks through marriage. Thus Rajputs say that such non-Rajput women have immolated themselves not out of devotion, but for ulterior motives; they cannot, therefore, be considered legitimate satis.

This point is crucial. According to Rajput women, merely immolating oneself does not guarantee that one will become a *satimata*. One has to have the proper motivation, which must be selfless. The aspirant must have no desire except to share her husband's fate. Because a Rajput woman naturally has this single-minded desire, she makes her *vrat* to die as a sati spontaneously. When she learns of her husband's death, she automatically (without consideration and without calculation) utters a *vrat* of sati, and so becomes a *sativrata*. Her intentions are selfless and her motives pure. Therefore, the Rajput *sativrata*'s death becomes a direct reflex of her character (*charitra*) and a manifestation of her goodness, her *sat*. This goodness or *sat* is presumed to build up easily in Rajput women because they have an inherent, caste-derived inclination to realize the role of the *pativrata*.[5] Being Rajput means knowing how to sacrifice; being predisposed to sacrifice makes Rajputs the very best wives.

This is especially significant in light of the primary meaning Rajput women attach to the sati's death: they believe that is serves as proof to the sati and to others that the sati has successfully led the life of a *pativrata*, a good wife. This proof is necessary because status as a *pativrata* is more or less uncertain during a woman's lifetime. Every wife and mother must make decisions that are unpopular. Many times a woman is unsure whether the course of action she is taking is right, particularly if it draws family criticism. By dying as a sati, however, she can be confident—and others can be confident—that she has, on the whole, made correct decisions and lived selflessly as a *pativrata*. Hence, the sati's death serves an important validating function.[6]

In the case of non-Rajput satis, however, immolation has not in and of itself served this function. For non-Rajputs, say Rajput women, validation requires additional evidence. This evidence is provided by the observed emergence from within a *sativrata*'s body of flames, which have been ignited by the fervor of moral goodness, *sat*. Here, one can see clearly that Rajputs understand goodness as being both a moral quality and a physical substance—moral fiber in the literal sense, "the right stuff." This substance manifests itself as virtue during life and as fire at the time of death.

The qualification that the wifely virtue of non-Rajputs must be seen to be believed raises an interesting practical problem. Usually a *sativrata* mounts a pyre that is already burning or is lit soon thereafter. Of course, if the *sativrata* is a Rajput, the presumption is that the fire that consumes her is not the fire lit by someone else's hand, but the internal fire of *sat*. If the *sativrata* is not a Rajput, such an assumption is not made. In that instance the flames of *sat* must be visibly distinct from the lit fire. This is a tall order, and an order seldom filled; hence, few instances of non-Rajput satis occur in Rajput tradition. There are occasional exceptions, however, and I will soon refer to one of them.

To summarize, the fundamental idea Rajputs have of the sati's death is that it represents a manifestation of the virtue of *sat*, a moral and substantive quality that is inherent but latent in the Rajput *pativrata*. *Sat* causes the *pativrata* to become a *sativrata* if her husband predeceases her, and it manifests itself in flames, which prove that the woman has been a *pativrata* even as they transform her into a *satimata*.

With this schema in mind, let us return to examine more extensively the liminal stage in the sati scenario, the *sativrata* stage. During this period a sati sets the terms of the relationship she will share with the family members whom she will later protect; she also teaches that the sati's will must be respected, and her desires remembered.

The Srap

The first way in which a *sativrata* may express her feelings is by issuing a curse. A *sativrata* pronounces a curse (*srap* or *shrap*) if she becomes angry while preparing to die. By cursing, she makes it known that some person or persons have behaved badly and that behavior of such a nature is unacceptable to her. The curse, which hangs over a family for a number of generations, usually seven, serves to encourage within it proper attitudes and activities. Some examples, stories drawn from my interviews with Rajput women in 1984–1985, follow.

The first illustrates a situation quite common in sati mythology: a situation in which someone misbehaves by interfering with a woman who has manifested her intention to die as a sati. The *sativrata* makes it clear that intervention is unacceptable, and in fact dangerous:

> There once was a *sativrata* whose relatives failed to provide her with a horse and a drummer for her sati procession. Every *sativrata* is supposed to proceed from her home to her husband's pyre in grand style. A horse and a drummer are absolute essentials. Enraged, the slighted *sativrata* cursed her husband's family to the effect that for seven generations whenever it might require a horse or drummer for ritual purposes, neither would be available.

The consequences of this *srap* were far-reaching. Both horse and drummer have always been essential to many important rituals, among them marriage and Dashara rituals.[7] Thus the sati's curse subjected the family to hardship, ableit justifiable hardship.

Besides stories that demonstrate the perils of interfering with a *sativrata*'s intentions, there are stories that tell of the fury that may be unleashed if bad behavior by a family member, even a husband, has been the reason that the *sativrata* has had to become a *sativrata*. The following narrative serves as an example:

> There once was a woman whose husband was fond of liquor. Rajputs are allowed to drink liquor. This husband, however, abused his prerogative by

overindulging regularly. This caused much unpleasantness within the family. One day while inebriated he fell off a roof and died. At that time his wife took a vow of sati. Before immolating herself, she pronounced a curse that from then on no male in the family would be allowed to drink liquor.

This story illustrates what might be called a conditional curse. It curses the family to be deprived of alcohol *or else*. Here the "or else" is an inexplicit, though apparently effective, threat. Family members say that, since the curse was pronounced, no one in their household has dared to drink. Like the first curse I described, this curse pronounces a punishment that teaches a lesson, but it is a lesson that promises further punishment if ignored or forgotten.

The third example involves a curse that is violated. As will soon be apparent, the secondary or conditional punishment implicitly established by the curse turns out to be quite severe. The story goes like this:

There once was a Rajput king who decided to get married. Not long after his wedding, he found that he liked being married so well that he wanted a second wife. When he returned home from his second wedding, however, his first wife, full of jealousy, sprang on him from behind the entryway and stabbed him to death. At that time the second wife, livid, took a vow of sati. Then later, before mounting her husband's pyre, she pronounced a curse. She said that from then on no king from that kingdom would ever be able to be married to more than one woman at the same time. Several generations later, however, a king from that family took a second bride while his first wife was still living. Not long after the wedding, he died. Since that time the curse has not been breached.

Ultimately this curse's consequence is serious: the foolhardy transgressor dies. Actually, the curse's impact is harsh even when the *srap* is not breached. Polygamy was an accepted practice, which even Rajput women today feel was necessary in times past to ensure that there would always be an heir to the throne. Back then, they say, wars, disease, and court intrigues (including not a few poisonings) depleted the population of royal heirs.

One particularly notable feature of the three *sraps* described here is that all had a major impact on women, whether or not the women were the direct cause of the sati's ire. In the first case, the absence of a horse and a drummer meant that future satis would be deprived of these. In the second, the prohibition on drinking by men caused women, although technically allowed to drink, to abandon the habit, lest their enjoyment of alcohol tempt their husbands to partake of it. In the third, the remarriage ban meant an increased possibility that adoption, one of the major sources of disharmony, intrigue, and general unpleasantness within the *zanana* (women's quarters or harem) of a traditional Rajput household—would be necessary.

Thus, the curse is not simply aimed at punishing men for what they have or have not done. It is also designed to instruct and influence women, because, as the sati paradigm teaches, a woman must always share her husband's fate. By way of further illustration, one could point to the fact that the most common curse pronounced by *sativratas* upon men with whom they are angry is infertility, yet Rajputs understand infertility as biologically a woman's problem. The result is that, however many times a cursed husband might marry, if he produces no offspring, his wives are deemed infertile. Regardless of who is targeted by sati curses, then, the lives of women are inevitably affected.

Usually when a sati utters a curse, she, targets her husband's family. In the three curses described earlier, the husband's family was targeted. Occasionally, however, satis aim their curses at other relatives. Sometimes a sati curses her husband's sisters or daughters. For example, in one royal estate, a sati cursed the daughters of her husband's family never to have both happiness and children. When the daughters married, their misfortunes traveled with them and plagued their husband's families.

Other times, a sati curses her father's family. A story that comes readily to mind is that of young girl, engaged to a prince of Mewar. Unfortunately, just after her engagement ceremony, her fiancé died. When the girl learned of his fate, she asked her father to take her to her fiancé's pyre. The father, however, was reluctant. He did not want his little girl to die.

The father and daughter argued with one another until finally the father, exasperated, said, "Very well, go ahead and kill yourself!" Then he rigged his bullock cart with a curtain so that the daughter could travel to Udaipur while maintaining *parda*, seclusion. By the time he had finished preparing the cart, however, his temper had cooled down and he was once again heavy-hearted. He simply could not bring himself to drive his daughter to Udaipur. Miraculously, however, the cart started up of its own accord and proceeded without a driver to the daughter's destination.

When the girl arrived in Udaipur, she dismounted the cart and circumambulated her fiancé's funeral pyre seven times. In this way she married her intended. Afterward, she ascended his pyre, sat down, and took her husband's head in her lap. As she did so, her body ignited spontaneously. Flames of *sat* consumed both her body and the body of her husband.

As the sati burned, she pronounced a curse on her father's family. Today no one in the family recalls the nature of that curse: family members simply say that it lasted seven generations and then lapsed. Evidently it no longer matters to them what the curse was. The important thing is that it instituted a tradition of venerating the *satimata* and of receiving the *satimata*'s protection, for the *satimata* has become its guardian.

In sum, while *sativratas* usually curse their husband's families, they may curse other related families if given cause. In either case, the *sativrata*'s curse is taken to be benevolent, instructing those whom she loves. Her curse discourages future bad behavior that would only cause the family greater heartache in the long run.

Thus, by cursing, the sati may well assume a permanent role as a protector of family health and welfare. Nevertheless, when a sati curses persons to whom she is not related it is understood that she punishes without providing protection. To outsiders, she is malevolent and vengeful. This point is illustrated beautifully by the following story told by women in one Rajput family about a Gujar woman who was a consort of one of their ancestors. When that nobleman died, the Gujar woman prepared to die as a sati. Skeptical, the daughters of the consort's family scoffed at her and said, "You won't go through with it. You're no Rajput." In effect, they felt that she lacked the requisite *sat*. Adding further insult to injury, the family priest, drummer, and barber also taunted her and refused to join her procession as they would a Rajput sati procession.

When the Gujar woman reached the *mahasatiyan*, the cremation ground, she cursed all who had ridiculed her, beginning with the daughters. She said that neither they nor daughters born to them would possess any of the three happinesses a woman wants: sons, wealth, and a decent husband. The crowd that had gathered to watch the sati's immolation was shocked by the severity of the Gujar's curse. It pleaded for mercy on behalf of the princesses. Moved, the sati reduced the sentence so that if a woman had two of these happinesses, she would be deprived of the third.

Today her family says that so far this curse has held true for six generations. It also points out that, although its daughters have suffered from this, both they and the entire family have benefitted from the sati's protection. The sati has been a good mother (*mata*) to them.

The sati also pronounced curses on the priest, the barber, and the drummer. She tailored each curse to fit its target. To the priest, who was a Brahmin, she said, " In each generation, your family will have one son and he'll be half-cracked." Brahmins are supposed to be intelligent; their traditional tasks required that they be learned if not wise. A halfwit Brahmin is thus worthless, professionally speaking.

To the barber she said, "Your family will have no sons." Many of the barber's chief ceremonial functions have to do with childbirth and its rituals. Hence once again, the curse is particularly appropriate to its target. Finally, to the drummer the sati said, "If you or your descendants are playing your drums at one end of the village, nobody will be able to hear your music at the other end of the village." All of these curses remain in effect today. The Rajput family says that it has received protection along with its problems, but the nonfamily targets have received only problems.

The last sati account is notable not only because it demonstrates the benevolence or malevolence of the sati according to the nature of her target, but also because it provides a rare example of a non-Rajput woman who is ultimately (although not easily) accepted by Rajputs as a legitimate sati. Thus the story is careful to record the witnessing of the Gujar consort's death by the crowd, who saw flames erupt from her body. Because of this testimony, the Rajput family venerates the Gujar woman as their sati. One might think that the undesirable consequences of the curse would be enough to convince the Rajputs of the Gujar's transformation, but here, as usual, the witnessing of *sat* flames is shown to be essential.

The explanation family members give of the Gujar woman's success in becoming a true sati accords with that given by Rajputs of all verified, non-Rajput satis. The Rajput family says that because the Gujar lived as part of their family and behaved as a Rajput wife—that is, as a woman selflessly devoted to her husband's welfare—she was able to improve her character, accumulate *sat*, and die as a sati in the Rajput fashion. Living in a Rajput environment, the Gujar became so "Rajputesque" that she acquired the power to die as a sati and thereafter to protect her Rajput family as a Rajput sati would. Her intentions were shown to be honest, her curse effective, and (for Rajputs) her power of protection real. Others whom she cursed were not protected. It was as if she had been adopted as a Rajput.

From these observations some conclusions can be drawn. First, we cannot understand the sati as malevolent simply because she utters a curse. We have to look at her intentions as they are understood by her protegés. In their view, the sati is malevolent toward outsiders who anger her; but she is benevolent toward insiders, relatives, for she is their mother and a mother is benevolent even when she punishes. The sati punishes to instruct her family and to correct its behavior. Her curses demonstrate her love.

Second, we must take into account the extraordinary extent to which intention is stressed by participants in the tradition. Even if a putative sati pronounces a curse that appears to be effective, the curse will not be deemed effective unless the *sativrata*'s motivations are demonstrated to be pure, either by her possession of Rajput blood or by her eruption into flames of *sat*. In short, according to the traditional perspective of Rajput women, a sati is a person impelled by virtue (*sat*) to follow her husband in death. Any other source of inspiration is thought to contaminate a woman's intentions and prevent her from becoming a true *satimata*.

The Ok

While not every *sativrata* becomes angry and pronounces a curse, every *sativrata* establishes an *ok*, which proscribes certain practices or possessions. By establishing an *ok*, a *sativrata* marks a household for protection. So long as the terms of the *ok* are remembered and respected, the sati, now a *satimata*, will ward off and dispel bad fortune.

Widespread *oks* include the following : (1) bans on the wearing of traditional colors that women wear as brides (red, rose, and magenta) and colors women wear after giving birth (bright yellow speckled with red); (2) prohibitions against certain types of jewelry associated with marriage, such as jingly ankle bracelets (*chaurasi*) and various other bracelets and bangles; (3) rules against using baby cradles. The objects that are prohibited by *oks* are almost always associated with being a wife and mother. Each of them connotes female auspiciousness, *saubhagya*. They represent marriage, sexuality, fertility.

Paradoxically, however, the observance of an *ok* is considered auspicious, for it brings a woman and her household under the protection of the *satimata*, who is, as we have seen, a paradigm of auspiciousness. On the one hand, observing an *ok* helps a woman be a *pativrata*, because worship of the *satimata* is an essential part of a woman's duty as a wife. Women are generally responsible for performing rituals that honor the *satimata* and for observing *oks*. On the other hand, observing an *ok* also causes the devotee to grow in goodness, *sat*, ultimately enabling her to become a sati should her husband predecease her.

This notion of giving up the auspicious to gain in auspiciousness is aptly illustrated by the following sati story, which combines the imposition of an *ok* with the pronouncing of a *srap*; the two are frequently, though not always, found in combination. As the tale goes, there once was a woman who, having learned of her husband's death, took a vow to die as a sati. She tried to persuade a co-wife to die as a sati with her. The co-wife replied, "I'd love to, really, but you see I have all these dishes to do, and we both know a good wife never leaves dishes undone."

The sati found this a weak excuse. She cursed the co-wife and all daughters-in-law that, from then on, no one would be able to do dishes after dinner. Here, obedience to the *srap* is also the observance of an *ok*. Doing dishes is a wife's task; it is auspicious work and an integral part of caring for a husband's family. Yet when an auspicious activity such as this becomes so important in and of itself that it interferes with a woman's vow (*vrat*) of loyalty and service to her husband, its status changes. What would have been auspicious becomes inauspicious.

The prohibitions demonstrate the assumption that items and activities associated with *saubhagya* (auspiciousness) are auspicious only if they reflect a woman's desire to fulfill her vow as a *pativrata*. If these items or activities, supposedly symbolic of *saubhagya*, are used or performed by a woman without sincere motivation to be a good wife, they become wholly inauspicious.

It is not that the items and activities themselves are inauspicious. Only their use or performance is so, for it reflects bad intentions, a lapse in the vow of total service to one's husband (*pativratya*). This distinction, subtle as it may seem, is illustrated candidly in the tradition: many items that are flatly prohibited by *oks* may actually be used if a woman's intention to revere her *satimata* is demonstrated in related way. Thus women whose families are not supposed to possess baby cradles almost always borrow baby cradles from others. The borrowing is understood as a tribute to the *satimata*. In borrowing rather than buying a baby cradle, the woman shows that she remembers her obligation to the *satimata*, and thus displays the purity of her motivation to be a good *pativrata*.

In a similar practice, women who are not allowed to wear certain kinds of jewelry may actually wear such jewelry if they receive it as a present from someone outside the conjugal family. In not buying the jewelry but waiting to receive it from her parents, say, a woman shows that she respects the jewelry *ok* and the *satimata* who imposed it and that she intends to be faithful to the ideal that the *satimata* represents.

In sum, the traditions of *srap* and *ok* require that family members remember and respect the sacrifices that satis have made. When I speak of sacrifice in this context, I do not refer simply to the *balidan* itself—"suttee," the ritual sacrifice in which a woman immolates herself. True, self-immolation is the central event that sati tradition celebrates, but it is not the only sacrifice venerated within the tradition. The act of self-immolation is really only the culmination of a series of sacrifices performed throughout life by a *pativrata* who has thus built up stores of explosive moral substance, *sat*. Similarly, through a network of *sraps* and *oks*, it creates occasions for many other sacrifices to be performed.

By remembering the sacrifices that satis have made, Rajput family members seek to imbibe the spirit of sacrifice that has encouraged men and women to perform their duties properly. Not only does the sati influence family fortune through direct intervention in its affairs, she also serves as a paradigm of selflessness. Thus, like the hero who falls in battle, the sati stands for a way of life, a way of life informed by values that are only slowly changing to suit changing social norms and circumstances.

Notes

1. More extensive treatment of traditional sati veneration in Rajasthan can be found in Harlan, *Religion and Rajput Women: The Ethic of Protection in Contemporary Narratives* (Berkeley: University of California Press, 1992).

2. The self-immolation of the Rajput village woman, Roop Kanwar, on her husband's funeral pyre in September 1987 has brought international attention to the ongoing veneration of *satimatas*, as in the present volume.

3. David Mitten has discussed a parallel dual locality of familial spirits in ancient Greek conceptions of the afterlife. See Mitten, "Aspects of Meaning in Greek Burial Customs," paper presented at the conference, "Representations of Death," Harvard University, November 4, 1988. For similar reflections on Maharashtrian tribal culture, see Günther-Dietz Sontheimer, "The Religion of the Dhangar Nomads," in Eleanor Zelliot and Maxine Berntsen, eds., *The Experience of Hinduism* (Albany: SUNY Press, 1988), p. 115.

4. Similar observations are made about other classes of ancestors in rural Rajasthan by Ann Grodzins Gold in *Fruitful Journeys: The Ways of Rajasthani Pilgrims* (Berkeley: University of California Press, 1988), p. 91. This collectivization of spirits does not occur in the case of aristocratic Rajput hero spirits (*jhunjhars* and *virs*). See Harlan, *Religion and Rajput Women*, p. 178.

5. For a general discussion of caste norms understood as being transmitted genetically, see McKim Marriott and Ronald B. Inden, "Towards an Ethnosociology of South Asian Caste Systems," in Kenneth David, ed., *The New Wind: Changing Identities in South Asia* (The Hague: Mouton Publishers, 1977), pp. 227–38.

6. For further discussion of the probative value of death scenarios, see Harlan, "Abandoning Shame: Mira Bai's Bad Behavior," paper presented to the Association for Asian Studies, Washington, D.C., March 17, 1989.

7. Dashara is a holiday celebrating the defeat of the demon Ravana by Rama, the hero of the *Rāmayāṇa*. The principal rituals performed on this day by Rajputs are the cleaning of weapons and the veneration of horses.

Comment:
Good Mothers and Bad Mothers
in the Rituals of Sati

KAREN MCCARTHY BROWN

In September of 1987, thousands gathered to watch Roop Kanwar, an eighteen-year-old Rajput woman, burn to death on her husband's funeral pyre. A shrine, built on the site in the town of Deorala, was for a time, at least, the center of intense devotional and political activity. The shocking nature of the event, as well as its obvious social and religious power, demands explanation. The sati of Roop Kanwar may be understood variously as an expression of Rajput chauvinism during a period of social and economic flux, an assertion of Indian traditionalism and nationalism against the forces of modernity and Westernization, and a handy means of enforcing social norms and keeping women in their place. Somewhat on the side, the revivification of the sati cult allows Marwari businessmen to make a profit, build important networks between their urban business centers and their rural homelands, and share in the machismo glory of the warrior caste, an increasingly important ingredient in the generalized male image in modern India. Thus sati is not simply a religious ritual; it is a confluence of religious, political, and social ideologies.[1]

Setting Roop Kanwar's death in a complex matrix of social, political, and economic forces, and then placing that in conversation with Rajput gender roles and certain Hindu beliefs appropriately demystifies the event. It sweeps away much of the smoke and shadow (often rank with sentimentality) and allows the rawer dynamics of the event to emerge. It makes Roop Kanwar's immolation an event within its time and place, but it does not explore the reasons for the gender roles and religious beliefs that allow a sati to function as the organizing metaphor for such varied problems and issues.

I am an outsider to Indian Studies. I have never visited India, let alone carried out field research there. Yet the first time I heard Roop Kanwar's story, it was not lack of understanding I experienced but an instant stab of recognition. Cultural relativity and the importance of understanding context are key principles for me in my own fieldwork situation in the Caribbean. I am much more flexible and tolerant with Haitians than I am, for example, with my own family or my university colleagues. I withhold judgment longer and work harder to understand the cultural context of actions that, on the surface, I find offensive. Yet there have been times when this carefully cultivated attitude could not staunch a rush of judgment. It happened once in Haiti when I witnessed a brutal instance of domestic violence. I reacted without a second's analytic pause. My reaction was equally quick when I read the *New York Times* account of Roop Kanwar's sati. I immediately saw it as an instance of a people acting out its deep-seated hatred and fear of women. While I never felt that the context was irrelevant, I did not think I needed to know much about it to make such a diagnosis.

Therefore, as the nonspecialist in this group, I have chosen to respond to Lindsey Harlan's rich phenomenology of sati in Rajasthan by addressing sati on common human ground. I want to consider it as an extreme example of misogyny—the cultural component that comes as close as any I know to being a human universal.

There is another way to describe what I propose to do here. I want to ask why and how the burning of a young woman could come to be a powerfully articulate symbol, one capable of drawing to itself—like a magnet—a diverse collection of social, political, and economic agitations and, in turn, making each of them more articulate. Answering this question requires beginning at a level of human universality. It requires looking at the special vulnerability that accrues to women because they bear and, for the most part, rear children. The specifics of childbearing and childrearing in India will then emerge as variations on a common human theme, variations that help explain the particular tone and direction misogyny takes in modern India.

We human beings, unlike other animals, are born almost entirely unprepared to deal with our environment. Our entry into the world is marked by a long period of profound and mute dependence, and a woman presides over this fearsome vulnerability. Dorothy Dinnerstein describes it this way:

> The mother is in a literal sense, not just a figurative one, . . . in charge of the most intimate commerce between the child and the environment: the flow of substances between the flesh and the world. The infant gets from her the stuff that goes into its body and gives to her the stuff that comes out of it. And the sense of her presence—carnally apprehended in rocking and crooning, in cuddling and mutual gazing—is what makes the world feel safe. Separation from the touch, smell, taste, sound, sight of her is the forerunner of all isolation, and it eventually stands as the prototype of our fear of the final isolation. . . . In the body's pain, which it is up to the mother to prevent, is all the terror of annihilation. The sinking sense of falling—loss of maternal support—is the permanent archetype of catastrophe.[2]

The mothers we all carry within us are, by definition, both good mothers and bad mothers:

> It is in interaction with woman that the child makes another basic carnal discovery: that the body's love of pleasure, and its vulnerability to deprivation and pain, can subject the person who inhabits it to the dominations of another person's opposing will. The least coercive of mothers must sometimes restrain an infant's movements, or make it wait against its wishes. . . .[3]

And from such inevitabilities, when experienced in the oceanic space of infancy—a timeless, wordless world of unbounded emotion—comes the image of mother as rapacious, polluting, and death-dealing.

A human being's attitude about the basic safety of the world is thus shaped in an intimate, fleshly, preverbal conversation with a woman's body. The maternal presence is, furthermore, so thoroughly enmeshed with the infantile world that a child's first experiences of pain and loss are, by default, experiences of her. As adults, we carry the inchoate memories of these primal moments of safety and panic, consolation and loss within us. They are the deep waters rushing through the basements of our carefully constructed edifices of culture and self.

It is not that these currents are more important than all others in shaping adult life. Most of the time we manage to stay on dry ground and act out of places in ourselves that can be influenced by later experiences, as well as by reason and personal and communal values. Yet, when stress mounts sufficiently, when fear grows and generalizes itself, and most of all when need for reassurance is profound enough, we plummet into these chaotic waters and the problems of the moment assume an aura of boundless infantile need and fear. At such times, something must be done about the Mother, and no other solution will suffice.

In the Marwari businessman's envy of the accouterments of *kshatriya* manhood; in the loss of Rajput hegemony as the larger world encroaches on Deorala; in the precarious jockeying for power characteristic of the nationalist arena; and in the disorientating incursions of Western culture and modern life—in such things begin the "sinking sense of falling" that Dinnerstein argues is always, at some level, felt as a loss of maternal support. When the immediate circumstances that cause those feelings cannot be controlled, there are always women around who can be. When it seems as if catastrophe might be lurking around the next corner, keeping women in their place—doing what they are supposed to be doing—can make the world feel safer.[4]

It is every woman's special vulnerability to carry (at least potentially) for every other human being in her world something of an aura of the mythic good and bad mothers. This is what makes women the frequent scapegoats of individual and social pathology. Turning women into scapegoats for needs and fears whose roots drink from the deep waters of helpless infancy produces complex ritual forms in which the victim is forced to act out good and bad mother roles simultaneously. Just as devotees insist that a widow's pure devotion to her husband propels her toward sati (if it is a "true sati"), so rapists frequently insist that their victims express pleasure and arousal. Yet both rituals are patently punitive at the same time. Just as a Hindu woman may be held morally responsible if her husband predeceases her, so the victim of rape is told by the rapist (and too frequently also by the general public) that she brought it on herself. The two-sided nature of both these "rituals" allows for punishing the bad mother while, at the same time, calling on the good mother to give assurances that the world is ultimately safe and the raging infant still lovable.

While sati and rape may share some basic psychodynamics, they are also profoundly different. Sati is a public event, a type of ritualized theodicy, a religious drama called into being by the most threatening of human realities, death itself. As such, the rare occurrence of sati can speak meaningfully about many different types of loss and do so to large numbers of people. A religious event, unlike a political or social one, directly addresses our multilayered selves. With touch and taste, sound and smell, image and act, religion can give solace to the screaming, preverbal infant as well as to the frightened adult. Religion binds the whole together. The richly sensual character of Hindu ritualizing adds an important nuance to this picture and suggests that Hinduism may be especially proficient at addressing the preverbal levels of psyche and society.

The particular forms of childbearing and childrearing in India add further nuances. In *The Inner World: A Psycho-analytic Study of Childhood and Society in India*, Sudhir Kakar argues that the bond between Indian mothers and children is especially intense and long-lasting for several reasons. First, the mother–child bond is strong because, in India, a woman's worth tends to be defined by her ability to bear children. The arrival of a child, particularly a son, saves a young bride from the suspicion and even open hostility that are frequently occasioned by her arrival in her husband's extended-family home. Women thus hold tightly to their children, because, to some extent, they experience them as saviors.[5] The second reason for such strong mother–child bonding is the prolonged period of infancy characteristic of Indian childrearing. Kakar says that the Indian child does not experience any significant separation from the intense, intimate, and exclusive bond it has with its mother until the age of four or five. These early years are characterized by the nearly constant presence of the mother and by large amounts of physical interaction with her. During this same period, according to Kakar, the father generally plays "no significant caretaking role."[6] The third reason concerns Indian women's attitude toward developmental tasks. Kakar says that Indian mothers tend to be relaxed and accepting of the vicissitudes of childhood, following the child's inclinations in such things as weaning and toilet training, rather than imposing rules and limits of their own. Indian children, Kakar reports, routinely breastfeed until the age of two or three, but "it is not uncommon to see a five or six year old peremptorily lift up his [sic] mother's blouse for a drink."[7] Kakar concludes: "the Indian infant's experience of his [sic] mother is a heady one, his contact with her is of an intensity and duration that differentiate it markedly from the experience of infancy in western worlds."[8] From this configuration of the infant's world, Kakar sees strong images of both the good mother and the bad mother emerging, and he traces each type to multiple locations in Hindu mythology.[9]

In India, the expectations placed on women to offer selfless nurturance are great. The Hindu ideal of the *pativrata*, the self-sacrificing wife, mythologically represented through such characters as Sita and Parvati, is an especially potent expression of this expectation. And as might be expected, the fear that the mothering one will not give food but, instead, turn others into food for herself (think of the rapacious Kali) is equally great.

When viewed from a psychological perspective, such as the one I have suggested here, the symbolic language of sati opens up in a new way. A dialectical tension between images of woman—nurturer on the one hand, devourer on the other—reveals itself to be at the heart of sati practice. The drama of sati is shown to take place in the midst of a dense choreography of images of the eaters and the eaten, the consumers and the consumed. These images are transparent to the sort of infantile vulnerability experienced by all human beings, but they also gain specificity and intensity from the prolonged breastfeeding and strong mother–child bonding characteristic of India. The data in Lindsey Harlan's paper offer abundant illustrations in support of this analysis. Harlan has provided a text that makes it possible to read this subtext clearly.

The good wife, the *pativrata*, stands at the center of the sati drama. According to Harlan, the good wife offers her husband two kinds of protection: service and ritual austerities. The latter are vows, "most of which involve fasting." Through these dual activities—giving to him and withholding from herself—the wife assures her husband (and herself) that she is a self-sacrificing nurturer, one who has no hunger, need, or will of her own that could interfere with her caring for him. In other words, she shows herself to be a good mother.

But the good wife becomes frighteningly anomalous without her husband. Whereas before whatever she consumed, literally and figuratively, could be understood as fuel for further acts of self-sacrifice, as a widow she threatens to become a consumer of family resources, literally and figuratively, in her own right and for her own purposes. Whereas before her will (another form of hunger) was contained by being subject to that of her husband, there is now a danger that it may break loose, untempered by larger family agendas.

And this is exactly what happens during the liminal period in the sati rituals when a woman is a *sativrata*, one who has taken a vow to commit sati but has not yet carried it through. For the short period of time during which she is a *sativrata*, the woman gains a power and autonomy she knew at no other point in her life. "During this period," Harlan says, "a sati sets the terms of the relationship she will share with the family members whom she will later protect; she also teaches that the sati's will must be respected, and her desire remembered." In the transformation that occurs when a woman becomes a *sativrata*, a powerful social secret is briefly vented. Good mothers can also be bad mothers. Women have wills of their own. The *sativrata* becomes dangerous (she is said to be literally too hot to touch) and punitive. Against anyone who angers her, she delivers a curse (*srap*). Furthermore, she is expected to place prohibitions (*oks*) on the activities of the very family that until recently confined and restricted her. But the secret of the bad mother is like a scary truth whispered quickly through a small crack in the ritual process. The bad mother fully emerges only for a brief moment and in ways that are ritually contained (she dies shortly after issuing her curses and proscriptions) and later rationalized (her curses are said to be blessings in disguise). As Harlan puts it, "a mother is benevolent even when she punishes."

On rare occasions a woman takes a vow to commit sati and is prevented from going through with it. This might happen because a family fears breaking the law or, in a few cases, because the woman is needed in the home. When the family prevents her sati, the woman may nevertheless become a "living *satimata*." Harlan tells a story about such a woman who proved her virtue by miraculously needing to consume no food. This widow, confined to a tiny room, resolutely refused to eat any of the food offered to her, but did give blessings to all who came to see her.[10] The woman earned the title of living *satimata* by acting out the part of a good mother. She denied herself but served others; she never took but always gave; she never consumed but nourished all who came to her.

When the sati event is actually carried through, as the *sativrata* mounts the funeral pyre, the dialogue between consumer and consumed, devourer and devoured becomes more convoluted and more highly charged. The bad mother, who made a brief appearance through the curses and prohibitions of the *sativrata*, has now retreated from the foreground. Her rapacious presence is still felt, however, beneath the increasingly intense images of beatific female self-sacrifice. For example, from the moment a woman takes a vow of sati, a process of self-devouring is said to begin. Harlan notes the belief that when a woman, on hearing of the death of her husband, utters the spontaneous vow that she will die with him, her *sat* (virtue) begins to heat up and "consume her body." This same *sat* is believed to ignite the funeral pyre and finally consume both husband and wife. But this does not happen until, as the devotional images of Roop Kanwar show, she mounts the funeral pyre and takes the body of her husband into her lap, in a breastfeeding posture. Then, as Harlan characterizes it, "her body explodes into flames, and these cremate her own body and the body of her husband."

As he feeds on her, she eats him up and, most important, devours herself as well. The nurturing woman and the devouring woman become one through a process in which fire transforms the rapacious, willful bad mother (who made an uncharacteristically direct appearance lest anyone should miss that she was there) into a self-devouring good mother. When woman's power is safely turned back against herself, the net result is that the bad mother gets burned up while the good mother survives. But the good woman who survives is very different from the one who mounted the funeral pyre.

The flames purge the actual woman of any blame in her husband's death. He did not die because her *sat* was insufficient. On the contrary, they both burned because her virtue was so great. Yet even as the good mother triumphs, the individual woman, who momentarily incarnated her, disappears. As Harlan reports, "satis are almost invariably referred to in the singular. What is important is not the individual woman who dies on a pyre but the transformative reality that her death symbolizes." The flames transform the untrustworthy, fallible, particular human woman into a safe, infallible, generalized, transcendent mother called Sati.

While much more detail could be added to this analysis, I think the point has been made: whatever else the rituals of sati are about, they are surely about "Mommy" and about putting Mommy in her place.

Notes

1. Sudesh Vaid and Kumkum Sangari, "Institutions, Beliefs, Ideologies: Widow Immolation in Contemporary Rajasthan," *Economic and Political Weekly* 26:17 (April 27, 1991), especially pp. WS-14–16; also, Madhu Kishwar and Ruth Vanita, "The Burning of Roop Kanwar," *Manushi* 42–43 (1987), pp. 15–25.

2. Dorothy Dinnerstein, *The Mermaid and the Minotaur* (San Francisco: Harper & Row, 1976), p. 131.

3. Dinnerstein, *Mermaid*, p. 132.

4. To some extent women, as well as men, support this maneuver. Women and men gathered to watch Roop Kanwar burn, and women are often eager devotees at sati shrines. Women have mothers just as men do, and they too hold deep in themselves a view of woman as a combination of a pure goddess, totally selfless and nurturant, and a polluting, rapacious witch. But women do not write the culture script (empathy alone might have prevented them from including the chapter on sati), even though they have to live (and sometimes die) on its terms.

5. Sudhir Kakar, *The Inner World: A Psycho-analytic Study of Childhood and Society in India* (Delhi: Oxford University Press, 2d ed., 1981), p. 79.

6. Kakar, *Inner World*, pp. 79–80.

7. Kakar, *Inner World*, pp. 80–81.

8. Kakar, *Inner World*, p. 80.

9. Kakar makes a connection between mythic images of the good mother and the extraordinary degree to which Indian women conform their lives to their children's needs. He also argues that these same childrearing practices create generalized Indian personality traits, principally trust in the world and openness to others. But Kakar attributes mythic images of the bad mother to a destructive pattern in which frustrated women overwhelm their children with needs that could more appropriately be met by their husbands, if it were not for the dense extended-family context in which marital life must be negotiated. While I find Kakar's connections between women's social roles and mythic images generally quite enlight-

ening, because of the near universality of the bad mother image, I find Dinnerstein's argument for the etiology of this image more convincing; it stresses the inevitability that a child will experience pain and frustration with even the best of mothering.

10. Lindsey Harlan, personal communication, September 27, 1988.

4

The Roop Kanwar Case: Feminist Responses

VEENA TALWAR OLDENBURG

On September 5, 1987, in Jaipur, Bal Singh Rathore and Sneh Kanwar discovered that their eighteen-year-old daughter Roop Kanwar—married only eight months before—had suddenly been widowed and then cremated along with the corpse of her husband in the manner of a sati in the village of Deorala, a two-hour drive away. They read this piece of information in the local Hindi language daily; they had not been informed either of the death of their son-in-law in a hospital in the district headquarters in Sikar, nor of their daughter's wish to die as a sati on her husband's funeral pyre. They were later persuaded by Roop Kanwar's in-laws that their daughter had, over efforts to dissuade her, chosen this way to die.

Under usual circumstances, this brief newspaper report would have caused little stir, not unlike the forty other cases of sati-style deaths recorded since 1947, when India became an independent and secular republic. Some twenty-eight of these have occurred in Rajasthan, mainly in and around Sikar district. What made the profound difference this time was the activism and concern of women. Arguably, the Roop Kanwar case has converted the idea that a woman can become (an alleged) sati—and be glorified for it—from a residual quasi-religious theme into a critical political issue on which women's voices were heard for the very first time.

In the colonial period it was chiefly men—Hindu reformers and British officials—who debated, and the East India Company that eventually legislated, to abolish the practice in 1829. The Maharaja of Amber and Jaipur followed the company's lead in 1846. He banned the practice in his kingdom, as did eighteen other princely states in the Rajputana Agency. The Indian Penal Code, as revised in the early 1950s, did not incorporate the East India Company regulation. The presumption was that its sections on murder and abetment to suicide (sections 302 and 306, respectively) would be enough to deal with such a happening, and therefore no explicit reference to the custom of sati was made.

This implicit redefinition of sati as a crime is accepted by women opposed to the custom—they deem it to be murder or abetted suicide—and sati has, quite properly, no separate place in the penal code of a secular state. The redefinition also ought to have eliminated the possibility of further debate on the authenticity of such an event and on whether or not it enjoys scriptural sanction, issues much discussed and presumably settled before legislation was hammered out in 1829. With the law in place and enforced, the act of committing sati—whether the widow's participation was voluntary or coerced— was shorn of all mystification, glory, glamour, and ritual significance, and adjudged to be simply a crime. Those implicated in it would be equally punished by death or life imprisonment. After its abolition and an initial upsurge of incidents, the practice of sati faded into a very rare crime; and statistically speaking, today it is rarer still. Nonetheless, satis did still occur. The Roop Kanwar death mobilized feminists and liberals to ensure that the present crime and all others like it be punished, so that even a single sati would become unthinkable in the future in Rajasthan or anywhere else in India. On the other end of the spectrum of opinion are conservatives who believe that Roop Kanwar heroically sacrificed her own life, in keeping with the ideology of sati, which finds honor and pride in the most painful and brutal of deaths—the burning of a woman on her deceased husband's funeral pyre.

The purpose of this essay is to summarize the Indian feminists' response to Roop Kanwar's death.[1] This response has come in the shape of active protests, detailed reports of the knowable facts, and a stream of analytical articles. I expect to tell the story of the event as it emerges from this literature, which is published in English, and to distill its substantive and interpretive points. Before proceeding, however, a caveat is in order, and a word of preparation.

First the caveat: I use the word *feminist* advisedly, although I am more than aware that it is not accepted by some of the women activists and scholars whose work is reviewed in this essay. It is rejected by these women on the grounds that the term has specific meanings that grew out of the experience of women activists in the West, and that it is therefore unsuitable in the Indian context. I believe this is mistaken. Feminism has a long history and is no longer monolithic; multiple feminisms abound, and *feminism* is capable of the same kinds of distinctions one would expect in any analysis of the word *patriarchy*. I define the word *feminist* in its simplest political sense, as a person (and not necessarily a woman) whose analytical perspective is informed by an understanding of the relationship between power and gender in any historical, social, or cultural context. To me, the argument against using the word *feminist* is weakened by the fact that terms and theories of equally Western provenance—*Marxist, socialist, Freudian,* or *post-structuralist*—do not arouse similar indignation and are in fact (over) used as standard frameworks for analyses of Indian society by Indian scholars. I rather suspect that gender analysis will one day trip off the scholarly tongue with the same panache as class analysis does now in Indian academic and activist circles; in the meantime, I will take my chances.

My second preliminary comment has to do with background. Historians are indispensable when a custom or tradition is being bruited about as a timeless phenomenon, and sati is clearly believed by many to be a Hindu tradition with such credentials. Therefore, before launching into my review of contemporary feminist reactions to the Roop Kanwar episode, I urge the reader to consult the account that has been provided by the leading historian of India, Romila Thapar. Her essay, entitled "In History," appears in the excellent issue of the journal *Seminar* which is devoted to sati (February 1988). This essay was prompted by Roop Kanwar's death; and although it does not deal directly with the event, it puts us in a position to appreciate both the discursive and material aspects of the response to it, providing a solid background to frame the contemporary event and gently but firmly clearing away the historical misinformation and misinterpretations that nonhistorians have produced in their own attempts to put the Roop Kanwar case into perspective.[2] Authoritative, rigorous, and elegant, Thapar's essay may be read in conjunction with my own historical construction of "The Continuing Invention of the Sati Tradition" in this volume. As one moves closer in time and space to the Roop Kanwar case, one should consult the work of Sudesh Vaid, whose detailed historical analysis of sati in the Shekhavati region provides the tools for best understanding the Roop Kanwar sati and the larger pattern to which her immolation belongs.[3]

After reading many reports of Roop Kanwar's death, it is possible to conclude that gender-sensitive scholars and activists in India—whatever their disagreements on a wide range of issues that concern women—are of one mind about the tragic end of Roop Kanwar. The consensus is profound; the analyses differ only in the method or details they choose to emphasize.

Feminists are united, first and foremost, in denouncing the event as one among many crimes against women. They do not admit any obfuscating rhetoric about whether this event was or was not an "authentic" sati;

coercion or consent is not really relevant to their formulations of the problem. Their concern is about the women involved—their lives, the pain they endure, the cruelty and barbarity they experience, and the resultant negation of the meaning of their separate existence. It is not far-fetched to say that feminists would be steadfast in their view of sati even if Roop Kanwar's volition could be established without doubt, by some magical replay of linear time. For them, sati as an issue was settled 175-odd years ago; the question is why it is still allowed to persist. Feminists unanimously reject the glorification that follows an alleged sati, what with the endowment of commemorative shrines and temples and the holding of festivals and anniversaries. They also continue to work hard to counter the propaganda in the media that represented Roop Kanwar as a symbol of an alleged ideal of Hindu womanhood—chaste, devoted, and able to sacrifice her very life for her husband. This propaganda is part of the agenda of the Bharatiya Janata Party, which has become the leading opposition party in the Indian Parliament by touting an essentialized and homogenized Hinduism while projecting itself as the defender of a beleaguered faith.

Another common strand is feminists' anger at the reactions of governments at the state and federal levels. Rajiv Gandhi's Congress government in New Delhi is sharply criticized, first for its apathy toward or tacit approval of the event, then for its ineptitude in trying to prevent the site of the sati from becoming a shrine for the offerings of the multitudes that converged on Deorala, and finally for its pernicious policy of giving in to demands by religious extremists to destroy the secular foundations of the constitution of India. All the reports also see caste more than class as the decisive factor behind the incident. They allege a conspiracy among the three dominant castes, which moved in swiftly to capitalize on the alleged sati. They blame Rajput men for using women's lives as the means of propping up old chivalric traditions in a time when they are otherwise disenfranchised. They censure the Marwari businessmen for imitating and supporting these traditions in their quest for status and power and for contributing their wealth and commercial acumen to perpetuate this custom. And they hold Brahmins responsible for lending an air of legitimacy to the ethos of sati as a way to bolster their own dwindling importance in the modern world. Through the efforts of these three castes, a combination of patriarchal values and opportunistic greed approves the event and orchestrates its aftermath by converting the site of the cremation into a shrine, inventing a *chunari* (veil) festival to glorify the painful death of a woman, and assisting a prosperous but undistinguished village to become a pilgrimage site. Finally, most feminists are agreed that, although each sati is projected as a rare and spontaneous happening, nonetheless all satis share a common plot or script, as well as the costuming and dramatization necessary to make sati a riveting spectacle for those who witness it. Witnesses affirm the nature of the event as religious; their gaze makes it sati. I would add that the event also reinforces the base appetites of the male members of the audience to see women suffer, while in women sati confirms the ideology that women's strength lies in the act of sacrifice and the endurance of untold pain.

Feminists have pointed out that, as the news media lost interest in the issue, the battle of words finally narrowed into a duel between pro- and anti-sati scholars, unwittingly mimicking the tradition-versus-modernity debate on what British bureaucrats termed "social evils" in India in the colonial period. That debate pitted orthodox Hindu religionists against Hindu liberal reformers and British utilitarian-evangelicals.[4] The former, who were temporarily eclipsed by the secular thrust of the Nehruvian era, have forcefully reappeared and been joined by scholars who defend sati as a widow's unique act of sacrifice incomprehensible to modern women. The latter groups have been replaced by feminists and secularists who are irate to see such a practice make a comeback, albeit in a modernized form.

All this has finally moved the sati debate from its familiar rut of profit and patriarchy onto new ground, where questions about women's subjectivity, about pain and suffering, and about culturally constructed and gendered notions of volition and sacrifice are explicitly asked. This last twist in the feminist argument has rescued the debate from being a mere replay of its nineteenth-century predecessor. The fact that women are now speaking for their sisters, who could not, may finally unmake the tradition of sati.

Feminists in Jaipur were alerted to the death of Roop Kanwar by the report of the first journalist who arrived in Deorala, Tej Pal Saini of the *Rashtradoot*, a newspaper that covers Sikar district.[5] He probably did not realize that he had fired the opening salvo of a debate that was going to rage in the print media for years. Interpreting his mission as the need to establish whether or not Roop Kanwar's death was a "voluntary" or "authentic" sati, he visited Deorala for a week, interviewing all the relatives, friends, and other inhabitants of the village, and firmly concluded that the act was indeed voluntary. *India Today*, a major fortnightly newsmagazine, sent out its hounds, who later confirmed this view. An early editorial in the Hindi daily *Jansatta*, widely distributed in north India, wrote a ringing approval of the live burning:

> Roop Kanwar did not become a sati because someone threatened her. . . . [S]he purposely followed the tradition of sati which is found in the Rajput families of Rajasthan. Even among Rajasthan's Rajputs sati is no ordinary event. Out of hundreds of thousands of widows perhaps one would resolve on a sati. It is quite natural that her self-sacrifice should become the centre of reverence and worship. This therefore cannot be called a question of women's civil rights or sexual discrimination. It is a matter of a society's religious and social beliefs. . . .

People who accept that this life is the beginning and the end, and see the greatest happiness in their own individual happiness and pleasure, will never understand the practice of sati. . . . The practice of sati should now be totally reexamined. But this is not the right of people who neither know nor understand the faith and belief of the masses of India.[6]

This editorial summed up the general pro-sati, anti-woman, conservative position. The day after its publication, about fifty angry women stormed into the offices of *Jansatta*, besieged the author of the article, and obtained the right to publish a rebuttal in the same paper. The ensuing debate was defined by these reports, and a nation of historical amnesiacs ardently resumed the old arguments about voluntary versus coerced sati.

Among the first feminists to respond to the event was Dr. Sharada Jain, an activist, scholar, and teacher based in Jaipur. She was part of the delegation representing three women's organizations that called on Hardeo Joshi, the chief minister of Rajasthan, two days after the event. They reminded him that sati was a crime and urged prompt and stern action against the culprits, but were coolly and quickly dismissed. They did not fail to press the view that, as Sharada Jain put it, "Roop Kanwar's death could not have been an act of free will. She was murdered."[7] In a chronology of the first few weeks after the event (including feminist responses to it), published in Bombay's *Economic and Political Weekly*, Sharada Jain and two colleagues pose what was to become the central question for feminists regarding the issue of sati:

Why was the burning of a girl [sic] described as "sati" and not as "murder" even in the first press reporting? Even if the overt "form" of a widow being dressed up and being take to the funeral pyre with ostentatious celebration camouflaged the crime for the simple-minded, tradition-oriented villagers, why was the official perception not that of a violation of a law? . . . [T]he episode cannot be viewed as emerging out of an "illiterate", backward situation. Ironically, not only are Roop Kanwar's family and Maal Singh's father educated (in the conventional sense of the word), but she too had received formal education up to class ten. . . . This exposes the hollowness of the entire educational engagement, which leaves basic attitudes untouched.

The climax of the horror story in fact lies not in Deorala, or even in other parts of Rajasthan. It lies in the elitist "distanced" quarters. It is from the urban-educated elite that the oft repeated question came: "Did Roop Kanwar commit sati of her own will or was she forced?" If, even at this level, the utter irrelevance of the question is not clear and if, even here, the condemnation or approval of the event depends on an answer to this question, then the focus of action has to be deliberated on with great care.[8]

These were the issues Jain and her delegation brought before the Rajasthan chief minister as well. They culminated in two unambiguous demands: one, that the alleged sati be named and booked as murder, and not abetment to suicide; and two, that the public celebrations planned for the *chunari mahotsav* (a ritual held on the thirteenth day after the cremation, when a red veil is placed on a trident at the site) be prevented. Both demands were ignored; but a case for abetment to suicide was registered the next day, and Roop Kanwar's fifteen-year-old brother-in-law was arrested. Yet the excitement over the planned *chunari* ceremony ballooned unchecked as news of the now "miraculous" sati, with burgeoning anecdotal evidence, spread from the village to the district, the state, New Delhi, and beyond. Several newspapers carried daily descriptions of the feverish anticipation of the *chunari* ceremony that probably served as unwitting advertisement for the action to come. Approximately 10,000 pilgrims were debouched daily from trucks, buses, and camel carts, and many traveled miles on foot to gather in the village of Deorala for the forthcoming ceremony, while the state government did nothing. The event also became a commercial opportunity, as crudely cut and pasted photographs of Roop Kanwar, often with her husband Mal Singh, were reprinted as lurid posters and icons for sale. Her marital home, particularly the bedroom she had shared with her husband, became consecrated as a site for pilgrims to view. Stalls selling sati memorabilia and snacks mushroomed, while thousands of handbills informing the visitors of the *chunari* ceremony were systematically distributed. An obscure village was ready for an obscurantists' carnival.

Four days before the *chunari* ceremony was to take place, seven women's groups in Rajasthan serving rural and urban constituencies came together for the first time to plan joint action. They agreed to condemn the barbaric murder of Roop Kanwar publicly and to appeal to citizens at large to demand immediate and appropriate action against the crime. They also planned to hold a public demonstration on September 14 to demand that the chief minister enforce the law and stop the planned celebrations on September 16. They sent telegrams to the prime minister, Rajiv Gandhi, and to Margaret Alva, the minister of state for Women's Welfare, since the state government had virtually abetted the glorification of sati by its silence and inaction. According to Rajasthan state's own standard procedures, the offenders should have been charged under the Indian Penal Code, and the worship of the sati and the collection of donations should have been prohibited. By allowing thousands to congregate in Deorala, by sending messages to permit restricted numbers to worship at the site, and by failing to forestall the *chunari* ceremony, the chief minister proved his credentials as a puppet of Rajiv Gandhi's central government, which was unwilling to offend the powerful Rajput lobby in Rajasthan.

The anti-sati demonstration in Jaipur on September 14 was a small affair in contrast to the milling, jostling crowds in Deorala. About 350 people, including members of thirteen women's organizations, journalists,

scholars, college and university teachers, students, actors, and other pro-
fessionals—people of all castes and creeds—marched in silence under a
relentless midday sun to the state legislature. Their memorandum was finally
accepted by a bureaucrat, because the elected leaders of the state (the chief
minister and his cabinet) were curiously unavailable; even the women
ministers showed little courage and did not meet the protestors, who waited
for hours for them to appear. And while the government displayed "a total
absence of political will" and disowned all responsibility to enforce the law,
a "culture of silence emerged among the prominent citizens and intellectuals
(barring the few who had joined the march)."[9] This deliberate occlusion
forced the next step: the feminist leaders decided to make a last-ditch appeal
to the Jaipur high court, before it closed at five o'clock that evening, to direct
the state government to prohibit the glorification ceremonies to be held two
days later in Deorala, on the grounds that they were illegal. The next day,
September 15, the advocate for the women's groups persuaded the bench to
admit the petition and to direct the state government to ensure that no public
function be held in Deorala.

This injunction finally elicited a statement from the chief minister. He
conceded that the act in Deorala had been "unlawful and improper."[10] But
this statement failed to spur a resolutely inert government to take any steps
to prevent the *chunari* ceremony; indeed, to the contrary, many members of
the Rajasthan Legislative Assembly proceeded to join the throng that had
gathered in Deorala. This provoked hitherto uncommitted scholars and
teachers to join the discussions that the women's groups were holding on the
subject of sati the same evening. Their indignation was compounded by the
fact that the state had accepted this murder as a matter of religious and
communal pride for the Rajputs. Rajput youth were out in force, brandish-
ing swords, to protect the site of the cremation. That the event in Deorala
was not a religious matter but a question of women's social identity and
status was the crux of the deliberations by the women's groups.

Margaret Alva chose to express her belated anguish in a telegram to the
Women's Studies Centre at Jaipur University after the festivities were safely
over, and Rajiv Gandhi despatched his minister of state for home affairs, P.
Chidambaram, to "inquire into the matter" on September 19. Chidambaram
delivered the government's assurances that the situation was now under
control, since the main culprits—Roop Kanwar's father-in-law and his three
sons—had been arrested, and that no temple would be permitted to be built
on the site to glorify the alleged sati. Later that afternoon he met with 500
or so young Rajput men, who had driven recklessly through the streets of
Jaipur in triumph and demanded an audience, uninhibited by the police.
The meeting was an angry one, since the minister held firm in his position
against the event, and the youths went away swearing to protect *sati*

dharma. Public opinion seemed to polarize along gender lines. Women activists abhorred the event as the murder of a young and helpless widow; and men saw it as a mark of Rajput high society. As activists, the latter formed the overwhelming majority. The Congress Party is often thought of as a bulwark protecting secular values in India, but it was Atal Bihari Vajpayee, the nationally important leader of the Bharatiya Janata Party, who called a public meeting and roundly and unequivocally denounced the glorification of the Deorala incident. The Congress Party acted only when embarrassed by reminders from feminist groups.

Sikar, where the district headquarters governing Deorala are located, lacked any women's organization that could raise consciousness and determine to prevent such acts in future; and indeed, only a few representatives of women's groups in Jaipur visited Deorala after the event. These were glaring omissions. Finally on September 25, a select group of women from the various women's organizations in Jaipur went to Sikar to help form a women's organization in that district. Local women who responded to this initiative "were very clear that the religious cover given to the entire episode was false. It was a clear case of murder and needed to be condemned in unmixed terms."[11] Meanwhile women's groups from other parts of the country began to call and express their solidarity with the women in Rajasthan; women journalists working for national dailies had also convened in Jaipur, meeting with the women's group to ensure better coverage of the steps taken to protest the event.

Unfortunate as Roop Kanwar's death had been, it seemed to have given women's organizations fresh impetus to come together and forge new alliances and put into place better networking procedures and strategies for mobilization. On September 29, the disparate women's groups in Jaipur formed a joint action committee. It formally condemned "all atrocities committed on women in the name of religion or community" and stated that "the basic issue in our struggle was that of women's identity and status." It also decided that signatures should be collected from those who supported the groups' stand, particularly among Rajputs. Further, it resolved to produce a pamphlet that would unambiguously spell out the groups' position on the issue of sati. This pamphlet would be distributed to the national media and to women's groups in other parts of India who were also in the process of forming anti-sati committees.[12]

These deliberations and exchanges resulted in plans for a large anti-sati rally on October 6, for which strict ground rules were laid down. It was agreed that the march would be silent, no political party or institutional banner would be allowed, and nobody would be paid even for transport; it had to be an entirely voluntary commitment. Selected people would speak, including a rural woman, a woman from an urban slum (*basti*), two men who had proved very supportive, and two Rajput women. It was also decided that no political party or outside person would be given a platform.[13] An open discussion at a local girls' high school on the eve of the rally attracted droves of new supporters, particularly male faculty from Rajasthan University and representatives of women's groups from Ahmedabad, New Delhi, Nagpur, and Pune. The decision to march without party banners and in silence is a recent departure for women's groups; from such small but significant strategic moves, a coherent feminist platform was built and shared by all groups, including male participants.

On October 6, 3,000 people marched through the streets of Jaipur. They represented some 25 organizations from Rajasthan and 31 from other cities. At the public meeting that followed, sati was proclaimed to be not just an issue that concerned women but a crime against women; it was seen as a move to manipulate religion and caste to exploit women. The state government was strongly indicted for its failure to enforce the law. Laxmi Kumari Chundawat, a Rajput writer and former member of the legislative assembly of Rajasthan, asserted that the burning of widows was a barbaric act and that no religion gave sanction to it; a Sanskrit scholar challenged anyone to prove that the *shastras*, the cultural repositories of Hindu legal wisdom, advocated sati. The feminist agenda for further thought and action on the matter of widow-burning emerged with clarity and force:

> A systematic and sustained dialogue on this issue of widows (should they always be described as widows?) and their status needs to be carried on at all levels just as much as the even more sensitive issue of religious sanction. Unless the matter is brought out in the open and talked about, its supercharged emotive character will not wear off and rational decision making will always stand in danger of being swept away by the mere chanting of a few words.[14]

When reminded by an interviewer that the women who participated in the march had been accused by Rajput critics of being overly Westernized, Sharada Jain spoke passionately. "It is totally false to say that we are Westernized women. The Rajputs have taken to Western ways much more than any other community. The sati was not a question of tradition against modernity." In some ways, she went on to say, it was just the reverse. The glorification of sati was to be seen as the sly revival of a shameful custom by the three most powerful castes in Rajasthan, whose investment in the process of modernization was the greatest: Rajputs, Brahmins, and Marwaris. Jain charged that these three had promoted the murder as sati for their own gain:

> Take the family that committed this murder. They are Rajputs. They pride themselves on their tradition of chivalry and valour. In villages throughout Rajasthan, the Rajputs were once the main landowners. Now there is little opportunity for deeds of chivalry, the government has taken away much of

their land, and so the Rajputs are in search of an identity. A sati by a woman of the Rajput caste was a tremendous boost to their morale and image. . . .

[The Brahmin priests'] approval was necessary before Roop Kanwar's sati could be accepted. Brahmins' prestige still depends on their priestly role. . . . They would certainly want to dip into something so unusual as a so-called sati. . . .

The banias [merchants, especially Marwaris] are a very rich and powerful caste. You could say that they are commercially very daring, but they are basically very superstitious. They are religious-minded but their religion is based on luck. They would want to touch the ground where a sati was committed because they would believe it would bring them luck. The banias have the economic power, the Rajputs the political power and the Brahmins the power of religious knowledge. Is it right that a woman's identity should be controlled by these vested interests?[15]

Sharada Jain's argument—albeit an oversimplification, because it attributes greater homogeneity of opinion to members of a caste than actually exists—contains the nucleus of the analysis that would be couched in more sophisticated language in several later articles by other scholars. Her question puts the central issue of woman's identity, autonomy, volition, and agency squarely into place: even if Roop Kanwar was willing, she would only have been responding to an internalized ideology. In that case she should be seen more as a puppet than as an agent. This line of argument, by no means new, finds its most detailed treatment in the work of Kumkum Sangari and Sudesh Vaid. These scholars have been investigating sati in the Shekhavati region for well over a decade; the Roop Kanwar sati spurred them to write a comprehensive article that collects and updates previous research and culminates in the Roop Kanwar case. They systematically expose the long collaboration between Rajputs and Banias in inventing a formula with an appealing blend of ideological, ritual, and commemorative elements for these periodic spectacles of sati. This formula judiciously borrows features from many traditions of goddess worship already prevalent in Rajasthan. They recount the earlier brutal murder of the young widow Om Kanwar, on August 30, 1980, ill-disguised by her in-laws as a sati and glorified through the erection of a shrine that has become a popular pilgrimage site in Jhardli, Rajasthan. From the details, they abstract what emerges as a model and horrifying inspiration for subsequent instances of sati. A chilling replay of this plot can be seen in the Roop Kanwar murder seven years later.[16]

In the weeks and months that followed the death of Roop Kanwar, a flood of articles on the subject appeared in newspapers, special numbers of journals, and independently produced reports and analyses. Every piece that lamented the event was matched by another that approved it. These pro-sati attacks, articulated by men who postured as keepers of a timeless Hindu tradition, such as the Shankaracharya of Puri, challenged the right of feminists to act as spokespersons on behalf of the alleged satis, and served to focus the feminist position sharply. Nationally known women's groups such as the Women and Media Committee of the Bombay Union of Journalists and the editors of the leading women's journal *Manushi* were provoked to conduct their own fact-finding missions to reconstruct a clear narrative of events in Deorala. Both groups' reports are worth examining at some length.

Three members of the Women and Media Committee visited Deorala in the last week of September 1987.[17] A part of their stated brief was to "examine the sequence of events that led to the sati and obtain a clear perspective on the debate on whether or not there was an element of coercion in the act." This may sound somewhat regressive, considering what has already been said about implicit coercion, but the Committee nevertheless unearthed some very startling facts. Its members had other purposes as well. They wanted to document the impact of the event on the village—"the communal overtones the incident had assumed" and the "socio-cultural influence of *sati* in the region, especially among the Rajputs"—and they wanted to analyze how this incident was reported in the mainstream press.[18] Their report, *Trial by Fire,* deals systematically with each item on their agenda, although much of the reportage contains no new analytical perspective. They faithfully catalog the doings of the women's organizations and analyze the sensational way the English-language press in India reported the event, with journalists feeling free to make the most obvious and insensitive puns and jokes about fire and burning.

But the real value of *Trial by Fire* lies in the nuggets of information it reports that appear to have been overlooked by the rest of the media. At first the authors seem dispirited at finding "a conspiracy of silence in Deorala."[19] Yet it was not quite silence, judging from the text that follows, although some residents refused to confirm that they had witnessed the event. This, of course, may be explained by the fact that a women's investigative team would be greeted with suspicion even if there had been no controversial event in the village.

Despite that "conspiracy of silence," the Bombay team amassed a wealth of amazing details showing how legends are made and how myths are perpetuated—the sorts of things Sangari and Vaid had assiduously tracked in other locations earlier, especially in the village of Jhardli.[20] The team also found some medical and material evidence in the police files that could eventually be used to cut through the mystique and solve the criminal case. The visual details recreate the scene. The now canopied *sati sthal* (cremation site) was raised into a brick platform, beside which was embedded a trident covered with Roop Kanwar's red *chunari*, which, they write, ominously resembled the figure of a woman. Seven youths bearing swords and chanting slogans circumambulated the site; two-hour shifts had been organized to make this an around-the-clock vigil. The Women and Media Committee team also noted the odd little artifacts on sale: wedding pictures of the couple; the sati photomontage; ribbons; toys; and all the paraphernalia needed to offer prayers at the site, such as coconuts and incense sticks. The alliance of religion, commerce, and patriarchy was evident everywhere.

The Women and Media Committee members also recorded the stories circulating in Deorala about Roop, her marriage, her character, and the miraculous nature of the event. They went to Roop Kanwar's home and peered into the lamp-lit room, adorned with large framed photos of various gods and a color television set. This room now served as a new version of a shrine for a modern sati. They could not meet the mother-in-law, who was in the house, obstructed in their intent by a male relative; her husband and two sons had by now been arrested, and she, understandably, was not feeling too well. Elsewhere in the village they heard, from women who claimed to have heard it from others, an account of the sati itself. Immediately before the event

> The girl, they say, acquired *sat*—a supernatural power which is akin to a trance-like state where the woman's body burns to the touch and her eyes redden and glow. No one dared dissuade her for fear of being cursed by *sati mata*. She is said to have led the procession, chanted the *gayatri mantra* and blessed people. Roop Kanwar, they say, had only raised her hands and the pyre lit itself.

This miraculous rendering of the event was not only believed by the villagers but also "shared by powerful Rajput politicians, her family and even the police."[21] Government investigations, tardy and inadequate as they were, were perceived as meddlesome and intrusive by most people in Deorala. Reporters and cameramen were treated with hostility.

The Bombay team also interviewed the parents of Roop Kanwar. While the couple appeared "disturbed," they seemed reassured that the in-laws' delay in informing them of their daughter's decision to die was understandable, considering that they were devastated by the loss of their eldest son. This telling excuse was made by Sneh Kanwar, Roop Kanwar's mother; she betrays the view that a son's death is more serious than that of a daughter-in-law or a daughter. In normal circumstances in any Hindu household, the parents would have been instantly informed of the death of their son-in-law, no matter how upset the bereaved family might be. In this case they would have rushed to the funeral, being only two hours away and having a car at their disposal. Instead of questioning this serious failure to notify them of their daughter's intentions, Roop Kanwar's parents gave the team a well-rehearsed summary of the pious character of their dead daughter: she was very religious, an indifferent student, a girl who preferred to play with idols rather than with toys, and a frequent visitor to the sati temple in Jhunjhunu. This evidently was intended to establish her predisposition to make the decision to commit sati.[22]

A counternarrative, which was also somewhat problematic, emerged from the "bits and pieces" in "eyewitness accounts" provided to the same team. A Congress Party worker (who had not witnessed the event, but whose relatives confirmed the account) claimed that Roop had actually hidden herself in a nearby barn as she "got an inkling" of the planned immolation.[23] She was found and forcibly put on the pyre at 1:30 P.M. "She screamed and struggled to get out when the pyre was lit, but Rajput youths with swords surrounding her made escape impossible." Her flailing arms, seen by the crowd, were "interpreted by the villagers, not as a sign of her struggling to get out, but of her showering blessings on them."[24] One witness claimed that she "was frothing at the mouth"; another, that she had been swaying all the way from her home to the cremation site while ringed by Rajput sword bearers. Because the scene was obscured by the plumes of smoke, clouds of red powder (*gulal*) flung on such auspicious occasions, and the pressing throng, few witnesses had a clear view of the cremation site itself; but there is no doubt that the younger brother of the dead man lit the pyre, because that is the ritual procedure in the case of a man who has no son. Given these circumstances, the team concluded that the crime committed was murder.[25]

The Women and Media Committee's report also contained a detailed study of what the police had done until then, and the group's members seem to have had very easy access to all levels of police officers and their documents on this case. The only variance between the police view and the team's own assessment of the event was that the police seemed to be making one crucial distinction: sati, in their minds and in the minds of the population they were dealing with, was something other than murder or suicide. While they had booked the offenders—the deceased man's father and brothers—under sections 302 and 306 of the criminal code, they expressed a clear wish that a law specifically banning sati should be promptly enacted to strengthen their hand. The police did not explain their own bumbling incompetence in failing to cordon off the site so as to prevent the *chunari* ceremony planned for the thirteenth day. Through sins of careful omission such as these, sati rites found new legitimacy in Deorala. Of the hundred or more people who were alleged to have witnessed the cremation, not one was willing to provide testimony for the police. Given the widespread fear of policemen and their tactics, and considering the danger of becoming embroiled in a matter that was being billed as a miracle, it was by no means easy to step forward and attest to the nature of the occurrence under oath. This explains the silence, the rumors, the myths, and the snippets of detail only heard from equally vague "others" who could not be named.

The police files yielded some intriguing material that other investigators seem not to have found, and it is surprising that the team did not work some of this into their conclusions or pursue a lead that might have answered the very first question on their list. These facts emerged from interviews with M. M. Meherishi of the Criminal Investigation Department (Vigilance Branch) and pertain to the medical history of Roop Kanwar's husband Mal Singh and the particulars of the dowry that she brought into his family at the time of their marriage. Meherishi spoke on the basis of information recorded in the police report.

Let us consider the medical history first. The circumstances of Mal Singh's death are even cloudier than those surrounding the death of Roop Kanwar. Meherishi asserted that the opportunity to collect valuable forensic information was lost because the police had not troubled to investigate the case after registering it. All they did was hand it over to the Criminal Investigation Department eighteen days after the event, when sufficient political pressure had been applied by women's groups. The Bombay team actually examined the police records, including the first information report (written on September 4, 1987), and took the trouble to verify the medical information in the police records directly from the medical personnel involved in treating Mal Singh.

Meherishi raised a brand new issue. He felt he had some facts and leads strongly indicating that the death of Mal Singh "appears to be suspicious." The evidence in support of this claim is as follows. Unaccountably Mal Singh, the acutely sick man, was taken to a hospital in Sikar instead of to one in Jaipur, which is not only closer to Deorala but has far better medical facilities. The doctors at Sikar were equivocal about the cause of the death. The initial diagnosis of gastroenteritis was later dismissed, since it was supported by symptoms recorded only as "acute abdominal pain" at the Sikar hospital. It was claimed that the patient arrived in a state of shock and with low blood pressure. The chief medical officer at Sikar, who later diagnosed Mal Singh's condition as pancreatitis, "felt that there was no need for a post mortem," and no autopsy was ever performed.[26]

To compound the gravity of such evidence, it was established that the patient had been suffering "from shock and depression" and had been under the care of a Jaipur neuropsychiatrist, Dr. K. G. Thanvi, only a few months before his death. Mal Singh, Dr. Thanvi said, had twice failed to pass the premedical examination to enter medical school; the news of the results of his second attempt at the examination reached him only two weeks before his death. Dr. Thanvi told the team that Mal Singh had been under his care from June 5 to July 1 in 1987. He "had complained of having lost interest in life and was suffering from androgynous depression. An outpatient, he had been prescribed the usual anti-depressants."[27] The doctor felt that the patient was "fully cured" but admitted the high possibility of a relapse. He added that he had not followed up the case and was only reminded of it when he was called up by some journalists in connection with the sati. A local doctor who was summoned to treat Mal Singh in Deorala and accompanied the patient to Sikar had in the meantime absconded, and the police were trying to locate him. He is also suspected by the police of having administered a strong drug to tranquilize Roop Kanwar prior to undergoing the live cremation ordeal so that she would go to her death without too much pain or obvious resistance.[28] This body of evidence would smell foul even to the most credulous of sati watchers. One suspicious death seems to have made the second one possible.

Now let us scrutinize the facts about the dowry. The police discovered that Roop Kanwar's dowry consisted of 40 *tolas* (a *tola* is approximately 11.6 grams) of gold, 30,000 rupees in fixed-deposit receipts in her own name, a color television, a cooking range, a refrigerator, and household furniture, apart from her personal wardrobe and other gifts. The police officers saw more significance in this dowry than did the Bombay investigative team, who merely saw it as "[a]nother aspect to be borne in mind."[29] The police officers were right. This is a very substantial dowry by Indian middle-class standards, a *tola* of gold being roughly worth 210 dollars in 1987. It was a fortune far beyond the dreams of a village schoolteacher such as Roop Kanwar's father-in-law. The team confirmed that the custom in the area was for a young, childless widow to return to her parents with all her dowry. The team saw the television set and the furniture that Roop Kanwar had brought, and the fact that her parents were very affluent is reported in several places. Yet none of the feminist reporters or scholars—not even the editors of *Manushi*—pursued this matter. The parents of Roop Kanwar would probably have been open to questions about how this marriage was arranged and what the wedding and alliance cost them in material terms.

It is incomprehensible that this very suggestive and potentially incriminating published information has been ignored or treated as insignificant by other feminists who reported on the case subsequently. Instead, implausible speculation about a supposed secret romantic past for Roop Kanwar and allegations of embarrassing ailments suffered by Mal Singh appeared in the press, eroding the possibility of ever getting close to what might have truly ailed Mal Singh and how he died. A story by a woman journalist in the Delhi paper, the *Hindustan Times*, published three-and-a-half weeks after Roop Kanwar's death, claimed that Mal Singh was being treated for impotency and that Roop Kanwar was having an affair with a man from a lower caste, presumably to explain why her in-laws forced her onto the funeral pyre.[30] Such unsubstantiated and irresponsible stories justifiably outraged the villagers at Deorala and increased their mistrust of women reporters, which may account for much of the hostility that various feminist investigative teams report they encountered.

It has been impossible for me, as a feminist historian, to read the evidence gathered by the Women and Media Committee without speculating about what might really have happened. My own research over the past several years for a book on dowry murders, in connection with which I have read innumerable police reports, not to mention case files in a women's resource center, intensify my urge to help clarify some of the mystery shrouding Roop Kanwar's death. So, here is how I read it.

* * *

The village school teacher and his wife find that their eldest son is not particularly bright, is unemployed, and is prone to depression. He has already failed his entrance examination to medical school—a serious matter, since one can only take the test a few times—and the prospects for achieving his family's ambitions for him to become doctor seem dim. Yet the situation is not hopeless: his failure can be shielded from public view for a while. To give the boy a sense of purpose and responsibility, and possibly to help him get over his depression, it might be best to find him a suitable bride while he still appears to have at least the potential of becoming a physician. Marriage is often proposed to cure young men who have strayed from the socially acceptable path and begin to gamble, drink, womanize, or show sexually "deviant" interests; depression, as in Mal Singh's case, probably invited such intervention even sooner. Hindu wives are famous for their endurance of lackluster husbands and for their therapeutic and nurturing qualities. A good match is found in Roop Kanwar, an attractive and educated girl (but only up to the 10th grade) from Jaipur.

They probably did not need to demand a dowry, but they are delighted that their future daughter-in-law is from a wealthy family. As for Roop's parents, they regard this young man as a respectable, highly educated son-in-law with the potential to earn a high income as a doctor.

The young man's condition, however, does not improve; nor do his prospects for a job. He makes another attempt at the medical entrance examination, but that only confirms for him the doubts he has about his own worth. His marriage to this hopeful and beautiful eighteen-year-old heightens his chagrin and possibly his frustration at his own inadequacy. When he failed the examination for the first time, he may have been depressed enough to want to end his life. Failure in examinations prompts many young students to take their lives in India. Waiting for the dreaded results for a second time might bring him to the brink of a nervous collapse. The seriousness of the situation—possibly even a failed suicide attempt?—now compels the family to seek the services of a "neuropsychiatrist" in Jaipur to treat their hapless eldest son. It is well known that resort to any kind of psychological help in India is seen as a drastic recourse and would be taken only in extreme circumstances. For a village family to go to the big city and seek this particular kind of help suggests that plenty more might have been wrong with the lad than even the Criminal Investigation Department knows.

In the meantime, Roop Kanwar spends most of her time with her parents in Jaipur. The Women and Media Committee team discovered that she had spent only twenty days with her husband after the wedding; she rejoined him only a few days before their deaths.[31] It is even conceivable that Mal Singh's psychiatric treatment was kept from his wife and in-laws so as not to alarm them. Another crisis might have forced them to send for Roop Kanwar. Perhaps he tried to take his life (again?) when the results of his failure came out, two weeks before he was to die. On the eve of his death, he is first treated by a local doctor—the one who later absconded and so could not be questioned by the police. Then he is inexplicably rushed to a hospital in Sikar, or so it is claimed. Mark Tully, incidentally, found a serious discrepancy in the story told to him by Mal Singh's family about this event: he personally checked and found that there is no record of Mal Singh's admission to the Sikar hospital.[32] So the role of the local doctor, who is alleged to have treated him at home, is a vital—and missing—piece of the puzzle.

Whatever may have actually transpired the night before, we do know for certain that Mal Singh was dead and cremated in Deorala shortly after midday on September 4, along with his wife. Mal Singh's death was probably a fate to which his parents were in some way already reconciled. Their problem suddenly was Roop Kanwar. She must have known what happened to her husband on the days just before he died. When death actually came, Roop Kanwar—as a young, attractive widow—would have presented them with two awkward possibilities. Either she could return to her parents' home, taking back her dowry and dwelling sorrowfully there (because widows find it impossible to marry in the class and circles to which she belonged), or she could opt to remain with her parents-in-law in Deorala. Either way, as time went on, her sexuality would pose problems and be perceived as a threat to the honor of both families; a sati would convert impending shame into glory. Therefore, persuading her to commit sati seemed an attractive expedient and a culturally acceptable solution. Young women are presumed to be vulnerable and obedient. In this instance, persuasion may have meant anything from brainwashing an already religious and sati-temple-visiting teenager to drugging her into compliance. The same local doctor would administer a drug, if needed.

The doctor's sudden disappearance from the village suggests culpability on his part: he may even have suggested the latter course to the distraught parents. Deorala, it is reported, had already been the site for two earlier satis. Whatever was done was done with speed, and Roop Kanwar took the story of her brief marriage to a troubled young man with her to her death. It was murder.

* * *

The above scenario, speculative and unspeakably evil as it may sound, would make sense of why Roop Kanwar's parents were not informed until too late. There really was no good reason for keeping Mal Singh's death and her resolve from them unless Roop Kanwar was not entirely persuaded and could not be relied on to go through with it. The presence of her own family—parents, brothers, possibly friends—would have made this act difficult, if not impossible. So the in-laws hastily decided that it would be best to inform the parents *after* the cremation; surely they would understand how grief and pain keep people from their worldly obligations. This, however, was also the case in all the preceding sati-style deaths in the Jhunjhunu-Shekhavati region: no parents were informed until after the cremation.[33] Prominent people in the village, who nostalgically approve of women's sacrifice and purity, came to the cremation ground in every case. They certainly would have done so this time, since the school teacher commands some respect in the village, and his circle of acquaintances certainly would have exceeded the hundred or more who did come. And so they stood there and watched and approved, with their chants and slogans, and added coconuts and buckets of *ghi* to the flames, as they beheld the spectacle of Roop Kanwar's flailing limbs showering blessings on them amid the smoke and *gulal*. This was not just a dowry murder but a doubly cynical and criminal act committed, not with the help of kerosene in the kitchen, but in the full gaze of an applauding and credulous multitude. As for Roop Kanwar's parents, they not only believed the story of their daughter's sacrifice, they donated 100,000 rupees toward its commemoration on its first anniversary. Are people capable of such self-serving evil? Yes, everywhere and in all cultures.

Madhu Kishwar and Ruth Vanita, editors of *Manushi*, were the next major team of women to visit Deorala. They arrived in the last week of October; by then, all the possible interpretive angles on the event were already in print, and a heated "modernity-versus-tradition" debate was in full swing. While they rightly condemned the sterility of this controversy, they ironically furthered it by arguing that this so-called traditional event is a thoroughly modern phenomenon. By preserving the binary opposition of traditional versus modern in their analysis, they unwittingly proved that sati has resurfaced on the scene in modern-day India with inevitable modern-day political (instead of religious) trappings.

In their subsequent report, Kishwar and Vanita insist on calling the Deorala happening a "modern day Sati," conceding thereby that it *was* a sati.[34] They reinforce this impression by carefully explaining the distinctions between a dowry death and a sati. Interestingly, in their analysis of the ensuing debate on sati, they criticize the argument made by "most reformers" that the Deorala event was a product of "blind superstitiousness and excessive religiosity" and "backwardness and primitiveness . . . preserved in our rural vastness," because this unwittingly supports the position of the pro-sati camp, which sees modernity as the enemy of traditional values.[35] In distancing themselves from the anti-sati campaign, the editors write that "Somewhere along the way" it became "counterproductive," and the campaigners "became characterised as a handful of anti Hindu, anti Rajput, antireligion, progovernment, antimasses, urban, educated, westernised people, and the pro-Sati lobby as those sensitive to the sentiments of the rural traditional poor." The "reformers," they feel, saw the Roop Kanwar case as a "product of an old tradition, whereas in its present form it is a new created cult [sic], organised by political, not by religious, leaders." They go on to say that it was also a mistake to enter into the debate "on the religiosity or otherwise of the Deorala Sati." It should have been demystified and seen as "a case of a woman being hounded to death under a specious religious cover, and of her death being made a symbol by certain power groups to demonstrate their clout." Petitioning the government, they say, only let the government "off the hook for its complicity in Roop Kanwar's death" and gave it the opportunity "to pose as progressive by introducing a repressive law."[36] They suggest that human rights and women's organizations should use Mahatma Gandhi's weapon *satyagraha*, nonviolent civil disobedience, to protest "the murder and its subsequent glorification."[37]

This sati was indubitably the creation of modern economic, political, and social forces. Deorala, the *Manushi* team points out, is a modern village of 10,000 inhabitants with a 70 percent literacy rate, electricity, and tap water—a relatively prosperous place dominated by Brahmins and Rajputs. It has brick houses, a large market well stocked with consumer goods, and inhabitants who dress as fashionably as their counterparts in the cities and who are not uninfluenced by the ubiquitous Hindi film manners and mores. Roop Kanwar's family is educated, as was she. Her father-in-law was a school teacher, her husband a science graduate, her brothers the owners of a thriving transport business in Jaipur. As for the sati event itself, Kishwar and Vanita show that it was no less modern than the setting in which it occurred. They list many crass adaptations from Hindi films, political rhetoric, and other aspects of popular culture that had been incorporated to valorize the sati. The slogans they heard voiced by youths near the cremation site were emended political slogans, shouted in a cheerleading

a religious ritual. The
village was traced to a
ati with the Beautiful
ted as a daily evening
hymn popularized via
n ritual performed for
hotsav, a carnival with
major attraction.
gely succeed in doing
not only modern but
though women would
ower wielders of the
tee for the Defense of
as dropped after the
rification of sati) are
tary, Narendra Singh
her-export business,
g women's colleges.
ds of young Rajput
creamed slogans "as

he construction and
Rajasthan and else-
omen in Rajasthan.
mple to the sati ideal
enth-century *bhakti*
h India. Her
ore integrally a part of
being created around
ders should choose a
jasthani womanhood
evidence that a major
themselves.[40]
ry rich article based
istrict published in
impressed with at-
t through the vested

in action of the state
hey assert that "our
ot even neutral. It is
er and profit are far

more important than human rights

that generalization. Particular acc

police, however, seem to be totally

journalists—notably the encounte

Deorala police discussed earlier.

attempts to challenge the cult are

the case are being suppressed an

tion."[43] They seem unaware of the f

in the last decade, and that only f

out.[44] The *Manushi* editors appear

police and Criminal Investigation

instead they claim that Deorala w

making it difficult for them to dist

as it may, it explains why the *Ma*

Singh's illness or Roop Kanwar'

A more trenchant critique of t

episode was published in the *Eco*

1987.[45] Using a broader perspecti

Jawaharlal Nehru University in

death as one more dramatic exam

by both Hindu and Muslim obsc

incident has happened," they w

because the government is not v

modern and civilized state."[46] In

isolated event nor as exclusively a

Rajashthani patriarchal pride a

nected complexity of recent com

sharp contrast to the past wh

consensus," write Imrana Qade

social forces have entered the ce

of the state."[47]

Imrana Qadeer goes furth

"Roop Kanwar and Shah Ban

explains how the prevarication

headed by Rajiv Gandhi, led

passions. In 1986, Rajiv Gandhi

in the Shah Bano case and to Hi

Ramjanmabhumi dispute prog

Briefly, Shah Bano, a 75-year-o

very affluent lawyer husband,

nance, which was granted. This

Muslims as undermining Mus

divorcee's right to maintenance. A prolonged and bitter fight of Muslim women, Indian liberals of all religions, and women's organizations ended in their defeat when Rajiv Gandhi's government overturned the Supreme Court's judgment by an Act of Parliament. The fundamentalist mullahs then cornered the powerless old woman and made her retract her demand for maintenance as a grave religious "error" and made her flout the judgment of the highest court in the land.[48] The Act of Parliament shredded the secular constitution of the country in the same way as did the government's irresponsible opening of the locked doors of the Babari Mosque while the dispute over its proprietorship was awaiting judgment in the local courts. In each case either Muslim or Hindu extremists were given an extrajudicial arena to play out the dispute, transforming what might have remained longstanding grumbling matches into a make-or-break deal for the opposition Bharatiya Janata Party.[49]

Qadeer describes the triumph of religious fundamentalists and militants who have brazenly exploited the tragic circumstances of powerless women in both Hindu and Muslim communities. She delineates the emerging trends as follows:

1. That fundamentalist forces are capitalising not upon an event or two but on a persistent feature of the social system: the position of women as second class citizens. This . . . strengthens their alliance with the ruling classes.
2. That fundamentalists have not only succeeded in capturing the imagination of the majority in their respective communities but also succeeded in confusing a section of their intelligentsia.
3. That the state not only gives in to their anti-secular demands but also justifies them—and its [own] actions—by changing the very definition of secularism. Then in the name of democratic practice it supports the majority view within religious communities.
4. That as a consequence of the above, the liberal democratic sections are becoming increasingly paralyzed and marginal.[50]

This was said in 1987; the situation of late has grown far grimmer, and Qadeer's verdict holds more true than ever before.

Now we can return to the issue of women's identity and autonomy in the context of sati. In a thought-provoking recent article, Rajeswari Sunder Rajan expressly addresses the question of pain and agency in an effort to counter the absence or transcendence of pain that is claimed as reality by those who argue in defense of sati. While the results of her attempt to theorize female subjectivity as agency in this particular situation remain tentative, one cannot gainsay her observation that "in the discourse of the anti-sati position, however, while pain is undeniably everywhere present, it is nowhere represented."[51] She looks for signs of pain in a large assortment of "social texts" produced by this event, such as newspapers, photographs, and documentary films, as well as in the law itself, and finds it only in a single feminist poster and in a consciousness-raising documentary. In the popular posters and commercial mementos of the Roop Kanwar sati, the woman's face and body show no marks of the experience of burning; the aforementioned photomontage (a version of which is Figure 1 in the present volume) shows her smiling as she sits serenely on the pyre in all her bridal finery while a small figure of a goddess beams down the magic ray to ignite it.[52] Sunder Rajan argues that the subjectivity of pain is important to stress because it

> needs to be conceptualized as a dynamic rather than a passive condition, on the premise that the subject in pain will be definitionally in transit towards a state of no-pain (even if this state is no more than a reflexivity. . . . [T]he affect produced by a body in pain—pity, anger, sympathy, identification—is an important consideration in formulating the politics of intervention.[53]

While Sunder Rajan has made the most valiant attempt yet, in the Indian context, to articulate the idea that a woman's pain is to be apprehended as subject-constitutive, the idea of a woman's agency in sati remains problematic at several levels. First, the belief in a woman's volition, her special power of *sat*—a "miraculous" driving force that enables her to shower blessings, heal the sick, and order the funeral pyre to ignite itself yet feel no pain—makes her the agent of her own destiny in the ideology and biographical narratives of sati. Sangari and Vaid point out the difficulties that arise in "squaring widow immolation as a product of the woman's own volition with the necessarily public and participatory nature of the funeral," in whose absence the miraculous nature of the event cannot be established.[54] In fact, one could go further and add that it makes female agency a very dangerous idea—one that sati perpetrators would be happy to appropriate in Deorala and elsewhere. Deeper still, even when agency can be forensically established, can the woman's act of self-immolation be judged to be a product of her own will, or must it be judged as a product of the very studious socialization and indoctrination of women (particularly for the role of wife) that shape her attitudes and actions from girlhood? At yet a fourth level, as Lata Mani points out, the current legislation on sati, by making a woman who escapes or otherwise survives the burning liable for attempting sati, implicitly conceives of her as a "free agent." The law is self-contradictory, in that case, for it cannot logically claim to locate coercion and agency in the same act. So the question of agency is delicate, complex, even contradictory, and it certainly cannot be conceptualized as neatly as it has been in liberal feminist theories in the West. In fact it might be better to settle for a provisional view of woman as victim until some way is found to resolve the question of woman's agency in this particular setting. As Lata Mani says,

> The example of women's agency is a particularly good instance of the dilemmas confronted in simultaneously attempting to speak within different

historical moments and to discrepant audiences. What might be a valuable pushing of the limits of the current rethinking of agency in Anglo-American feminism, may, if not done with extreme care, be an unhelpful, if not disastrous move in the Indian context.[55]

Perhaps the last word on "agency" should belong to a Rajput woman, Rani Chundawat, who has spoken eloquently against sati and is a prominent Rajasthani public figure. In commenting to the editors of *Manushi* on what Mal Singh's family maintains was Roop Kanwar's decision to commit sati, she poses a series of rhetorical questions that challenge the notion of woman's agency very profoundly in the context of sati: "How many women have the right to decide anything voluntarily?" If a woman does not choose her husband and does not decide matters such as her own education or career, how can she choose in a matter as imperative as that of life and death? Given that a woman's status is generally determined by her relationship to men (as daughter, wife, widow, mother), "can any decision. . . . particularly such a momentous decision, really be called voluntary and self-chosen?"[56] The answer to the last question is, of course, no. Therefore, it may be ill-advised to seek female agency in the act of committing sati.

The question that has not come up anywhere in the literature and remains a silent subtext in other equally harrowing situations, whether dowry murders or other widow immolations in the Shekhavati region, is the question of the fear of a young woman's sexuality. If we see few images of her pain, we see even fewer images of her desire; and in the concept of sati, both the pain and the desire that arise in a woman's body are erased. Sati is about transcendent states, not embodied ones. For feminists it has been enough to invoke patriarchy, that umbrella term that serves as an explanatory backdrop for all crimes against women, including the punitive control of female sexuality. Like the wordless language of pain—flailing arms, screams, tears—desire is smothered at the source in the body language of modesty and in silence. It is easier to trot out the material reasons for sati and other violent crimes against women than to venture into the psychosexual realm of human motivations. The idea of a desirable and desiring widow whom no one will marry and whom many will want to exploit remains unexpressed—oddly, even more so than in the case of pain. This is true both with respect to the perpetrators of sati and with respect to its critics, opponents, and analysts. The need for a more forthright discussion of this issue is urgent. Feminists will have to take the lead in demolishing this blank wall.

But what of feminists' achievements so far? What have been the results of feminist intervention in Roop Kanwar's case? A law, called the Commission of Sati (Prevention) Act of 1987, has been inserted into the statute book. Vasudha Dhagamwar, a professor of law and an activist, offers a capsule history of the legislation that has attended the custom from the earliest legal debates of 1805 to the present.[57] She recounts that the clamor for fresh and separate anti-sati legislation (which in her view was redundant with the existing Indian Penal Code) came entirely from anti-sati activists who were drawn into the debate on whether or not this event could have been voluntary. She pleaded, along with others, that there was no such thing as "voluntary sati" and that a law against murder already existed and simply needed to be enforced. After a fractious interlude, which Dhagamwar describes with zest, Parliament enacted comprehensive anti-sati legislation outlawing not only sati but its glorification in any way, shape, or form. Yet this piece of legislation was not drafted by feminists, and a close inspection of its many sections would please them little. It has replicated, in some parts verbatim, many of the prejudices, caveats, and ambiguities of the East India Company Regulation of 1829, and it adds a few complications of its own by attempting to define sati. In fact, if I may put a gloss on it, instead of making a law that prohibits an incontestable crime against women, the framers of the new law succeeded in defining sati as a woman's crime. Dhagamwar points out that, in refusing to distinguish between voluntary and involuntary sati, they have in effect managed to "treat all sati as voluntary. That is why the woman is punished and that is why those who kill her are punished for abetment, and not for murder."[58] So, should a woman by some chance manage to escape the pyre, she would be culpable first and foremost. This is not exactly a giant step forward for womankind, and it can be lamented as yet another inroad into the secular terrain of the Indian Penal Code.[59]

What did this law achieve in the case of Roop Kanwar's death? Before it was promulgated the police had arrested her father-in-law and her two brothers-in-law; the village doctor had absconded. Then the law was enacted, but even so the culprits were eventually released without bail. The case against them is pending, but the frustrating reality is that they will not come up for trial; and no one quite knows or cares to determine the whereabouts of the doctor. Thus the case has effectively stalled; and as far as I am able to find out, no one plans to reactivate the charges. On the other side of the ledger, the glorification of sati has been curtailed to the extent that some sati temples find worship interrupted on occasion by a policeman on duty. Yet we will have to wait until the next festival season—or the next—to see what impact the anti-glorification legislation really has on popular reverence for sati. In the meantime, the silence is deafening. When in January 1993 a foreign traveler asked how he could get to Deorala, he was told, "Why do you want to go to Deorala? There is nothing to see."

Acknowledgments

I wish to thank Arati Rao for our many discussions on feminism and for the bibliographic suggestions she made while work on this article was in progress.

Philip Oldenburg, my captive editor and critic, helped in his usual manner with careful and constructive comments.

Notes

1. This is not the entire range of responses. Ashis Nandy's chapter, which follows this one, represents quite a different side of the debate, and I will respond to it subsequently. For brief feminist analyses of the various political positions—liberal, conservative, and feminist—see Lata Mani, "Multiple Mediations: Feminist Scholarship in the Age of Multinational Reception," *Feminist Review* 35 (Summer 1990), pp. 24–41, and Rajeswari Sunder Rajan," The Subject of Sati: Pain and Death in the Contemporary Discourse on Sati," *Yale Journal of Criticism* 3:2 (1990), pp. 1–23.

2. Romila Thapar, "In History," *Seminar* 342 (February 1988), pp. 14–19. For example, Ashis Nandy had claimed, in the *Indian Express* on October 5, 1987, that there had been only three historical periods when sati had become an epidemic. Without fuss, without even mentioning his name, Thapar offers a well-documented explanation for Nandy's misperception in the case of Vijayanagara in the sixteenth century (p. 17).

3. Sudesh Vaid, "Politics of Widow Immolation," in *Seminar* 342 (February 1988), pp. 20–23. This essay remains the clearest statement of the historicity and world view of sati in the Shekhavati region.

4. Lata Mani has written extensively on the colonial discourses on sati, and I refer liberally to her work in my response to Ashis Nandy's article in this volume. Her observations on the discursive continuities between the colonial and the present debates on Roop Kanwar in her "Multiple Mediations" are exceptionally pertinent here.

5. The information in the following paragraph is based on Mark Tully's chapter entitled "The Deorala Sati" in his book, *No Full Stops in India* (New Delhi: Viking Penguin India, 1991), pp. 210–36; also published in *The Defeat of a Congressman and Other Parables of Modern India* (New York: Knopf, 1992), pp. 191–215. His interview with Sharada Jain, the sociologist and women's rights activist who spearheaded the women's protest against the valorization of the sati, captures both her anger at and her analysis of Roop Kanwar's murder very well.

6. Prabhash Joshi, *Jansatta*, September 18, 1987, as translated in Tully, *No Full Stops*, p. 228.

7. Tully, *No Full Stops*, p. 222.

8. Sharada Jain, Nirja Misra, and Kavita Srivastava, "Deorala Episode: Women's Protest in Rajasthan, "*Economic and Political Weekly* 22: 45 (November 7, 1987), p. 1894. The following account is abstracted from this chronology, pp. 1891–94.

9. Jain et al., "Deorala Episode," p. 1891.

10. Jain et al., "Deorala Episode," p. 1893.

11. Ibid.

12. Ibid.

13. Jain et al., "Deorala Episode," p. 1894. The entire chronology is taken from this source and checked against other newspaper reports.

14. Ibid.

15. Tully, *No Full Stops*, p. 223.

16. The article referred to here is their most recent piece, "Institutions, Beliefs, Ideologies: Widow Immolation in Contemporary Rajasthan, "*Economic and Political Weekly* 26:17 (April 27, 1991), pp. WS-2–18, which subsumes earlier publications.

17. These three were Meena Menon, Geeta Seshu, and Sujata Anandan, and they produced a 33-page report entitled *Trial by Fire: A Report on Roop Kanwar's Death*, published in Bombay by the Bombay Union of Journalists. It has no date of publication but states that the authors visited Deorala, Sikar, and Jaipur between September 24 and 30, 1987, after the *chunari mahotsav* had already taken place. They must have written their report not long afterward.

18. Menon et al., *Trial by Fire*, p. 1.

19. Menon et al., *Trial by Fire*, p. 2

20. Sangari and Vaid, "Institutions, Beliefs, Ideologies," pp. WS-3–6.

21. Menon et al., *Trial by Fire*, p. 3.

22. Menon et al., *Trial by Fire*, p. 4.

23. Menon et al., *Trial by Fire*, pp. 4–5.

24. Menon et al., *Trial by Fire*, p. 5.

25. Ibid.

26. Menon et al., *Trial by Fire*, pp. 6–7.

27. Menon et al., *Trial by Fire*, p. 7. The term "androgynous depression" is unusual but not explained. It may be a euphemism for repressed homosexual desire or for impotence caused by a lack of enthusiasm for heterosexual activity, such as Mal Singh might have experienced after marriage; it certainly merits further investigation.

28. Ibid.

29. Ibid.

30. Tully, *No Full Stops*, p. 215.

31. Menon et al., *Trial by Fire*, p. 1.

32. Tully, *No Full Stops*, p. 216.

33. This fact raises questions about the conventional view of the natal family's callousness toward daughters in India, especially after marriage—a view that has wide currency among feminists in the West.

34. Madhu Kishwar and Ruth Vanita, "The Burning of Roop Kanwar," *Manushi* 42–43 (1987), p. 15.

35. Ibid., p. 16. These "reformers"—a puzzling usage at best—are not named, nor are the direct quotes used in the article attributed to any particular "reformer." The editors' report makes no mention of the other fact-finding teams' analyses of political slogans, although these had been published long before the *Manushi* team visited the site, and although these had argued in much the same way. *Manushi* is a leading feminist journal and carries many scholarly articles, yet its editors seldom practice the art of scholarly attribution of borrowed ideas. Their report develops the sati-as-a-modern-phenomenon argument more fully than did Sharada Jain et al.

or the Women and Media Committee report, among others, but the editors waste no space on acknowledgments to suggest the provenance of the many themes they bring to a fullness in their own much later report.

36. Kishwar and Vanita, "Burning," p. 24.

37. Kishwar and Vanita, "Burning," p. 25.

38. Kishwar and Vanita, "Burning," pp. 16–18, 24.

39. Kishwar and Vanita, "Burning," p. 18.

40. Kishwar and Vanita, "Burning," p. 20.

41. Kavita, Shobha, Shobita, Kanchan, and Sharada, "Rural Women Speak," *Seminar* 342 (February 1988), pp. 40–44. The authors of this piece (who, like most feminist activists, do not use their family names) are affiliated with the Women's Development Programme in Rajasthan.

42. Kishwar and Vanita, "Burning," p. 21.

43. Kishwar and Vanita, "Burning," p. 22.

44. Rajeswari Sunder Rajan, "The Subject of Sati," p. 3.

45. Imrana Qadeer and Zoya Hasan, "Deadly Politics of the State and Its Apologists," *Economic and Political Weekly* 22:46 (November 14, 1987), pp. 1946–49.

46. Qadeer and Hasan, "Deadly Politics," p. 1947.

47. Ibid.

48. Considering that Shah Bano succumbed to religious pressure to recant in the full glare of national multimedia publicity, one can imagine how easy it might have been to convince an eighteen-year-old widow in the privacy of her marital home in an obscure village in Rajasthan to immolate herself.

49. Briefly, Hindu militants claimed the soil as their god Rama's birthplace and wished to build a temple to him on the site where a Rama temple is believed to have once stood. This alleged space was since 1528 occupied by a mosque built by the Mughal Emperor Babar's general. The critique is even more pertinent if we consider the habit of dangerous vacillation inherited by Narasimha Rao's government. The same apparent inertia overwhelmed it when throngs of hoodlums destroyed the Babari Mosque in Ayodhya on December 6, 1992, and an eminently preventable act became the signal for thousands to go berserk and bloody the face of a secular republic.

50. Imrana Qadeer, "Shah Bano and Roop Kanwar," *Seminar* 342 (February 1988), p. 33. In this essay Qadeer incorporates some of the points discussed in her other cited piece, but she goes much farther in producing a cogent and gender-sensitive analysis.

51. Sunder Rajan, "The Subject of Sati," p. 7.

52. Sunder Rajan, "The Subject of Sati," pp. 14–15. She discusses the very important ideas of Elaine Scarry, *The Body in Pain: The Making and Unmaking of the World* (New York: Oxford University Press, 1985) and in the process has stimulated discussions among Indian feminists about the inadequacy of current theory on the subjectivity and identity of women.

53. Sunder Rajan, "The Subject of Sati," p. 9.

54. Sangari and Vaid, "Institutions, Beliefs, Ideologies," p. WS-10.

55. Lata Mani, "Multiple Mediations," p. 38.

56. Kishwar and Vanita, "Burning," p. 21.

57. Vasudha Dhagamwar, "Saint, Victim or Criminal," *Seminar* 342 (February 1988), pp. 34–39. Apart from being a compact piece of legal history, this essay is valuable for its very careful comparative analysis of the Rajasthan and central government statutes on sati occasioned by the Roop Kanwar incident.

58. Dhagamwar, "Saint, Victim or Criminal," p. 38 (emphasis in the original).

59. The first was made in 1986 when the Shah Bano case led to the exemption of Muslim husbands from the requirement to pay maintenance for their abandoned or divorced wives under the Penal Code section designed to prevent vagrancy. This exemption, for Muslims only, was enacted separately as the Muslim Women's (Protection of Rights on Divorce) Act.

5

Sati as Profit Versus Sati as a Spectacle: The Public Debate on Roop Kanwar's Death

ASHIS NANDY

The peculiar mix of fascination, fear, dramatics, moral self-righteousness, and anger with which India's Westernized middle classes reacted to the sati committed by Roop Kanwar at Deorala in Rajasthan in 1987 should have been a psychologist's delight. Evidently, the very idea of suicide on the funeral pyre of one's husband—or the possibility that someone might exploit this ancient and rare rite to hide the murder of a young widow—had its own strange fascination for the modern mind. For a small minority of thinking Indians, however, the middle-class reaction to the sati only deepened the tragedy of the death of a teenage widow.

This minority could not forget that during the previous decade, a number of such instances of sati had taken place in Rajasthan without arousing the same passions in urban India. These people remembered their discomfort at the unconcern with which most social activists and journalists greeted instances of sati even a few years before. Such events were almost invariably reported in the inside pages of the national dailies, usually as a form of esoterica that had survived the juggernaut of progress. A large majority of those who were ready to throw epileptic fits at the mention of the word *sati* after Roop's death, did not care to write even a few standard letters to the editor when, for instance, the last sati took place only a year earlier, even though that case, too, was duly mentioned in the English-language press.[1]

Were the passions aroused by the Roop's death only a matter of heightened moral awareness, or was there something more to it? Why was this particular instance of sati, at this particular point in time, so provocative to the Indian middle classes?

Both questions relate to the politics of public consciousness in contemporary urban India. To that extent, one would think, journalists, social scientists, and activists should find them relatively easy to handle: they concern a familiar clientele. Other important questions about the incident demand answers that have to be teased out of a mass of tangled data and from an unfamiliar world. Who organized, witnessed, or applauded the rite? What is the symbolic meaning of sati in contemporary times? And what is the structure of self-interest that characterized those who were involved in the act and/or derived material benefits from it?

Yet answers to these latter questions have been attempted—by Veena Oldenburg in the present volume, for example—while the question of the impact of the Deorala sati on the politics of public consciousness has been little discussed in India's English press and in scholarly journals. Does this tell us, the urban, Westernized Indians, something about ourselves? I believe that this is the first question about sati that we must ask ourselves. And it is the first question that we must answer, however imperfectly, before proceeding any further. For me, a psychologist, insight begins at home.

My tentative answer to the question is as follows. I suspect that two contradictory social-psychological forces are operating in India's middle-class culture of politics. On one side is the growing political power of the mass culture through which urban, middle-class Indians have begun to influence the political process. This pan-Indian mass culture, increasingly a part of global mass culture, is strengthened by a number of social forces, among which are the growing reach of the media, urbanization, industrialization, geographical mobility brought about by changing occupational patterns, and technological growth. On the other side is the democratic process, which threatens to consolidate further the political presence of nonmodern India in the public sphere. In an open system, in however distorted a form, numbers count.

In such a system, the only way moderns can retain the legitimacy of their social and political dominance is by setting themselves up as the final bastion of rationality and as the vanguard of social change. They have to seek sanction for their disproportionate political power from what they see as the symbols of their superior knowledge and morality. Thus it is not surprising that in recent years the Westernized and semi-Westernized middle classes have tended to justify their political power by playing up in the media the spectacular technological and organizational achievements of the Indian state and the modern sector, or the equally spectacular evidences of backwardness and irrationality in nonmodern India. Together the two sets of spectacles endorse the culture of modern India and justify its status in the higher reaches of Indian public life. Hence the feigned panic and the hyperbole that followed the Deorala sati. Hence the remarkable contemporaneous claim by the Harvard-trained Minister of State for Home Affairs that hundreds and thousands of Roop Kanwars have been killed in India. In so claiming, P. Chidambaram ignored that in the last fifty years, cases of sati have mainly been confined to one state, and within that state to one region. He also neglected to point out that the figures involved do not match the rate of homicide in even the smallest of Indian towns.[2]

One suspects that this search for grand spectacles of evil has shaped much of the middle-class response to Roop's sati and has led to an avoidance of the basic issues raised by her death. For only as a search for evidences of the inferiority of the other India can one explain the tenor of public debate on the subject: those who declared the Deorala sati to be a "pure case of murder" attacked, in the same breath, Indian traditions, village superstitions, even the *Mahabharata* and the *Ramayana*. As if a pure case of murder could not involve greed pure and simple and could not be handled under the existing Indian penal code, without reference to the larger cultural factors.

This ambivalent response, depicting sati as simple murder, yet as something more than murder, has already created strange anomalies in Indian public life. First, thanks to the supposed legal reforms brought about by anti-sati activists—the new statute against the glorification of sati—there can now be systematic attempts to pass off cases of sati as cases of murder, since cases of murder now give the accused and the police more room for maneuvering than do cases of sati.[3] For instance, abetment to murder does not invite the death penalty, but abetment to sati now does.[5] Second, there is the danger that a draconian law like this, passed by legislature as a public gesture against a social pathology, may become available to the state for misuse against political opponents, or even for the simpler purpose of extorting money through law-enforcement agencies.

In the following pages, I shall try to rescue for discussion four "undiscussable" issues that have fallen victim to the new mystifications produced by the public debate on sati in metropolitan India. The issues I have chosen to reproblematize are the nature of coercion in sati, the glorification of sati, the roots of sati in the traditional role of woman, and the use of the state to stop the practice of sati.

Four Issues Problematized

First, the matter of coercion. The earliest reports on the Deorala sati did not mention any coercion. Some people, including Roop Kanwar's parents and their relatives staying at Deorala, seemed sure that none was used. (As one knows from cases of wives who are killed by their in-laws for failing to bring satisfactory amounts of dowry from their parents, the victim's parental family are usually the first to challenge a suicide theory floated by in-laws.) In the second week, stray reports of coercion began to come in, but a majority still did not speak of any direct use of force.[5] By the end of the third week, however, the large majority of journalists were fully convinced that Roop's death was a clear case of cold-blooded murder. One newspaper gave lurid details of how she had run away and hid in a barn and was pulled out from there to be burnt.[6] Nine months later, coercion was so obvious that at least one reporter in a major national newspaper—as well as some policemen—had come to the point of lamenting that torture could not be used to extract information from some of the witnesses.[7]

Now, I believe that suspicion as to coercion should be exercised in all cases of sati. I say this not merely because I am doomed to be a skeptic in matters such as these, but also because I once studied the epidemic of sati in eastern India in the early years of British rule.[8] During that period, nearly all cases of sati for which the data are recorded suggested direct or indirect coercion. That experience has left its mark on me. For the moment, however, I am concerned not with the empirical reality of the sati at Deorala but with the certitudes of middle-class commentators on that reality.

I believe it was naive on the part of some journalists and social workers to assume at the beginning that there had been no coercion. In the main, their information was provided by some of the same villagers who had applauded the rite in the first place. It was equally naive for others, who later came to believe that the Deorala sati was a clear case of homicide, to trust the same villagers who had earlier denied any coercion. In both cases, there being no outside observers when the sati took place, a little healthy skepticism about the constructions of the villagers would have done no harm. Traditional Indian villagers, when dealing with their modern urban compatriots, can be remarkably devious, cautious, and secretive, and can demonstrate a sharp instinct for survival. Many of the same Rajput youths who bared swords at Deorala in 1987 to defend the sacred place of sati against its opponents were later seen hedging their bets, after the Indian state reaffirmed the illegality of sati. To trust such defenders of the faith as informants may reveal one's confidence in human nature, but not one's political acuity.

In any event, direct physical coercion was hardly the central issue. Did those claiming that Roop's death was a case of murder really mean that, if force had not been used, the rite would have been justified? If so, theirs was essentially the position of the Shankaracharya of Puri and local politicians such as the Janata Party chieftain in Rajasthan, Kalyan Singh Kalvi. They, too, said that sati was unjustified when force was used; but they concluded that, since force had not been used in this instance, Roop's sati was blameless. There may have been disagreement about the facts of coercion, then, but in the public debate there was perfect agreement between most supporters and opponents of sati as to the principle involved. Few raised the crucial question: was the sati justifiable if no direct physical coercion occurred?

The answer to this question must be based on an awareness that no religious event of this kind can remain uncontaminated by our times. None is safe from the secular cost-calculations and market morality that have now filtered their way into even the remote interstices of Indian society. Many of the Rajputs protesting the new anti-sati legislation are refusing to acknowledge this triumph of secularism and modernity. Some of them are convinced, like many Sikhs, that the rest of society is trying to get them. In reaction, they are trying to defend a rite that they believe remains pure, an aspect of the traditional religious world view.

Today, even when a widow independently decides to commit suicide, that independence cannot but be imperfect. For one can never be sure that her family, her village, and her caste, motivated by common greed and the hunt for higher status, have not pushed her into it. They need not even be self-consciously greedy or status-hungry. It is possible to push a person to self-destruction by creating the right atmosphere—without being aware that one is creating such an atmosphere.

Even if one assumes that no force was used in Roop's case, it is clear that the family and village did nothing to persuade her to reconsider her headstrong decision. Nothing they did encouraged her to pull out of the depression caused by her husband's death. In fact, they colluded with her self-destructive desires. The sati was organized within a few hours, even before Roop's parents could talk to her. There is no record of any serious effort by her in-laws to dissuade her from the self-immolation; and Roop's parental family, confronted with a *fait accompli*, did not create a fuss. But this proves only their pragmatism, not the authenticity of the sati. Both sides of the family knew that the sati would pay them—the relatives, the villagers, and the caste—handsome, long-term dividends. It is pointless to argue that they did not know beforehand the full extent of the profit they would reap. They must have known in a general way, and one suspects that, as denizens of the *kaliyuga*—our final, fallen age of human history—they knew more than that.

The second question is: does the recent government enactment proscribing the glorification of sati really make sense? Can it be effective, given its point of departure, or is some other course possible?

To begin with, what are its limits? Does the new law mean that children will be forbidden to read about or admire Rani Padmini's self-chosen death in medieval times? Does it mean that the part of the *Mahabharata* which describes Madri's sati will now be censored? What about Rabindranath Tagore's awe-inspiring, respectful depiction of sati and Abanindranath Tagore's brilliant invocation of the courage, idealism, and tragedy of sati in medieval Rajasthan?[9] Do we proscribe these works, forgetting that the Tagores were at the forefront of the movement against sati during the colonial period? And what about Kabir, who, over the last four centuries, has remained the ultimate symbol of nondenominational spirituality and interreligious tolerance in India? After all, as Coomaraswamy points out, he constantly used the impulse to sati as an image for surrendering one's ego to God.[10] Finally, what does one do with the original sati? Does one ban the celebration of Durga Puja or, for that matter, the reading of Kalidasa's *Kumarasambhava*, following the logic of two young activists who have been keen to get the *Ramayana* declared unconstitutional so that it could not be shown on government-sponsored television? That these questions may not in the future remain merely theoretical or hypothetical is made obvious by the fact that the Indian History Congress felt obliged to adopt a statement critical of the TV *Ramayana* in its 1988 convention.[11]

One possible response to such questions is to *presume* that in the mythical past sati was a rare, fearsome, but moving ritual that symbolized the reaffirmation of the purity, self-sacrifice, power, and dignity of women, and the superiority of the feminine principle in the cosmos. This posture has a certain provisional logic, in that it calls into question the ill-educated assumption on the part of decultured Indians (not to mention foreigners) that classical or mythological instances of sati demonstrate the degradation of women. Such people would do well to read what is probably the twentieth century's most spirited defense of the philosophy of sati, the one offered by Ananda K. Coomaraswamy.[12] I always recommend it to shallow, pompous progressives and feminists who believe that one ought only to immolate oneself for secular causes like revolution and nationalism, not for old fashioned religious or cultural causes.

The asymmetry between sacrifices for secular and nonsecular causes, to which Coomaraswamy drew our attention, is now being systematically propagated through the Indian media as the last word on the subject. In the third week of November 1987, when the debate on sati was at its height, the self-immolation of a DMK party worker in Tamilnadu for the cause of Sri Lankan Tamils was mentioned without any fanfare in the inside pages of virtually all the national dailies. It is no surprise that there was not even a murmur of discomfiture on the part of the newspaper-reading public.[13]

Whatever one may presume about the nobility of sati in the mythical past, its status in real, contemporary times—in the deep *kaliyuga*—is a different story. Sati as observed is a rite that has been corrupted by modern market forces and by the idea of negotiable social status. In real time, it is safer to presume that sati is a perverted form of sacrifice, if not homicide, than to allow for the contrary possibility. To borrow a phrase from criminal law, it is better to prevent a hundred authentic satis than to allow one inauthentic sati to occur.

This differentiation between the idea of sati and its practice, between sati in mythical time and sati in historical time, between sati as an event (*ghatana*) and sati as a system (*pratha*), between authentic and inauthentic sati is not my contribution to the understanding of the rite. This distinction was already implicit, for instance, in the writings of Rabindranath Tagore, who aggressively opposed sati as practiced in contemporary times, yet treated the ideas behind it respectfully. It is implicit in folk culture in many parts of India. It may also be implicit in the difference between the simple faith of the pilgrims who thronged Deorala after the sati and the actions of the main organizers of the event, who profited so greatly from it.[14] And certainly it is implicit in the contrast between the monuments that have attended a sati such as that of Roop Kanwar and the absence of such monuments in the wake of the virtual epidemic of satis that occurred in eighteenth- and nineteenth-century Bengal.

While more than a hundred sati temples and hundreds of *chhatris* (memorials) are spread over large parts of India, to the best of my knowledge no such temple or *chhatri* exists in honor of any one of the thousands of women who committed sati in that late eighteenth- and early nineteenth-century epidemic. Now there are a few sati temples in Bengal, set up mainly by Rajasthanis, and someone may discover one or two of them to have developed a connection with mythologized satis from the early years of colonialism. Yet the paucity of temples commemorating these nineteenth-century satis (there were five per day at the height of the epidemic) tells us something, as does the comment of a priest in one of the few existent sati temples in Bengal that true sati is impossible in our times. Evidently, at some level, an awareness exists among common Indians that the satis in colonial Bengal were not authentic and therefore did not deserve to be honored. It is not all a matter of superstition and blind faith. Traditional Indians do discriminate; they do make moral choices.

One acquires the right to talk of the inauthenticity of satis in the *kaliyuga* only after respectfully admitting the authenticity of the values that speak through the acts of sati recorded in the epics and myths—or behind the mythologized accounts of satis in historical times, as for example in the medieval satis recounted by the balladeers and folk-singers of Rajasthan. The two Tagores, Rabindranath and Abanindranath, showed us how to do it, by writing with great sensitivity and a touch of tragedy about sati in mythologized history, even though they were proud that their own family had consistently fought for the abolition of sati in contemporary times.

If such discrimination is not shown, modernist criticisms of sati are likely to have the same impact that criticisms of child-marriage have so far had on village India—namely, none at all. The reasons for this are obvious. The ideas represented in the myth of the original sati, as reaffirmed in epics, folktales, and ballads, continue to live in the ears and minds of millions of Indians. These ideas constitute part of the basic substratum of Indian culture. They cannot be wiped away by angry letters to the editors of newspapers.

Once one evinces respect for the ideas of sati at the mythological level, one acquires the right to criticize all individual instances of sati, even those put forward in the myths themselves. One can even say that Madri in the *Mahabharata* or, for that matter, Parvati should not have committed sati, and that what took place at Deorala was not sati but murder. Such criticisms will make sense to many of the 300,000 pilgrims to Deorala, in the same way that similar criticisms by great Indians made sense to earlier generations. After all, criticisms of sati that began many centuries ago in a traditional context have continued to resonate up to modern times, even if not in a tone audible to self-styled modernists.[15]

In this respect sati is part of a larger picture. Rammohun Roy could be heard when he ridiculed Krishna for killing Putana; and Tagore when he criticized the way Sumitra was treated in the *Ramayana* or when he made Karna, not Arjuna, the hero of a verse-play. Both had precedents in premodern times. Madhusudan Dutt made Rama the villain of his epic and Meghnad the hero; and he, too, was said to have been partly inspired by much earlier texts: Tamil and Jain *Ramayanas*. These great Indians viciously attacked aspects of tradition that did not fit in with their concepts of an ethics appropriate to their age (*yugadharma*), and few challenged their right to do so. Because they understood and revered the values enshrined in the tradition as a whole, they were felt to deserve an audience when they attacked or reinterpreted certain figures in the Indian epics or even made fun of them. Only a few illegitimate children of the British Raj—self-proclaimed, semi-Westernized defenders and comic-strip satraps of Hinduism such as the Shiv Sena's Bal Thackeray and the Hindu

Mahasabha's Vikram Savarkar, whose feelings of cultural inferiority cause them to semiticize Hinduism—have challenged this right of dissent in recent years and gotten away with it, and only in metropolitan India at that.

Third, there is the question of the alleged degradation of women in the ideology of sati. The existing literature on sati—broadly understood, not just in its Hindu form—indicates that the idea of sati was associated with convictions about the sacred and magical powers of woman, both right-handed (straightforward) and left-handed (sinister) kinds. These associations went with fears of woman, her power, and her special status in the cosmos. As a carrier of the ultimate principle of nature and the cosmic feminine principle, a woman was conceived to be the natural protector of her man. It was taken for granted that a man could not match her in piety, power, or will. To moderns, the mythology of the rite seems an insult to women, but that is mainly because these meanings are lost to us. We cannot in the same breath blame traditional India for being organized around religion and also claim that the religious power women enjoy in Indian society is meaningless.

In recent times these noneconomic powers of women have not only declined but been devalued. Like men, women in India, too, are assessed more and more in terms of their productive capacity and the market value of that capacity. Wherever that market value is low and market morality infects social relationships, the chances of sati—now more appropriately called widow-burning—increase.[16] They also increase when women have access to economic power within the family but family relationships become largely interest-based as a result of large-scale breakdowns in cultural values.

It was such a combination of circumstances—and the one-dimensional valuation of women that it produced—that precipitated the only large-scale epidemic of sati we have witnessed in the last 300 years. The Bengal epidemic of sati was a logical culmination of rational, secular cost-calculation against the background of a large-scale breakdown in traditional values. In colonial Bengal, sati was certainly an expression of the degradation of woman, but traditional values were not at all the cause. If anything, modern values, not traditional ones, were to blame.

Finally, there is the question of social intervention through the state. V. N. Datta in a recent book has tried to sum up the attitudes of Muslim rulers of India, especially the Mughal emperors, towards sati.[17] The Mughals were hostile to sati, and some of them saw it as a by-product of Hindu idolatry. But they did not use the might of the state to suppress it. Instead, they insisted on prior government permission for performances of sati as an insurance against coercion. By delaying such permission, supposedly to screen out genuine satis from inauthentic ones, they put obstacles in the way of the prospective sati. The aim, as reported by the traveler Bernier, was to wear down the patience of the widows. That this usually worked is partly indicated by Jean de Therenot's remark that the relatives of prospective satis sometimes sought to bribe Mughal officers. Women with children were in any case not allowed by the Mughals to burn themselves, because they were expected to look after and educate their children. One emperor, Jehangir, required those wishing to commit sati in regions near the capital to appear before him personally to obtain permission. Promises of gifts and land were made to them to dissuade them from the act.

Ultimately, such tactics probably worked because, paradoxically, the Mughal hostility to sati went with a deep respect for the values represented by the rite. Coomaraswamy reminds his modern readers of the poem of Muhammad Riza Nau'i, written in the reign of Akbar, on the sati of a Hindu girl whose betrothed was killed on the day of marriage:

> This Musulman poet, to whom the Hindus were "idolaters," does not relate his story in any spirit of religious intolerance or ethical condescension. . . . He does not wonder at the wickedness of men, but at the generosity of women. . . .
>
> This Hindu bride refused to be comforted and wished to be burnt on the pyre of her dead betrothed. When Akbar was informed of this, he called the girl before him and offered wealth and protection, but she rejected all his persuasion. . . . Akbar was forced, though reluctantly, to give his consent to the sacrifice, but sent with her his son Prince Daniyal who continued to dissuade her. Even from within the flames, she replied to his remonstrances, "Do not annoy, do not annoy, do not annoy."[18]

The last word of Nau'i on the subject is as follows:

> Teach me, O God, the Way of Love,
> and enflame my heart with this maiden's Fire.[19]

As for the colonial period, it is not widely known that Rammohun Roy (1772–1833), the social reformer whose name is most closely associated with the struggle against sati in historical times, was himself ambivalent toward a legal ban on sati; according to some, he opposed such a ban.[20] Horror of horrors, he also showed respect for the values unpinning the mythology of sati by pointing out that the rite presumed the superiority in the cosmos of the feminine principle over the masculine and recognized the woman's greater loyalty, courage, and firmness of spirit. Perhaps he wanted a reform movement rather than the colonial state to be the main instrument of social change. Given that he also saw the social values constituting the philosophy of sati to be an endorsement of the superiority of the feminine principle over the masculine, it could even be hypothesized that he saw his society as perfectly capable of handling the pathology of sati with the help of its own cultural resources. After all, he did sense that the epidemic of sati he was seeing around him was a product of colonialism, not of traditions; and that the epidemic was a feature of exactly the part of the society—the Westernizing, culturally uprooted, urban and semi-urban Indians—that was most dismissive toward the rest of the society as a bastion of superstition and atavism.[21]

This is a reading of sati for which I once, fifteen years ago, tried to give some direct and indirect evidence. Some secular-rationalists and modernists have virulently objected to the reading, but they have not, I believe, put forward an alternative explanation that links the social context and empirical reality of sati to the understanding of it that motivated policymakers and social activists to fight against it during the colonial period. When it comes to criticisms of modernity, the rationality of the rationalists all too easily collapses!

Interestingly, many contemporaries of Rammohun Roy acknowledged the modern, colonial connection. They included some who were aggressively anti-Hindu and would have loved to blame Indian traditions for the outbreak of sati in Bengal—for instance, the Baptist missionary Joshua Marshman. Even those who were unable to see the direct colonial involvement often identified the distorted remnants of tradition as the main culprit, and saw that sati was not a problem when such traditions flourished undisturbed.

Probably one can sum up the argument in retrospect by saying that, even if one takes a consistently modernist view, sati, when it was a discrete event (*ghatana*), was an instance of individual pathology and remained thus primarily in the domain of clinical psychology and psychiatry; sati, when it became a system (*pratha*), became primarily a social problem and entered the domain of social psychology and social psychiatry. The state comes in as an important actor mainly in the second case.

The Modern, Neocolonial Critique

Blurring the two categories—sati as event and sati as a custom or epidemic—is essential for those seeking to adapt the colonial discourse for internal use, both as a political strategy and as a psychological defense. It is remarkable how, since the Deorala event, there has been a revival of efforts by anglophone, psychologically uprooted Indians—exactly the sector that produced the last epidemic of sati in eastern India—to vend sati as primarily a stigma of Hinduism, not as one of the by-products of the entry of modern values into India. (A truer reading would emphasize the role played by the absolutization of contractual social relationships, the productivity principle, and market morality.) At one time, most such efforts were closely associated with attempts to justify British rule in India. Now, as a cultural projection of a new form of internal colonialism, these efforts are primarily associated with the rootless, Westernized, Indian *haute bourgeoisie* who control the media, either directly or through the state.

At least one scholar has expressed her anguish that the criticisms of sati since the Deorala event have borrowed so heavily from colonial discourse.[22] What she has seen is correct, and such borrowing is to be expected. Colonialism has to try to discredit the cultures of the colonized to validate the colonial or quasi-colonial social relationships that it itself has created. Culture can be resistance, and those seeking hegemony in the realm of political economy cannot afford to leave that area alone. The self-declared social engineers in the Third World and their support base within the tertiary sector of that world know this fully. One indicator of that awareness in India today is that Roop's sad and unnecessary death has become for the urban Indian bourgeoisie another marker of the cultural backwardness of the traditional Indian, even though responsibility for the death should be shared by social forces to which these Westernized Indians have contributed handsomely. These forces constitute the kind of attack on more traditional life-styles that has produced epidemics of sati in the past.

Nothing reveals the clay feet of middle-class progressivism more clearly than its attack on any toleration of the values that prompted Indians to remember and venerate premodern satis over the centuries. These values cut across Indian society, challenging barriers posed by caste, class, gender, age, and even religion. The available data show that veneration of sati continues to be a characteristic of Indian society as a whole.[23] Many middle-class social critics and radicals call such respect "glorification of sati" and want it to be banned. They believe it contributes directly to instances of sati in contemporary times. People who hold this view often style themselves Marxists, yet when it comes to sati and village India, they forget the relevance of materialist interpretations of history and the socioeconomic determination of social pathologies. Too often they speak as if the ideology of sati itself produced sati.

In much that I have said, I have drawn a comparison between contemporary middle-class and earlier colonial reactions to sati. Even closer comparisons can be made, however, to the reaction of the urban bourgeoisie to the Muslim Women's Bill in 1986—the Shah Bano affair—and to a not so widely known plea that some Bengali intellectuals addressed to the West Bengal government at about the same time, to the effect that it should suppress Santhal witch-doctors. As the agitation against the Muslim Women's Bill is likely to be better known than the Santhal case to readers of this essay, I shall confine my comments to it.

The protest against the Muslim Women's Bill, like that against Roop Kanwar's sati, was meant to resist the victimization of women and was justified as such. But those who spoke so loudly against the victimization of the single woman involved—Shah Bano, who had been divorced and left in penury by her well-to-do Muslim husband—failed to appreciate (or tried to whitewash) the larger victimization of the community involved. They pretended that the Shah Bano case could be discussed without taking into account the fact that a large proportion of Muslims have been discriminated against, frequently subjected to violence, and pushed increasingly into urban ghettos by the encompassing Hindu society. They behaved as if one did not have to recognize that, in this discrimination and violence, the Indian state and its law-enforcing agencies—two main actors in the Shah Bano case and the self-declared agents of social change on behalf of Muslim society—had played a growing role, whether deliberately or by default.[24]

In their insecurity, fear, and sense of being cornered, a large section of the Muslims were bound to see the court's judgment in favor of Shah Bano as another attack by the same state machinery against their identity and culture, which was, in fact, their last line of defense. No wonder they closed ranks and supported even the more obscurantist and fanatic elements among them. It was eerie to see how well this closing of ranks suited the Westernized middle-class Indians who opposed the Muslim cause; it was as if they were waiting for just that. The moment some of the more atavistic elements in Muslim society joined their voices in protest, the chorus was interpreted by a drove of near-hysterical social analysts as final proof of the moral and cultural decadence of Muslims, as another of the stigmata of Islam itself. Notorious Muslim-baiters began to shed copious tears over the plight of Muslim women, much as some well-furnished drawing rooms in urban India were soon to reverberate with lamentations over the plight of rural Rajasthani women such as Roop Kanwar.

Let me conclude by admitting a central problem that every critic of modernity must face up to. Every culture has a dark side. Sati in the *kaliyuga* actualizes some of the possibilities inherent in the darker side of India's traditional culture, even if this actualization has been made possible by the forces of modernity impinging on and seeking to subvert the traditional culture. After all, the tradition of sati exists in some cultures, not in all, and the kind of pathological self-expression

found in some South Asian cultures is not present in other parts of
the world.

However defensive one might be in public, and whatever might be
one's position on issues such as sati, one does know both sides of the picture, although it is often painful to admit that knowledge. For modern
Indians, there are professional colleagues and friends to be considered, and
the fear of being shamed in the metropolitan centers of dominant global
culture. For nonmoderns, there are loyalties to caste and community, and
the pathetic attempts to reaffirm a faith that has become shaky within.
When modern urban Indians froth in anger at Roop's death, it is partly
because they suspect that her sati was a matter not merely of blind superstition but of rational cost-calculation superimposed on nonrational faith.
They suspect that some individuals invested in and profited from Roop's
death. That is what arouses such deep anxiety and free-floating anger in
them: they are horrified to see the villagers of Deorala applying their kind
of secular, instrumental rationality in order to extract the maximum profit
from the nonrational traditions of Indian villages. Such moderns see mirrored in the in-laws of Roop Kanwar their own faces, distorted by what
to them are odd aspects of Indian tradition.

The absence of that particular mix of the rational and nonrational
makes the Indian middle classes relatively callous toward dowry deaths in
urban India—crimes in which recently married women are usually burned
by husbands and in-laws who calculate that the brides have brought in
insufficient dowry. The dowry deaths reflect rational cost-calculation and
profiteering through and through. Although the greed for dowry does
hang on the peg of what is allegedly a pan-Indian tradition—I say allegedly because it is often said that bride-price was more widespread in India than dowry until the earlier decades of this century—no scope for any
mystery is left in the practice. That is why the hundreds of dowry deaths
(the average for New Delhi in the mid-1980s was roughly 150 deaths per
year) cannot match the impact of one sati. As a letter to the editor of *The
Times of India* pointed out soon after the Deorala event,

> On November 1, *The Times of India* reported the death of five women by
> burning. All the incidents were from Delhi. What is shocking is that it is
> almost a daily feature now, with only the numbers varying.
>
> The sati incident at Deorala pales into insignificance before this pheno-
> menon. . . . These are not mishaps; these are planned deaths. . . . When will
> women's welfare organizations and the Central and State governments wake
> up?[25]

To some, the question may seem to have a certain poignancy.
Surely, it draws attention to an asymmetry that may not be obvious
to urban Westernized Indians but was all too obvious to some Deorala
women, who sarcastically pointed out to the visiting women journalists

that burning to death in a West Delhi lower-middle-class concrete slum was no less painful than burning in a Rajasthani village; and that Deorala women were not accustomed to burning their daughters-in-law to death the way urban women did. Perhaps I should also add here that, if Roop's death was a case of murder through burning, there is no dearth of modern Indians who either kept silent about or colluded in the burning of thousands of Sikhs on the streets of Delhi in 1984. Some national dailies that later published strident condemnations of the Deorala sati were then busy censoring news of the anti-Sikh pogrom, lest the role of the Indian state and the ruling Congress Party become apparent.

Sociologically, dowry deaths are clear cases of murder, for no one supports them — not even the neighbors. Sati is different, inviting a mixed response. It arouses anxieties in modern Indians because the idea of self-immolation makes little sense in a world where self-interest is the ultimate currency of public life. That is why, after saying that sati is nothing but unalloyed murder, moderns worry not about the nearly 3,000 people getting murdered every year in Bihar's countryside in land-related disputes, but about the few cases of sati in Rajasthan. Moderns can understand that sati might be exploited for profit, but they nervously remember the 300,000 people who went to Deorala on pilgrimage after Roop's death with no interest in profit at all. Their faith was real and not feigned, and it tells Westernized Indians something they do not like to hear.

Yet modern societies do not lack their own rituals of imposed or forced self-immolation. Why is it not troubling to see teenaged soldiers goose-stepping to their death in war, in a society that has militarized spectacularly during the last decade? Instead of opium, the soldiers are given alcohol; instead of fear of a widow's going back on her decision to commit sati, there is fear of desertion. Moderns have argued that any mention of conjugal loyalty in the context of sati is sexist, because men do not immolate themselves on the death of their wives. But just because self-immolation in war is a male preserve, does this mean that women are incapable of a comparable loyalty? As in sati, so in war there is a charged atmosphere and a ritual fervor that makes self-immolation seem justified; there are even priests, secular and nonsecular, to smooth one's journey to the other world. Above all, there are profits to be made from wartime self-immolations, and the scale of profits to be made in war today would put to shame both Roop's in-laws and their political supporters.

Can one expect a hundredth of the enthusiasm that journalists and the media have shown about sati if one invites them to take a position on the culture of armaments and war? If the answer is no, is it a part of the intellectual's moral responsibility in contemporary India to inquire why this is so? Is the comic anti-hero in *Monsieur Verdoux* correct when he insists that if one kills a few one is a murderer, but if one kills a million, one

is a hero, for number sanctifies? Can it be that war is more forgivable because it is not a proof of the superstitions of the defeated cultures of Asia
and Africa but a respectable instrument of diplomacy and a profession on
which the modern world is built?[26]

What are the psychological forces that numb social sensitivities
thus? Are they the same that prompt the apologists of sati to blind
themselves to the fact that Roop Kanwar was an eighteen-year-old girl
whose mental state, after her husband's death, was hardly what would
be needed to set a responsible course of action? Are these insensitivi-
ties comparable to those that kept anyone from helping the young girl
at Deorala move out of her depression, instead of pushing her into self-
immolation even before her parents could meet her? It has been very
difficult for moderns reacting to the sati of Roop Kanwar to ask such
questions, but these are the questions — questions about oneself—with
which one ultimately has to deal.

Notes

An earlier version of this essay was published in *The Illustrated Weekly of India*,
January 17, 1988. That version was written as an intervention in a public debate
and addressed to Indians living in India. Naturally, the tone of the essay was less
than scholarly. I regret, through not very deeply, that a touch of that tone has
persisted in this version, too.

1. For instance, Chinu Panchal, "1,500 Witness 'Sati' Ritual," *The Times of
India*, October 6, 1986.

2. P. Chidambaram, quoted in Tavleen Singh, *Indian Express*, May 29, 1988.
On the broad sociology and "epidemiology" of sati, see the special issue of *Seminar* 342 (February 1988), on the subject.

3. See the case of Shakuntala Yadav, reported in Rahul Pathak, "Confess to
Murder, Cops Tell Family," *Indian Express*, January 13, 1988; Minu Jain, "Sati
or Murder," *Sunday Observer*, January 18, 1988. See also "Sati or Suicide," *Indian
Express*, January 12, 1988; and "Another Sati Reported in U.P. Village," *The
Statesman*, January 12, 1988.

4. Maja Daruwala, "Overkill of Sati Bill," *The Statesman*, January 21, 1988.
For the text of the new sati legislation, see *The Commission of Sati (Prevention)
Act, 1987 [Act No. 3 of 1988] with Short Notes* (Lucknow: Eastern Book Co.,
n.d.).

5. For instance, Shabnam Virmani, "The Spirit of Sati Lives On," *The Times
of India*, September 12, 1987. According to her, it was "unlikely that Roop
Kanwar was coerced into it by relatives," and that the villagers were "tight-lipped
and wary of press reporters and the public." Within two weeks the same newspaper published Sunil Menon's "Roop Kanwar's Act was not Voluntary" (*The Times
of India*, September 25, 1987). Roop Kanwar's parents have continued to deny that

she was coerced. See Sanjeev Srivastava, "Deorala Revisited," *The Illustrated Weekly of India*, May 22, 1988, pp. 20–23.

6. "Dragged to Pyre for Sati," *The Statesman,* October 21, 1988.

7. Sanjeev Srivastava, "Doctor Elusive about Deorala Incident," *The Times of India*, June 4, 1988. Srivastava wrote wistfully:

> Some of the police officials associated with the investigation of the case also feel handicapped in their efforts to extract more information as no "third-degree methods" could be used during the interrogation of Dr. Singh.

8. Ashis Nandy, "Sati: A Nineteenth Century Tale of Women, Violence and Protest," *At the Edge of Psychology: Essays in Politics and Culture* (New Delhi: Oxford University Press, 1980), pp. 1–31.

9. E.g., Rabindranath Tagore, "Vivāha," *Kathī o Kāhinī*, in *Racanābali* (Calcutta, Viśvabhāratī, 1987), vol. 4, pp. 71–73; and "Ma Bhaih," *Kathā o Kāhinī*, vol. 3, pp. 676–79; Abanindranath Tagore, *Rājkāhinī* (Calcutta: Signet Press, 1956).

10. Ananda K. Coomaraswamy, "Status of Indian Women," *The Dance of Shiva: Fourteen Indian Essays* (Delhi: Munshiram Manoharlal, 1982), pp. 115–39. See p. 128.

11. Only one scholar to date has critically assessed the modern discomfort with the TV *Rāmāyaṇa*, arguing that the discomfort comes from moderns' lack of access to the epics and inability to use them creatively. See G. P. Deshpande, "The Riddle of the Sagar Ramayana," *Economic and Political Weekly*, October 22, 1988, pp. 2215–16.

12. See note 11.

13. The reaction of modern India to the self-immolation of a Jain man of religion at about the same time was also minimal: the death was viewed as the foolish self-destructiveness of a slightly senile religious enthusiast. The reaction to the self-chosen death of Vinoba Bhave some years earlier was not much different.

14. When I first made a distinction between sati as a *ghatana* or event and sati as a *pratha* or system or practice in this and an earlier essay ("Sati in Kaliyuga," *Indian Express*, November 1987), there were howls of protest and hysterical outbursts in some journals and news weeklies. It was seen as direct support for sati; and some, not knowing that I was not a Hindu, even found in it indications of Hindu fanaticism. One called it a *dharmic* support of sati (Sudhir Chandra, "Sati: The *Dharmic* Fallacy," *New Quest* 68 (March–April, 1988), pp. 111–14). Another found the use of the "Hindu" fourfold division of *yugas* itself a clinching evidence of my real self: Kumkum Sangari, "Perpetuating the Myth," *Seminar* 342 (February 1988), pp 24–30. My faith in the practical wisdom injected or imposed by involvement in the politics of social reform was restored when two women activists, troubled by the sati bill, subsequently wrote the following comments:

> The bill assumes sati is a practice, whereas it could be described as a kind of rare and frightful event which reveals, in a flash, several of the problems of

our time. In other words, we might do well to consider whether it is now being given the sanctity of tradition and practice, and if so by whom and with motives. In order to do this, we must first distinguish between sati as an act, sati as an ideology, and sati as a source of political and financial profit.

> There is . . . a difference between those who organize the event of sati, . . . those who eulogize the principle of sati underlying one particular incident hundreds of years ago but repudiate the act of sati today, . . . and those who glorify the act in self-interest, be it practical or financial. (Latika Sarkar and Radha Kumar, "Flaws in New Sati Bill," *The Times of India*, December 15, 1987)

The only thing I might add here is that Sarkar and Kumar seem to be unaware in their discussion that sati is being associated with "the sanctity of tradition and practice" not merely by religious fanatics but also by a large section of India's modern literati, with a different set of motives and interests. Cf. S. Sahay, "Perspective on Sati," *The Telegraph*, January 26, 1988.

15. Cf. Arvind Sharma, *Sati* (Delhi: Motilal Banarsidas, 1988), pp. 15–17; and Romila Thapar, "In History," *Seminar* 342 (February 1988), pp. 14–19.

16. Nandy, "Sati."

17. V. N. Datta, *Sati: A Historical, Social, and Philosophical Enquiry into the Hindu Rite of Widow Burning* (New Delhi: Manohar, 1987), especially pp. 13–14.

18. Coomaraswamy, "Status," pp. 128–29.

19. Coomaraswamy, "Status," p. 129.

20. Ramesh Chandra Majumdar, *Glimpses of Bengal in the Nineteenth Century* (Calcutta: Firma K. L. Mukhopadhyay, 1960).

21. For a fuller treatment of this subject, see Nandy, "Sati."

22. Veena Das, "Strange Response," *The Illustrated Weekly of India*, February 8, 1988.

23. "Roop Kanwar Did the Right Thing," *The Times of India*, December 11, 1987. This survey showed that 63.4% of the respondents—63% of women and 41.5% in the age group 25–40—supported sati, and that 50.8% refused to accept it as a crime. This, 160 years after sati was legally banned.

24. Cf. B. C. Parekh, "Between Holy Text and Moral Void," *The New Statesman*, March 24, 1989, pp. 29–33.

25. Satish Gogia, letter to the editor, *The Times of India*, November 5, 1987. Also see Pradeep S. Mehta, letter to the editor, *The Times of India*, December 5, 1988.

26. In the entire debate on sati during 1987–1988 in India's English-language press, probably only Bill Aitken in his "Abomination (Private) Limited" (*The Statesman*, March 30, 1988), had the honesty to confront the issue of priorities, first raised by Ananda Coomaraswamy in the 1930s. Aitken raised the issue in response to the shallow, crypto-racist, bogus anthropology of George L. Hart in "Sati Just a Form of Human Sacrifice" (*The Statesman*, March 29, 1988). There have been more human sacrifices in this century, Aitken says in response to Hart, than in the 2,000 years leading up to it.

Aitken also recognized that Hart's article was a crude attempt to placate India's Westernized elite, provoked by his protegé Patrick D. Harrigan's two articles: "Tyranny of the Elect?" (*The Statesman*, November 5, 1987), and "Is Tradition Ridiculed by Western Values?" (*The Statesman*, March 5, 1988). Both dissented from the views popular among India's modern elites, although the dissent was steeped in innocence about the political sociology of traditions in contemporary India.

Comment:
Widows as Cultural Symbols

AINSLIE T. EMBREE

"Be very careful o' widders all your life," Mr. Weller advised his son in *The Pickwick Papers*, thus articulating a sense—if not universal, at least very widespread—that widowhood was a peculiar aspect of the human condition, characterized as a misfortune both for the widow and for the society in which she lived. According to the Oxford English Dictionary our English word *widow* is cognate with a series of Indo-European terms with such meanings as empty, separated, lacking, and destitute. The reason why a woman attains this state is clear: deprived through death of the protection of her husband, she has become an object of charity, a burden on society, and, very frequently, vulnerable to exploitation by the heartless and the powerful. At the same time, as in Dickens's story, she is a threat to social order, a *memento mori*, who, if she remarries, is likely to cause her husband to conclude, as Mr. Weller did, that "it's a great pity that she ever changed her condition."[1] Indian culture, however, with its marvelous capacity for logical solutions to intractable social problems, devised a practice that enabled a woman whose husband had died to avoid the horrid status of widowhood. Instead, she could choose to become a sati, to attain a transformed condition as an alternative to widowhood.

Ashis Nandy's essay in these pages focuses on the changed condition brought about through what he calls the *ghatana*, or event—the actual ritual of immolation—as well as its *pratha*, or meaning within the cultural system. His point of departure is a specific event, the death of a young woman that gained extraordinary attention in India in 1987. He chose to "reproblematize," as he puts it, four related issues: the place of coercion in the act of self-immolation; the veneration given to the person who performs the act; its roots in the Indian ethos; and the function of the state in forbidding the practice. The unifying themes of the essay are, however, his interpretations of the reaction of India's Westernized, urban middle class to the event at Deorala and, to a much lesser extent, the reaction of its organizers. Here, as well as in his other writings on the subject, Nandy finds in the practice of sati a dramatic occasion for a searching criticism of modern Indian society.[2] He asks and gives a very forceful answer to the query, "What is the symbolic meaning of sati in contemporary times?"[3]

For Nandy, one symbolic meaning of the reaction to the sati in Deorala is that it demonstrated the nature of the conflict between the Westernized elites, whom he also speaks of as "decultured Indians," over against the masses of non-modern India. He does not use the terms, but he trembles on the verge of referring to these rural masses, in the fashion so beloved of foreigners, as "real Indians," and the elites as "brown Englishmen." The Westernized elites, Nandy says, "froth in anger" at the Deorala sati but are relatively restrained in the face of greater horrors, such as the hundreds of "dowry deaths"—the young brides either deliberately burned to death because they did not bring sufficient dowry for their greedy in-laws or murdered by the thousands in land disputes in Bihar. The Deorala sati, he argues, exposed the anxieties of the elites, by suggesting that beneath the surface of Indian life are values and concerns that cannot be squared with their acceptance of a rational, cost-calculating world. The event, in Nandy's reading, with its appeal to forces that the elites see as superstitious and regressive, threatened their social and political dominance in modern India. Not surprisingly, this interpretation, when voiced on earlier occasions, subjected Nandy to a barrage of criticism from the elites he had excoriated.[4]

Another of Nandy's readings of the meaning of the Deorala event—and one no less controversial than his views regarding the attitudes of the Indian elites—is his argument that sati occurs because of attacks on traditional value systems by new forces from outside. In this essay and in other writings, Nandy argues that the well-known occurrence of many cases of sati in Bengal in the early nineteenth century is to be explained by the intrusion of the British as rulers into Indian society. Sati at that time arose, as he put it in another essay, out of the "pathology of colonialism, not of Hinduism."[5] British rule had introduced "rational, secular cost-calculation" into Indian society, leading to a breakdown of traditional values. The result, according to Nandy, was an "epidemic" of sati that was largely confined "to those groups made marginal by their exposure to Western impact."[6]

Nandy's reasons for stressing the direct relationship between British rule and the "epidemic" of sati in the first decades of the nineteenth century are fairly explicit in this essay, as well as in his other writings on the subject. One obvious and perfectly understandable reason is that he is reacting to the virulent criticism of Indian society that was such a prominent feature of Western writing on India in the early nineteenth century; this leads him to argue that the hundreds of cases of sati reported in Bengal were responses to foreign rule. He does not say (as some of his critics have suggested he does) that there were no sati events before the British intrusion, but he argues that in the premodern period they had a very different symbolic meaning within the society.

The Deorala sati, like those in the early British period, has been interpreted by foreigners—and by modern Indian feminists—as insulting and degrading to women; but this, Nandy insists, is because the original meanings are lost. In traditional society, the mythology of sati was grounded in a belief in the power of women: "As a carrier of the ultimate principle of nature and the cosmic feminine principle, a woman was conceived to be the natural protector of her man." The act of immolation symbolized the conviction of the society that women were stronger, more pious, and more virtuous than men; and sati was a freely performed sacrifice. It was only under the influence of alien forces that sati was transformed into an act of violence against women, because they began to be assessed in economic terms. Sati, now more appropriately called widow-burning, becomes common in times of crisis under foreign rule as the cash nexus enters social relationships and women have access to economic power.

In his writings on sati, Nandy has identified two periods prior to the nineteenth century when "epidemics" of the practice arose, owing to crises within the social order produced by foreign intrusions. One was in Vijayanagara, the great medieval kingdom in South India that was defeated by the Muslim sultanates of the Deccan in the late sixteenth century. The other was in Rajasthan, when the Rajput kingdoms were falling under the control of the Mughal empire.[7] In both cases, evidence about the extent of the custom and about the classes that practiced it is far from clear, since most accounts come from Muslim chroniclers or European travelers, neither of whom had much access to its inner symbolism. The emperor Akbar spoke for most such commentators when he said

> It is the ancient custom in Hindustan for a woman to burn herself, however unwilling she may be, on her husband's death and give her priceless life with a cheerful countenance, conceiving it to be the means of her husband's salvation.[8]

While Akbar did not ban the practice, local officials were ordered to prevent women from being burned against their will. Just what coercion means in a specific case is, as Nandy points out, difficult to define. And if there is no coercion, is sati justifiable? Akbar is unlikely to have had this view in mind; he thought, as did the later Mughal rulers, that the custom was barbarous but that to ban it would provoke the Hindus to rebellion, as they would see such a prohibition as an interference with their religion.

Nandy does not emphasize in his essay here that the incidence of sati in Vijayanagara and the Mughal empire followed on the dislocation of social relationships by foreign rulers, but the complicity of the British is central to his thesis in discussing sati in the early nineteenth century. Using data collected by East India Company officials in the first two decades of the nineteenth century, Nandy argues that precisely the same sector of society—the "anglophone, psychologically uprooted Indians"—that led the agitation against the Deorala sati also produced the epidemic of sati in Eastern India in the early nineteenth century. This is a rather startling accusation for a serious and well-regarded scholar to make against a class whose members, as Nandy would no doubt readily admit, included the leaders of the nationalist movement and (since 1947) the architects of India's political freedom and modernization. Therefore, one must examine, even if cursorily, the validity of his argument—first as regards his analysis of the nineteenth-century situation in Bengal, and then in connection with his interpretation of the symbolic meaning of sati in contemporary times. To support his argument, he draws heavily on empirical data from the period and from the writings and career of one of the most distinguished and familiar figures of modern Indian history, Rammohun Roy.

As far as the empirical data are concerned, Nandy summarizes here (and frequently refers to) the important work he published earlier on sati.[9] At the end of the eighteenth century, in the urban world of greater Calcutta that grew up as a result of the commercial and political activities of the East India Company, upper-caste Bengalis (the group often referred to as the *bhadralok*) experienced, according to Nandy, a deep sense of anomie, of being cut off from their roots in the traditional society. Nandy then makes a statement that I find puzzling. The colonial system, he says, created this anomie by "forcing them to maintain their traditional social dominance on almost new grounds."[10] How this was done and what advantage the new rulers gained from it are not made clear, but in any case Nandy's statistics show that, while the upper castes (the *bhadralok*) constituted only 11 percent of the population, they accounted for 55 percent of the cases of sati. "The rite was becoming popular not among the rural poor or the small peasantry, but among the urban *nouveaux riches* who had lost part of their allegiance to older norms and had no alternative commitments with which to fill the void."[11]

But Nandy provides other statistics that seem to undermine his argument that the Bengal elite, composed of Brahmans and other high castes, were weakened by the imposition of British rule. These Hindu elites, making up 11 percent of the population, he notes, "continued to own three-quarters of all the estates in Bengal, dominated both politics and administration, and controlled most of the trade in the hands of Indians."[12] How the East India Company could have "forced" them to accept such positions of dominance is hard to imagine, but it is reasonable to suppose, as historians have long argued, that these groups used their knowledge of bureaucratic procedures, their entrepreneurial skills, and their status as the traditional elite to become dominant in the society.

The losers were the Muslim elites, displaced by the alliance of the Hindu elites with the British. Rammohun Roy, of whose thought and role in Indian history Nandy in this essay and elsewhere is a distinguished interpreter, gave such a reading of Indian history. Under the Muslim rulers, the natives of Bengal (by which Roy clearly only meant the Hindu population) had had their property plundered, their religion insulted, and their blood wantonly shed. With the establishment of British power and the creation of the city of Calcutta, Roy said, the people came into "possession of such privileges as their forefathers never expected to attain [and] have been gradually advancing in social and intellectual improvement."[13] This may sound sycophantic to modern ears, but Roy was seeing what seemed to him to be the opening of a door to new possibilities for families like his own, who, as he said, had given up their role as spiritual guides in the late seventeenth century for "worldly pursuits and aggrandizement."[14] If this is a true account, his family—and no doubt many others—had begun to "modernize," to shift their social goals, long before the British even dreamed of ruling Bengal.

Nandy gives far too much credit to British officials for shaping the course of Indian history, and far too little to the creative contribution of the elite forces within Indian society. When the West intruded, groups were ready to appropriate from it what was useful to them and to shape what they took to patterns derived from Indian culture itself. The new political India was being born, and the intellectual descendants of the dominant elites in Bengal are the groups whose attitude towards the Deorala sati in 1987 Nandy finds patronizing and destructive.

Nandy has made an important contribution to an understanding of Rammohun's role in the discussion of sati in the first three decades of the nineteenth century. This culminated in the decision in 1829 by the Governor-General, Lord William Bentinck, to forbid the practice of sati in Bengal and the other territories under the control of the East India Company and to make participation in its performance an act of culpable homicide.[15] However, I do not understand Nandy's statement that, despite Roy's close association with the struggle against sati, "it is not widely known that Rammohun Roy . . . was himself ambivalent toward a legal ban on sati; according to some, he opposed such a ban." On the contrary,

I would have supposed that Roy's opposition to passing a law making sati illegal was well known at the time and had usually been referred to by writers on the subject.[16]

In his remarkable Minute giving his reasons for banning sati, despite the opposition of many of the leading officials of his government, Bentinck noted that Rammohun Roy, "that enlightened native," who hated the custom, as well as "all other superstitions and corruption," opposed taking legal action, since the Hindus would interpret this as an attempt by the British to force their religion on the conquered people.[17] No one understood this argument better than Bentinck, since he had been dismissed as Governor of Madras in 1806 because of a mutiny in the army caused, it was alleged, by the fear among Indian soldiers that British officers were interfering in their religious customs. This argument no doubt carried weight with Roy, as it did with many of the British officials, whose greatest concern was that any interference in religion might provoke an uprising.[18] Roy's main reason for not supporting Bentinck's decision, however, was probably his conviction that it was society's attitude toward widows that had to be changed. Making sati illegal would not change the attitude and belief systems that produced the custom; that could only be done through education.

I do not find in Roy's writings or in contemporaries' comments about him much support for Nandy's contention that Roy believed that "the epidemic of sati he was seeing around him was a product of colonialism, not of traditions," nor that it was "a feature of exactly the part of the society—the Westernizing, culturally uprooted, urban and semi-urban Indians—that was most dismissive toward the rest of the society as a bastion of superstition and atavism." I do not think the evidence available to us supports the claim that the increased incidence of sati took place among the "Westernizing" urban groups of Bengal after 1815; and furthermore, it is surely improbable that at the time such a group would have been large enough to supply the 839 women who were reported to have immolated themselves in 1819. My reading of Roy's works leads me to conclude that he would have shared the anger of the "Westernized" elite in 1987 over the death at Deorala. I will even venture to suggest that Roy would have responded to Nandy's query as to why the Westernized elite showed so much more passion over the Deorala incident than they do over dowry deaths by observing that what was horrifying about Roop Kanwar's death was that so many thousands celebrated it. By contrast, no one celebrates a bride-burning or claims religious sanction for it. Roy was genuinely convinced that sati was neither prescribed not sanctioned by the brahmanical tradition, but was a perversion of it—one of those customs that, as he put it in a telling phrase, "destroys the texture of society."[19]

Nandy claims that his critics have not put forward an alternative explanation for the increase in sati in the early period of British rule in Bengal, but in fact a number of explanations seem quite plausible. It is not altogether clear, for example, that the increase in the number of recorded cases of sati from 378 in 1815 to 839 in 1818 was not simply due to more careful counting on the part of the police.[20] A plausible explanation of why there were more satis in Bengal than elsewhere is that the legal system of inheritance known as *dayabhaga*—which gave women the right to inheritance—was used there. As Romila Thapar has suggested, sati provided a convenient way of eliminating an inheritor.[21] She also points out that the fact that so many Brahmin widows became satis may be explained by the practice among elderly Kulin Brahmins in Bengal, for a variety of cultural reasons, of marrying a number of wives, which would naturally lead to more Brahmin widows.

By his insistence in the present essay on the alien government's responsibility for the increased incidence of sati, Nandy weakens, or at least overlooks, the most persuasive element in the analysis he gave in his earlier work on the Bengal situation. His focus on Indian cultural responses to women and widowhood, with arguments derived from Indian social condition, applies equally well, I think, to the Deorala situation, in contrast to the political and economic ones. In the cultural analysis he put forward in his earlier essay, he met some of the criticisms that a number of writers, particularly feminists, have made of his present work—that it is derived from Hindu chauvinism. Sati, he argued, "expressed the culture's deepest fears of—and hatred towards—woman and womanhood."[22] One aspect of this was the belief that a husband's death was owing to his wife's failure to fulfill all the duties and obligations of her marital status; another was that, without the firm control of a husband, a widow would yield to sexual passions, disgracing herself and the family. Through immolation on her husband's pyre, a widow could transform herself, remaining a faithful wife. Nandy made another generalization that is surely relevant to Deorala in saying that the immolation "reduced the sense of guilt in those confronted with their rage against all women."[22] While this is an important insight, it is somewhat misleading, for one suspects that in India, as elsewhere, widows were a special subset of dangerous women and thus required special attention.

While it is easy to push a psychoanalytic analysis of group behavior to a point where it becomes self-parody, Nandy's emphasis on the importance of asking what groups participated in the sati performance as spectators and defenders of the practice is very valuable. The media, particularly television, showed, probably quite unintentionally, that the crowds celebrating the Deorala sati seemed to include a disproportionate number of young men. The same appears to be true of the participants in most incidents of violence that have a religious component—most obviously among the Sikh militants in the Punjab in the movement led by Sant Bhindranwale, and in the uprising in Kashmir from 1990 onward. In these outbreaks, as in virtually every communal riot in India, one gets the impression that these young men are primarily from urban areas, are employed in low-status occupations, and have a sense of being marginal to (and of not profiting from) changes taking place around them. They sense that those who are profiting are precisely the groups Nandy identifies as the Westernized, modernizing elites. The suggestion that the subversion of the old values of religion by these groups is the cause of their frustrations makes an easy appeal. If violence is called for, religion legitimates it, whether it is the armed violence of Kashmir and Punjab or the violent spectacle of sati, whether in Bengal in 1815 or in Deorala in 1987. Nor of course is the legitimation of violence by religion confined to India; pictures of the groups involved in illegal actions against abortion clinics in the United States have curious resemblances to those in the Deorala processions.

In his discussion of Rammohun Roy's views on sati, Nandy does not, I think, give sufficient attention to the fact that the status of widows who did *not* immolate themselves was Roy's central concern. While he was greatly moved by the suffering of the women as they underwent the fiery ordeal, and while he was repelled by the brutish behavior of the spectators, he saw sati as a dramatic summary of society's attitude toward women in general. He presented these views in the form of a dialogue between an advocate of the practice of burning women alive and an opponent of the practice. While the opponent is of course given all the best lines, the advocate's arguments probably echo those that were commonly used. The point of Roy's argument is that widow-burning was necessary for the community because of the place assigned to women—not, in his understanding, by the true Hindu tradition, but by its corruption. As the advocate pointed out, a widow was required by the scriptures to live "a purely ascetic life," but this was impossible since as a woman she was "subject to passions and void of virtuous knowledge." Not only would her existence be miserable for her, but inevitably she would yield to base sensual passions and bring disgrace on her community. Therefore, the logic of the situation demanded that girls be taught from their infancy that their becoming a sati would ensure them of "heavenly enjoyments in company with their husbands as well as the beatitude of their relations, both by birth and marriage, and their reputation in this world."[23] The logic is irrefutable, but Roy denied the premise on which it is based—that is, society's understanding of the nature of women. After providing a mordant listing of the ways in which society had assured women an inferior position by denying them opportunities, Roy admitted that women have one important fault, "which is, by considering others equally devoid of duplicity as themselves . . . they suffer much misery, even so far that some of them are misled to suffer themselves to be burnt to death."[24]

To return to Nandy's question about the symbolic meaning of sati in contemporary times, I think the answer is indeed given in Rammohun's analysis, although not in the reading that Nandy gives it. He did not see it, as Nandy suggests, as a symbol of colonial oppression, but as a symbol of the society's treatment of widows, founded on its understanding of the nature of women. And if I read correctly what the "Westernized elite" had to say in the media, this is why they reacted with what Nandy calls "feigned panic and hyperbole" to the Deorala sati. The sati was a symbol for them in the ordinary dictionary meaning of the term: something that stands for something else, a material object that represents a quality or an abstraction. But a somewhat more specialized meaning of symbol is used in theological discussions, where a symbol is a formal summary of a belief, a creed, a confession of faith, a statement of what a society believes at the deepest level. It is possible that the "Westernized elite" saw the Deorala sati as a symbol in this sense—a symbol of the rejection of the modern world.

Alasdair MacIntyre, the philosopher, in discussing the place of a culture's tradition in the life of the present, says that traditions from the past have survived "so as to become not only possible, but actual forms of practical life within the domain of modernity."[25] I suspect that what Nandy and his critics are arguing about is the domain of modernity, and many of the critics are quite certain that neither sati itself nor the values it represents can find a place in modern India. Modernity is of course a slippery term, but minimally it means the answer Immanuel Kant gave in 1784 when he asked his famous question, "What is enlightenment?" It meant, he said, our "emergence from self-imposed nonage," from being bound by the authority of the past, especially from beliefs and traditions that claim religious sanction. This vision of society, which has been called "the hidden agenda of modernity," has come in for much criticism in the West, as well as in India.[26] Nandy's critics, especially some feminist ones, sense that his arguments, although stated with sophisticated elegance, constitute a retreat from Enlightenment, which, in India as elsewhere, is threatened by the dark irrationality of religious discourse. The glorification of the Deorala sati was a startling challenge to those whom Nandy describes as "decultured" and "Westernized elites"; Nandy's arguments are a reminder to them that the domain of modernity is not secure against those who want a return to the ancient verities and traditional values of Indian culture.

Notes

1. Charles Dickens, *The Pickwick Papers*, chapter 20.

2. Ashis Nandy, "Sati: A Nineteenth Century Tale of Women, Violence and Protest," in V. C. Joshi, ed., *Rammohun Roy and the Process of Modernization in India* (New Delhi: Vikas, 1975) pp. 168–193; *At the Edge of Psychology: Essays in Politics and Culture* (New Delhi: Oxford University Press, 1980); and "The Sociology of Sati," in the *Indian Express*, October 5, 1987. In my remarks here, I use the term *sati* interchangeably for both the actor and the act; Nandy seems to do the same in his own writing.

3. From the present essay by Nandy, as are other quotations without footnotes.

4. "Sati: A symposium on widow immolation in its social context," in *Seminar* 342 (February 1988).

5. Quoted in Kumkum Sangari, "Perpetuating the Myth," *Seminar* 342 (1988), p. 27.

6. Nandy, *At the Edge*, p. 7.

7. Sangari, "Perpetuating the Myth," p. 27.

8. *A'īn-i-Akbarī*, quoted in V. N. Datta, *Sati: A Historical, Social and Philosophical Enquiry into the Hindu Rite of Widow Burning* (New Delhi: Manohar, 1988), p. 11.

9. Nandy, *At the Edge*, pp. 2–31.

10. Nandy, *At the Edge*, p. 4.

11. Nandy, *At the Edge*, p. 5.

12. Nandy, *At the Edge*, p. 26, footnote 6.

13. Quoted in Stephen Hay, ed., *Sources of Indian Tradition*, vol. 2 (New York: Columbia University Press, 1988), p. 19.

14. Hay, ed., *Sources*, vol. 2, p. 20.

15. *Parliamentary Papers*, 1830, vol. 28(2), paper 550, p. 4, Regulation XVII, 1829.

16. Most writers on the subject, whatever their points of view, use as their basic sources the voluminous materials sent from India or given as testimony at hearings before committees of Parliament. My own analysis of these materials is in "Some Aspects of the Indian Administration of Lord William Bentinck, 1828–1835," unpublished M.A. essay, Columbia University, 1955.

17. Lord William Bentinck, "Minute on Sati," in *Speeches and Documents on Indian Policy, 1750–1921* (London: Oxford University Press, 1922), vol. 1, p. 214.

18. Ainslie Embree, *Charles Grant and British Rule in India* (New York: Columbia University Press, 1962), pp. 237–49.

19. Quoted in Hay, *Sources*, vol. 2, p. 23.

20. *Parliamentary Papers*, 1821, vol. 18, paper 749, pp. 98, 175, 211, and 242.

21. Romila Thaper, "In History," in *Seminar* 342 (February, 1988), pp. 17–18.

22. Nandy, *At the Edge*, p. 8.

23. Nandy, *At the Edge*, p. 9.

24. Rammohun Roy, "Second Conference Between an Advocate for and an

Opponent of the Practice of Burning Widows Alive," in Kalidas Nag and Debyajyoti Burman, eds., *The English Works of Rammohun Roy* (Calcutta: Sadharan Brahmosamaj, 1945–48), Part 3. The portions quoted here appear on pp. 53–54 of the reprint of the "Second Conference" offered in Mulk Raj Anand, ed., *Sati: A Writeup of Raja Ram Mohun Roy About Burning of Widows Alive* (Delhi: B. R. Publishing Corp., 1989).

25. Roy, "Second Conference," pp. 124–27.

26. Alasdair MacIntyre, *Whose Justice, Whose Rationality?* (South Bend, Ind.: University of Notre Dame Press, 1988), p. 391.

27. Stephen Toulmin, *Cosmopolis: The Hidden Agenda of Modernity* (New York: Free Press, 1990).

Comment:
The Continuing Invention of the Sati Tradition

VEENA TALWAR OLDENBURG

The art of repackaging women's murders as suicides has reached a new high in the several recent satis in Rajasthan. A wide spectrum of responses, from religiously fervent approval to strong condemnation, has greeted the most recent of these, the death of Roop Kanwar on September 4, 1987, in Deorala. Murder is perceived as miracle by the throngs of witnesses, and misogyny as woman-worship. Outraged feminists join other protesters and strongly deplore the sensibility that undergirds the event. The opposing positions taken by feminist scholars (discussed in a review of their work in this volume) and by Ashis Nandy constitute a new phase in the age-old dispute over the rite of sati. Their quarrel furthers the debate over sati, which promises to remain the most controversial social issue in Indian historiography. The clash of these two perspectives has stimulated some of the comments that follow.

Nandy's research on sati, as his first foray into the field signifies, was limited to explorations of the sati "epidemic," as he called it, in colonial Bengal. He focused especially on the role of Rammohun Roy in urging that the practice be banned, as it ultimately was in a regulation of the East India Company promulgated in 1829.[1] The centerpiece of Nandy's argument must be kept in mind while one reads his response to the Roop Kanwar episode. In this essay on the Bengal satis, Nandy propounds what he believes to be the "folk theory" of sati, which he says emerged in the new psychological environment brought about by colonialism. This theory maintains "that the husband's death was due to the wife's poor ritual performance and was her self-created fate. . . . [T]he wife brought about the death of the man under her protection, by her weak ritual potency and by deliberately not using or failing to maintain her latent womanly ability to manipulate natural events and fate."[2] He goes on to say that the tenacious piety of the mythological figure of Savitri, the wife who won back her deceased husband from the god of death, is an important part of the cultural identity of women in India, an identity that widowhood patently belies. "All widows consequently seemed . . . instances of homicidal wishes magically coming true." This "demonology" was associated with the rationalizations of the rite:

> The first was expressed in the fear that, without the authoritarian control of the husband, the widow would stray from the path of virtue; the second in the imputation that women were virtuous only because of external rewards and punishments and not because they had internalized social norms. The contemporary pro-sati literature repeatedly mentions the frailty of women, their "subjection to passion," lack of understanding and quarrelsomeness, and their "want of virtuous knowledge." All three allegedly made them untrustworthy and fickle.
>
> Sati was therefore an enforced penance, a death penalty through which the widow expiated her responsibility for her husband's death. Simultaneously, it reduced the sense of guilt in those confronted with their rage against all women. Punishment by authority became, in an infantile morality, a proof of culpability. It perpetuated the fantasy of feminine aggression towards the husband, bound anxiety by giving substance to the vague fears of women, and contained the fear of death in a region where death struck suddenly and frequently. . . . On the other hand, to the extent women shared these fantasies about their ritual role and responsibility for the death of their husbands, sati was also associated with the introjection of the terrorizing maternal aspects of femininity, guilt arising from this self image, and the tendency to use the defence of turning against one's own self in atonement.[3]

This is clearly the best psychological, albeit Freudian, explanation of sati that I have encountered and it incorporates an undeniably powerful critique of sati. It constitutes no apologia for sati as high tradition; instead, it presents sati as a rigorously historicized folk tradition— and clearly not one that would see the rite as the wish of the sati, the good woman. On the contrary, it is the punishment for the evident failure of woman as wife. Nandy also spells out, in no uncertain terms, the misogynist nature of the custom and the punitive intent toward the woman who has outlived her husband. Here he is at his original, provocative best, and no feminist would disagree with a single word. In fact his argument, once shorn of the components peculiar to nineteenth-century Bengal, fits the Roop Kanwar death brilliantly; but entirely inexplicably, he seems to cast it aside in responding to the events of 1987. This is my first and foremost quarrel with a scholar whose mind and work I intensely admire.

Nandy, in this scholarly mood, would agree that sati is not a frozen tradition; it can be embellished, reinterpreted, and virtually reinvented to suit the purpose for which it is being staged. The making of Roop Kanwar into a goddess, in the manner of the many satis in Rajasthan since 1947, with recognizably adapted Shaivite symbology (a trident covered with a red veil) and calendar-art iconography, signify not the performance of an ancient rite but a grim pathology that reifies women's bodies, rather than deifying women. Meanings of key concepts are equally pliant. *Sat*, which once meant "essence" and therefore "truth," is now spoken of as physically ascertainable high body temperature, which in turn becomes the proof of the magical power of the sati. She can perform miracles. She wills her wedding clothes (which she must don for the immolation) to rise to the top of the trunk in which they are stored, and the pyre becomes a self-igniting pile as she calmly reposes on it. The witnessing throng is a major actor in the completion of the rite, transforming it into a faith-affirming spectacle.[4] Small desert townships, economically ravaged by several years of drought, sprout gaudy shrines and become booming pilgrim sites; impoverished petty Rajput families win god, gold, and glory by murdering their teen-aged widowed daughters-in-law; local politicians win another election. In many profound ways, I would argue, Nandy and many of the feminists are saying the same thing, for they refer to economic pressures in colonial Bengal and in present-day Rajasthan as being the backdrop for the immolation of widows.

At the conference on "New Light on Sati" at Columbia University, there was also much new heat. I was happy to respond as designated commentator on Ashis Nandy's oral presentation. Although the revised written version of Nandy's views published here eliminates some of my minor objections, the main objections I had as a feminist historian remain now as then. While his argument is organized around four different questions, his answers are grounded in the central assumption that sati, as a practice of widows to immolate themselves on their husband's funeral pyres, was underpinned by a set of religious values and occupies a special place in a timeless Hindu tradition and culture. Nandy's piece not only addresses but actually represents the binary split between secularist moderns and religious traditionalists in the large circle of academics and writers who have articulated their views on sati: he becomes, in an oblique way, one of the traditionalists. Instead of forging ahead with the kind of analysis that he offered us about historical satis, he remains happily mired in the tradition-versus-modernity debate and chooses to make the major focus of his paper the protest against the Deorala event and the role of the state as a social legislator.

Nandy does not condone the event in Deorala; he concedes that it was probably murder. The burden of his argument lies elsewhere. He sees in the public attack against the concept of sati an attack "in the same breath, [against] Indian traditions, village superstitions, even the *Mahabharata* and the *Ramayana*." Confessedly persuaded by Ananda Coomaraswamy's essay on the status of Indian women,[5] Nandy makes a disappointingly contradictory case this time around. In the first part of his essay, he dismisses educated middle-class urbanites who protested against the Roop Kanwar murder as moderns and feminists who are ill-educated, decultured hysterics reacting in panicked self-interest to an event that surpasses their understanding. He also sees these moderns and feminists as reiterating the colonial discourse on sati "both as a political strategy and as a psychological defense," with added froth at the mouth, to retain the mantle of power they inherited from their colonial masters. He then implies that his respondents at the sati conference at Columbia (the room was dotted with Indian academics and students who disagreed with him vehemently) were merely defensive in their anti-sati opinions because "there are the professional colleagues and friends to be considered, and the fear of being shamed in the metropolitan centers of dominant global culture." He distances himself from such people—for an urban, middle-class, postcolonial, Western-educated male from a Christian family, this is quite a trick—by implicitly counting himself among "a small minority of thinking Indians."

Nandy might never have indulged in name-calling in the first place if he had not studiously ignored work by historians (surely, Romila Thapar is a "thinking Indian"?)[6] that would have saved him from concluding that sati was an uncontested and timeless element in an equally timeless Indian culture. Instead, he refers to his earlier essay on sati and points to colonial rule as the context in which the custom became a pathology. I agree that the nineteenth-century epidemic of sati in Bengal was pathological, but I feel that Nandy confuses the issue by blaming the *kaliyuga* for making sati inauthentic through coercion and profit-making—features that have marked colonial and recent satis. As a historian, I find no evidence that there ever was an institution of "authentic" sati. (It would have helped if Nandy had also said that colonialism is the chief symptom of the reality of *kaliyuga*, but that conclusion would let the colonialists off the hook and would bring the whole question of human agency under a different kind of scrutiny.)

In what follows, I hope to point out the contradictions in Nandy's case and to provide some speculative answers that might help to disentangle the roles of tradition, modernity, and colonialism, thus enabling us to grasp more firmly the conceptual nettle of sati. Let us begin, in chronological fashion, with traditional Hindu mythology. Nandy claims that, if you show respect to the concept of sati at a mythological level, you gain the right (*adhikara*) to criticize sati in its corrupted colonial and contemporary versions. Where then does he situate the sanctioning myth? The authoritative myth that would give this pyschosocial custom religious sanction is conspicuous by its absence—as early Hindu critics of the practice, colonial officials, and present-day historians have repeatedly established. Coomaraswamy offers us Parvati, the spouse of Shiva, as the prototype, and Nandy happily goes along; but this is sloppy mythology. Actually they both have in mind the eponymous Sati, also the spouse of Shiva, who flung herself into a fire (not a pyre) to protest the insults her own father had heaped on her husband, Shiva. In one version of the myth she is promptly *rescued* from the flames by Shiva, and in another she is not; but she is patently never a widow, nor does she burn. Moreover, her act did not signify piety toward a husband but willful protest against a father. So the Sati myth really cannot qualify as the inspirational myth for sati. And what may we do with myths that serve as powerful counterexamples and shake our construction of Hinduism as a unified set of values? What, for instance, may we do with great goddess Kali, another incarnation of Shiva's spouse, who slays him and dances on his corpse in glee?

The Rukmini–Krishna story is not a very clear-cut precedent either. Rukmini is in love with Krishna but is refused permission to marry him by her brother, whose friend Krishna has slain. Instead, she is betrothed against her will to another neighboring prince; but on her wedding day she is abducted by Krishna and carried off to Dwaraka, where they wed. Rukmini, the chief queen among Krishna's wives, leads several co-wives (the number is variously given as five or seven) to a fiery end after Krishna dies from an arrow-shot wound in his heel. They immolate themselves not on his pyre but in a separate fire prepared for this purpose.

Even if we discount their grief as widows and their vulnerability to possible revenge at the hands of a thwarted brother and rebuffed suitor as motives for their collective action, the deaths of Rukmini and her co-wives scarcely serve as a convincing mythical precedent for sati. Krishna's several hundred liaisons make a mockery of the institution of marriage, particularly since he is best known and loved for his adulterous love affair with Radha, a married woman, whom he never weds. Radha, the adulteress, is popularly venerated, while Rukmini, the good queen, is scarcely remembered. Although it is useless as a template for sati, this myth might yield a clue to the Rajput rite of *jauhar*, and that, in turn, might help shed rather a different light on sati than the one Nandy directs at it.

Etymologically, *jauhar* is a compound of the words *jiva* (life) and *har* (to destroy, take away). It is defined in the authoritative Platts' *Dictionary of Urdū, Classical Hindī, and English* as

Taking one's own life, committing suicide;—fighting desperately to the death;—*jūhar* (or *jauhar*) *karnā*, To kill oneself together with wife and children. (When the *Rājpūts* are attacked by an overwhelming force, they sometimes slaughter or burn their wives and children, and then sell their lives dearly on the field of battle.)[7]

The origin of the term is interesting because today *jauhar* is understood to mean the same as the Persian word *gauhar* ("gem, worth, virtue"), arabicized to be written as *jauhar*. No one has spotted the anomaly of ignoring a rather straightforward Indic etymology in favor of a Persian one. Moreover, it is anachronistic to use a Persian (and therefore Muslim) name for what is unquestionably an ancient custom of Hindu (this time to use a another Persian word where no indigenous one existed) warrior-kings of the northwest. The conflation, it appears, occurred not because there is any similarity in meanings, but because the two words *jivhar* and *jauhar* are written in precisely the same way in the Persian script, the letter *vow* serving as both *v* and *u*.

The act of transliterating *jivhar* into the Arabic script clearly led to confusing the sound for the substance. Thus, the meanings of the Persian *jauhar*—a gem, jewel, pearl; essence, merit, virtue, worth—are most ironically (and mistakenly) imputed to the rite of Rajput suicide. One possessed of *jauhar* becomes a person of bright, shining qualities and the act comes to savor of valor rather than of desperation. It is therefore a mistake to think of the act of suicide, chosen by a warrior-king's co-wives to save themselves from being taken captive and raped by the conquerors, as a bid for posthumous glory. I would further argue that commemorative stones picturing the warrior and his wife on separate or single stones, as found in various places, are mistakenly understood to signify a proud and heroic death chosen by a prominent woman; to me they are markers of memorable tragedies. The eroded and neglected appearance of most such extant stones suggests that they were not intended for worship or for the glorification of the suicide victim.

My understanding of historical *jauhar* is clearly at variance with the common (mis)perception of *jauhar* as heroic death. *Jauhar* was committed for the sake of the defense of territory (and therefore economic interests) and for the purity of royal lineage, not for the chastity and wifely devotion implied in sati. Like polygyny, *jauhar* was a royal or noble prerogative: queens whose husbands were slain in battle had the prerogative to opt for collective suicide. It happened rarely and in exceptionally dangerous circumstances. I would compare it to the poison pill in the hollow tooth of a modern spy: a last resort. In spirit it was not unlike harakiri in Japan. Chivalric suicide has been seen as obligatory rather than heroic or glorious in many cultures.

Several obvious dissimilarities exist between *jauhar* and sati. *Jauhar* was committed by the queens of defeated Rajput kings on a *chita* or pyre with the husband's corpse nowhere in sight. Sometimes the fate of the husband was unknown to these wives; only their own capture was certain. The aim was to avoid becoming booty for the captor; therefore widow-hood was not an essential condition for *jauhar*. Women's resistance to rape, torture, and other ignominies inspired these very rare self-immola-tions. It was probably a pragmatic solution—cremation, as Hindu canons prescribe—invented by the women in the context of defeat rather than prescribed by men or scriptures. Inspired by the nationalistic self-interest of queens, it probably generated the social ideal of Rajput women's strength and courage, rather than the other way around. Internecine war-fare among the Rajput kingdoms almost certainly supplied the first occa-sions for *jauhar*, well before the Muslim invasions with which the practice is popularly associated. Padmini, the queen of Chitor who has been im-mortalized by the balladeers of Rajasthan, is sometimes thought to be the best-commemorated example of sati; but actually her death was by *jauhar*, and that is quite a different thing.

The geopolitics of the northwest, whence a succession of invaders entered the subcontinent, made of Rajasthan a continual war zone, and its socially most respected community was therefore not the Brahmins but the *kshatriya* or Rajput castes, who controlled and defended the land. This history predates the coming of the Muslims by more than a millen-nium. Commemorative stones unearthed and dated in Rajasthan and Vijayanagara mark the deaths of both sexes. Their dates, which can be reliably determined, match perfectly the times and zones of war, a point to which Vidya Dehejia draws attention in this volume. Rajput martial values were a product of their own historical circumstances, although they were later exploited and molded into a supposed racial identity by colo-nial bureaucrats who had their own purposes for doing so.

It is very likely that the Brahmins of the northwest—and particularly of Rajasthan, Punjab, and Kashmir—emulated the Rajput castes in their visible and status-bestowing practices. I propose that the Brahmins bor-rowed the practice of *jauhar* from the Rajputs and modified the concept over time to suit their own Sanskritic gender ideology of the good rather than the brave woman. This ideology probably became the phenomenon the British saw as "suttee," trasforming *sati*—"the pure wife"—into the common name for the rituals that were intended to elevate the social prac-tice of lower-status Brahmins to that of social groups at the upper end of the scale. The fact that no textual injunction demands sati, while an explicit proscription forbids Brahmin widows from practicing this custom, shows that such emulation was looked at askance by many Brahmins. Nevertheless, sati established itself, and the rite of a widow's self-immolation on her husband's funeral pyre spread to other nonwarrior castes—probably for reasons of prestige or for its practical use in enhancing a family's profit. Then, as now, Rajasthani Bania or merchant castes supplied the capital for temples that valorize sati and even produced a handful of satis of their own. M. N. Srinivas, with an understandable Brahmin bias, coined the word *sanskritization* to describe a plethora of such instances of status-enhancing bids in Indian social history.

My theory of the origin of sati may seem to be undercut by the fact that Megasthenes, the Greek chronicler, first documented a historical instance of widow-burning in the fourth century B.C. This is long before any account of the Rajputs appears. Yet this Greek report supports my theory, since the Greeks were a conquering army who captured many indigenous women and established the Greco-Indic colony in Gandhara. They might even have served as the catalysts for this variant of the custom. In any case, the notions of *jauhar* and sati have clearly reinforced each other over time, and this continues to be so even though *jauhar* is no longer practiced. In my view the Roop Kanwar episode can be best described as a hybrid of the ideologies of *jauhar* on the one hand and of sati (as understood in colonial Bengal) on the other.

To summarize, then, the practice of sati was originally grounded in a nonreligious, ruling-class, patriarchal ideology and later gilded with notions of valor and honor. *Jauhar* was reserved for queens in the context of war and defeat, and was not meant for plebeian widows. The prohibition of sati for Brahmin widows in the twelfth century was probably related to the reassertion of the social and political dominance of the Rajputs against Muslim invaders.

Nandy ignores this complex and substantial history in insisting that a definable long-lived religious ideology underpins sati as the custom of widow self-immolation. He goes further in his ahistoricism by conflating the notion of a cosmic principle that exists in nature with the female gender as constructed within Hindu society. According to him, woman traditionally was seen as the more powerful gender: "As a carrier of the ultimate principle of nature and the cosmic feminine principle, a woman was conceived to be the natural protector of her man." Yet—and Nandy sees no problem here—the chaste and devoted wife who prays and fasts for the longevity of her husband is simultaneously perceived as ritually ineffectual, inauspicious, and a social and cultural failure. She is rendered totally powerless yet held morally responsible for the event if her husband happens to predecease her. This outcome is indeed probable, since Hindu women are usually several years younger than their husbands and statistically live longer. Her *vrats* and *pujas*—fasts and prayers—come to naught, and it would be understandable, given the cultural constraints, if she felt a natural impulse to immolate herself on the pyre of her dead husband.[8]

Another contradiction lies hidden in Nandy's argument, as well. If we accept his assertions that Hindu society was religiously organized and that women's religious power was therefore not meaningless, then logically we must also construe the self-sacrifice of the sati as motivated by a self-interested desire for spiritual gain. This is no more high-minded than the motives of the organizers of modern satis who look for material gain in our materialistic times. For such a widow would escape social reproach, humiliation, and an austere life, and would convert her failure into a cultural and spiritual triumph. She would win the spiritual sweepstakes, attaining *moksha* for two—freedom from the chain of rebirth, the highest liberation in the Hindu schema. She would enjoy celestial bliss for many thousands of years with her man. In a more spiritual age, such inducements were probably as powerful as the material gains from the events at Jhardli and Deorala.

As we see in the conception of *sat* as magically burning body heat, a notion that has been insinuated into the rite of sati in relatively recent times, the tradition itself is fabricated over time out of myths that are only suggestively or obliquely related to the practice of sati and do not actually sanction it. The quote that Coomaraswamy offers, in his aforementioned article, provides an example of what I mean. He cites a dialogue between Shiva and Parvati, in the *Mahabharata*, in which Shiva asks the wise, beautiful, insightful Parvati to expound to him "the duties of a woman in full." Let me, in turn, cite Parvati's alleged answer as I find it in Coomaraswamy:

> The duties of woman are created in the rites of wedding, when in the presence of the nuptial fire she becomes the associate of her Lord, for the performance of all righteous deeds. She should be beautiful and gentle, considering her husband as her god and serving him as such in fortune and misfortune, health and sickness, *obedient even if commanded to unrighteous deeds or acts that may lead to her own destruction.* She should rise early, serving the gods, always keeping her house clean, tending to the domestic sacred fire, eating only after the needs of gods and guests and servants have been satisfied, devoted to her father and mother and the father and mother of her husband. Devotion to her Lord is woman's honour, it is her eternal heaven. . . .[9]

Nandy, who recommends and builds on the article that enshrines this passage, does not question the authenticity of the woman's voice in this male-constructed text. Yet a feminist reading would challenge it as a fabrication that betrays the wishful thinking of a male authorial voice. Let me propose alternate ways of reading this text:

1. Shiva is sitting with Parvati on his knee, not engrossed in a dialogue but practicing the most skillful ventriloquism; Parvati has agreed to play the dummy.
2. Parvati, knowing what an irate and eccentric husband she has, gives him the answer she knows he would love to hear.
3. Parvati is performing as a mouthpiece, reciting the internalized expectations of what an "essential" woman was expected to be by the norms of gods and men.
4. This is an instance of Parvati being ironic or playful since their relationship does not warrant such self-effacement on her part.
5. The author is employing dramatic irony whereby the female readers know what is really being said, but Shiva and male readers miss the point.

Only the literal reading of this as "the truth" leaves one stumped. What would Nandy do with equally compelling values inherent in counterexamples from the Shaivite lore? What can one make of the myth of Kali's dance on the still-warm corpse of Shiva?

The literal notion of the good wife is reinforced by the denouement of that popular epic, the *Ramayana* of Valmiki, which has given us an ideal conjugal pair and individual ideal types of male and female in the figures of Rama and Sita. Sita's well-known trial by fire (*agnipariksha*), an ordeal by which she proves that she has had no improper contact with her demonic captor Ravana, is a victory for Sita's truth in which the witnessing masses believe. Predictably she emerges cool and radiant from the fire; the marriage can go on a bit longer. Somewhat later the ideal man, Rama, plagued by a fresh round of gossip about Sita's sojourn at Ravana's palace, chooses to dispatch her to the forest. Less memorably, and in defiance of her essentialized portrayal as the good wife (in banishment, she follows her husband; in abduction, she resists her charming abductor; and in her final exile, she raises twin sons with sound patriarchal ideas), Sita finally and unequivocally rejects Rama's offer to go back with him to his kingdom. Instead, in perhaps the strongest autonomy-affirming gesture allowed to this good wife, she invokes her mother, Earth, and disappears into a fissure—her natal home?—for good. (Would someone please note this as a useful originary myth for Hindu divorce—one that existed long before the colonizing West supplied other models?).

In rewriting the epic, the sixteenth-century poet Tulsidas dealt with this vivid example of female resistance against patriarchy quite disingenuously. He simply excised it from the plot altogether. Tulsidas substituted for it the familiar fairytale cop-out: Sita is never sent away in the first place, so Rama and his wife live happily ever after. The two endings of Valmiki's and Tulsidas's epics give opposite meanings to the behavior expected of the good woman. The existence of a plethora of oral and written subversive and folk variants of better-known classical texts shows that myths, texts, authoritative laws, and values have always been contested by the groups they sought to render powerless.[10] One must therefore see the self-sacrificing, self-immolating widow as a social and historical construct with mythological resonances, and not a mythological one with social and historical distortions and corruptions.

The contentious debate on sati did not begin with the coming of the British, or even of the Muslims, or of the Mughal emperor Akbar; sati never enjoyed widespread currency or approval as a practice, occurring only at very select moments in time and space. Furthermore, its fiercest critics have come from within the tradition. When Nandy accuses the middle-class Indian response of being anti-tradition and therefore pro-colonial, or when he speaks of another scholar's "anguish that the criticisms of sati since the Deorala event have borrowed so heavily from the colonial discourse," I must beg to differ. In rebuttal to this kneejerk post-colonial-ergo-propter-colonial response I offer three counterarguments.

First, it makes for very sloppy history. Lata Mani, whose rigorous and lucid paper on the production of knowledge about sati by colonial officials is the only serious, detailed, and intelligent discourse analysis on sati to date, concludes that

> [S]everal interlocking assumptions informed this discourse. Chief among these was the hegemonic status accorded by colonial officials to brahmanic scriptures in the organization of social life. The corollary to this was to assume an unquestioning submission of indigenous people to the dictates of scripture and thus to posit an absence of conscious individual will. . . . Whatever their views on the feasibility of abolition, all colonial officials shared to a greater or lesser degree three interdependent ideas: the centrality of religion, the submission of indigenous people to its dictates, and the "religious" basis of sati. Those against abolition argued that prohibition of sati was likely to incite native resistance. . . . Officials in favour of abolition. . . developed arguments reflecting the view of Hindu society generated by these same assumptions. . . . [They argued that] the contemporary practice of sati bore little resemblance to its scriptural model as a voluntary act of devotion carried out for the spiritual benefit of the widow and the deceased.[11]

It is hard to deny, after reading the case Nandy makes for sati as a system (*pratha*) located in a generic set of Hindu values, that it is he, rather than those he excoriates as decultured fools, who shares these colonial assumptions about Hindu society. His essay revives another famous colonial debate over who the "real" Indian was—the tradition-bound villager or the imperfectly modernized, ill-educated urbanite who imitated the white *sahib*? In characterizing the protagonist groups in this way, Nandy seems not only to have appropriated colonial assumptions about sati but to be presiding over the debate among the natives (traditionalists versus reformers) like a colonial officer. In seeing "the faith" of the throngs of pilgrims to the shrine at Deorala as "real" and untainted with political self-interest, and in thereby distinguishing such genuine villagers from members of the political elite who come to bless the enterprise and from moderns who reel in disgust, he unwittingly affirms the worst of colonial assumptions about the mindless religiosity of the Indian masses. Why can we not give these "traditional" villagers credit for their own brand of political strategy? They vote and dislodge regimes; democracy is their weapon. Have they alone remained uncorrupted in the *kaliyuga?* Nandy's lengthy analysis of the event misses a crucial point, since it neglects the element of self-conscious, self-interested, rational cost-calculation on the part of those who constitute a very powerful voting bloc in village Rajasthan. The future of *hindutva*, the ideology of a resurgent Hindu nationalism passionately espoused by the Bharatiya Janata Party, depends on this very brand of religiosity.

Second, although he grants that internal criticism is a proud Hindu tradition, Nandy ignores any critiques of the custom from within the tradition, while at the same time selecting Muslim and colonial critiques to bolster his argument. Actually the present anger against the custom is quite similar to what one can find in precolonial, even pre-Muslim times. Bana, a seventh-century author, was the most "vehement, determined, and rational" opponent of this practice.[12] Of sati he says:

> The custom is a foolish mistake of stupendous magnitude, committed under the reckless impulse of despair and infatuation. It does not help the dead for he goes to heaven or hell according to his deserts. It does not ensure reunion since the wife who has uselessly sacrificed her life goes to the hell reserved for suicides. By living she can still do much good to herself by pious works and to the departed by offering oblations for his happiness in the other world. By dying she only adds to her misery.[13]

I have no difficulty in imagining a student a Delhi's elite St. Stephen's College expressing much the same sentiments, if by some miracle Roop Kanwar had acted voluntarily.

In the tenth century, Medhatithi, while commenting on Manu, condemned *anumarana* (the Sanskrit term for what we now call sati) as *adharma* (anti-religious) and *ashastriya* (nonscriptural). This is what the Indian feminists, too, have said, among other things. Another medieval author, Aparaka, writing in the twelfth century, cites Virata (who unambiguously prohibited the custom) and points out that, if the widow survives and offers him the prescribed oblations, she might actually do the deceased some good; if she ascends the funeral pyre, she incurs the sin of suicide. Another twelfth-century commentator, Devanabhatta, from South

India, maintained that this custom was a very inferior variety of *dharma* and did not recommend it at all.[14]

The *Mahanirvana Tantra* carries respect for the feminine principle from the realm of myth to social reality by enjoining a whole day's fast upon the man who speaks rudely to his wife, and by encouraging the education of girls before marriage. (Present-day feminists would endorse this heartily; Victorian colonialists would have blanched at the thought of fasting or of educating their women!) This *Tantra* forbids even the immolation of female animals. And the *Shakta Tantras* as a group explicitly banned the custom of sati and condemned to hell those who played a role in having a widow burn with her dead husband. This is surely good precedent for the Indian government's having made it a capital offense to aid and abet an alleged sati. Tantrics have long seen in any form of ill-treatment of women their devaluation, and in sati the worst form of ill-treatment; and this attitude persists today. In Jhardli, the ashes on the pyre of Om Kanwar had to be guarded for thirteen days by young armed Rajput volunteers out of fear of tantrics and local lower-caste villagers, who vigorously opposed the act. These spirited protests from within the tradition vindicate those of us today who unequivocally condemn all varieties of violence against women, whether culturally sanctioned or not.

Finally, a third point: By dismissing feminist scholars and activists along with the rest of his unfavorite people, Nandy refuses to hear a new and powerful analysis of the colonial construction of women's issues and women's status in India. Indian feminist scholars have been rigorously demolishing the colonial constructions of women in India as exotic victims of benighted cultures, whether Hindu or Muslim. This they have done by systematically raising the question of women's subjectivity and urging a discrimination between agent and victim in male-dominated discourse about an essentialized womanhood. Of this new and influential literature, let me mention only writings that focus on sati: Lata Mani's various articles and her forthcoming book; Gayatri Chakravorty Spivak's, "Can the Subaltern Speak?: Speculations on Widow-Sacrifice;" and Rajeswari Sunder Rajan's, "The Subject of Sati: Pain and Death in the Contemporary Discourse on Sati."[15] These writings underscore the only too facile dismissal of feminists and their work by Nandy; he is being fair neither to them nor to himself.

One point that Nandy himself makes very clear can be agreed upon by all: What may appear as a revival of an ancient custom is really the symptom of a modern pathology rooted in a stubbornly patriarchal society with burgeoning economic problems. Roop Kanwar, the hapless eighteen-year-old, was not a sati. Hours after her husband died she was murdered and burnt to death by a bunch of cunning and greedy in-laws. If colonial satis founded modern Indian women's consciousness and launched a social reform movement in nineteenth-century India, then Roop Kanwar's "sati" will, I hope, generate the movement that will give our society a genuine respect for women, not only in Hindu mythology but in the here and now.

Notes

1. Ashis Nandy, "Sati: A Nineteenth-Century Tale of Women, Violence and Protest," in his collection of essays entitled *At the Edge of Psychology* (Delhi: Oxford University Press, 1980), pp. 1–31.

2. Nandy, "Sati," p. 9.

3. Nandy, "Sati," pp. 9–10.

4. Kumkum Sangari and Sudesh Vaid, "Institutions, Beliefs, Ideologies: Widow Immolation in Contemporary Rajasthan," *Economic and Political Weekly* 26:17 (April 27, 1991), pp. WS-2–18, passim.

5. Ananda K. Coomaraswamy, "Status of Indian Women," in *The Dance of Shiva* (Bombay: Asia Publishing House, 1948), pp. 115–38.

6. Romila Thapar, "In History," *Seminar* 342 (February 1988), pp. 14–19.

7. John T. Platts, *A Dictionary of Urdū, Classical Hindi, and English* (New Delhi: Munshiram Manoharlal, 1977 [orig. 1884]), p. 399.

8. The impulse to suicide is seen in many who perceive themselves as moral or social failures; in India several male and female suicides are reported after the annual examination results are published. But to cite Kabir, as Coomaraswamy does, as the poet who "so takes for granted the authenticity of the impulse to sati that he constantly uses it as an image of surrender of the ego to God" ("Status of Women," p. 128) is to do precisely what a feminist reader would question. At least in a male-dominated society, female subjectivity is constructed differently by women themselves than by men such as Kabir. Does Nandy, with his psychoanalytical bent, subscribe to the notion that there is a natural masochism of the female?

9. Coomaraswamy, "Status of Women," pp. 115–16; emphasis added.

10. In regard to the *Rāmāyana* alone, see Paula Richman, ed., *Many Rāmāyanas: The Diversity of a Narrative Tradition in South Asia* (Berkeley: University of California Press, 1991).

11. Lata Mani, "Production of an Official Discourse on Sati in Early Nineteenth Century Bengal," in *Economic and Political Weekly* 21:17 (April 26, 1986), pp. 32–35.

12. Arvind Sharma, *Sati: Historical and Phenomenological Essays* (Delhi: Motilal Banarsidass, 1988), p. 15. The finest recapitulation of the historical critiques by Sanskrit scholars of the custom of widow self-immolation is to be found in Romila Thapar, "In History," *Seminar* 342 (1988), pp. 14-19.

13. Sharma, *Sati*, p. 15.

14. Sharma, *Sati*, p. 16.

15. Lata Mani, "Contentious Traditions: The Debate on SATI in Colonial India," *Cultural Critique* (Fall 1987), pp. 19–56, and *Contentious Traditions: The Debate on Sati in Colonial India, 1780–1833* (Berkeley: University of California Press, 1993); Gayatri Spivak, "Can the Subaltern Speak?: Speculations on Widow-Sacrifice," *Wedge* (Winter/Spring 1985), pp. 120–30; Rajeswari Sunder Rajan, "The Subject of Sati: Pain and Death in the Contemporary Discourse on Sati," *Yale Journal of Criticism* 3:2 (1990), pp. 1–23.

Afterword:
The Mysteries and
Communities of Sati

JOHN STRATTON HAWLEY

Over the years, the idea of sati has been unusual in its ability to hold multiple antinomies in close tension, and the flood of events unleashed by the sati of Roop Kanwar shows that it still does so today. Like a piece of quartz or crystal, sati draws its power to refract light from its density and many-sidedness. By the same token, however, the light flashes out in very different directions. As one begins to sense the huge number of angles from which sati may viewed, the thing itself comes to seem almost impenetrable— a substance too densely packed to be visible to the eye of any given beholder; a mystery, whether in the criminal sense or the religious. No wonder sati is so hard to name.

Those who would claim sati as their own—treating it as an issue capable of analysis from a single, consistent perspective—will surely resist this description. Feminists, for example, often take quite the opposite tack, aligning sati with other issues in such a way as to empty it of any illusory depth. Thus to illustrate their article in *Manushi*, Madhu Kishwar and Ruth Vanita created a collage of newspaper clippings that told, when juxtaposed, an obvious story. Their titles: "Female Infanticide," "Matricide," "Unnatural deaths among women in MP [Madhya Pradesh] high," "A shocking story of suffering," "Husband douses wife in acid," "3,208 dowry cases in Delhi in 1985," "Suicide or homicide," " 'Discipline' takes daughter's life."[1]

Yet even in feminist treatments of sati one sometimes finds a reluctance to reduce sati to its lowest common denominator—misogyny—and dismiss it. In part this is because the subject is difficult, and women themselves have differed on how to evaluate it. In part, though, it seems that feminists, like their traditionalist opponents, need sati to be a dense symbol; it points to both the crudeness and the subtlety with which patriarchal mystification can operate. I have sometimes thought that Indian feminist intellectuals feel obliged to comment on sati in much the way that Vedantin philosophers were expected to produce commentaries on certain critically difficult texts such as the *Brahma Sutras*. (The difference, of course, is that this is commentary meant to blame, not praise). By thinking about this common, complex object, feminists speak not only to the world but to each other. While they push back the boundaries of external ignorance, they also establish boundaries that define and clarify their own group.

The obviousness of sati as a topic makes it a useful tool in that enterprise. But so does its difficulty, as one particularly senses in feminist essays addressed to the issue of a sati's lost subjectivity. When Gayatri Spivak asks, in her title, "Can the Subaltern Speak?" the answer is clear, and in treating the sati as the epitome of this mute female subaltern, she implicitly justifies the need for a florid discourse that will compensate for the silencing of the sati herself. At the same time, however, Spivak necessarily highlights an element of mystery in the event of sati.

It will not do to suggest, as some have done, that feminists are foolish to invest such great energy in combatting a practice that only rarely occurs. Sati is important for feminists not just because a single, irreplaceable life is lost each time it occurs, but because it stands as a symbol of so much else. What matters is that in sati the death of a woman is celebrated, not mourned. Fortunately or unfortunately, this was substantially the perspective articulated by colonial critics like Edward Thompson, author of the book *Suttee* (1928). Thompson was the sort of person who would have been the logical opponent of Ananda Coomaraswamy, his contemporary. Writing in a defensive vein, he said

> It may seem unjust and illogical that the Moguls, who freely impaled and flayed alive, or nationals of Europe, whose countries had such ferocious penal codes and had known, scarcely a century before suttee began to shock the English conscience, orgies of witch-burning and religious persecution, should have felt as they did about suttee. But the difference seemed to them this— the victims of their cruelties were tortured by a law which considered them offenders, whereas the victims of suttee were punished for no offence but the physical weakness which had placed them at man's mercy.[2]

This was the moral voice that justified colonial intervention, and proponents of sati resent hearing it again in what feminists and their allies have to say. They resist the idea that sati is anybody's business but their own, which amounts to defining sati as a regional issue or a Hindu issue or both. To them, feminist critics from Delhi or even Jaipur are outsiders contaminated by the spirit of imperialism. Over against such people, and in part because of their opposition, the issue of sati functions as a symbol powerfully able to express a collective selfhood. As Kalyan Singh Kalvi suggested, it binds together "motherland, religion, and woman."[3]

Like his opposite numbers in the feminist camp, Kalvi also cultivates a mental collage of data to put sati in its place. For him, as for them, the issue is not only sati itself but something broader—in his case, not the persecution of women but the persecution of Hindu religion. The items he holds alongside sati are a Jain monk's death by self-willed fasting and a Buddhist monk's death by immolation (presumably in a religious cause, as in Southeast Asia). Such deaths, he points out, are typically extolled, not criticized; no right-thinking government would make an effort to intervene. In like fashion, when Muslims faced a challenge from feminists and secularists in the Shah Bano case, the central government took their side. Such parallels establish for Kalvi that Hindus are being treated unequally: persecuted for being the majority in a country whose laws are designed to coddle minorities. To Bhakti Lal, his comrade-in-arms, it was subliminally obvious that such a system could only have been designed by outsiders—the legatees of colonial power—and Rajiv Gandhi's marriage to an Italian (not to mention his family's alleged Swiss bank accounts, which Bhakti Lal might also have mentioned) proves the point to his satisfaction.

For people like Kalyan Singh Kalvi and Bhakti Lal, a woman who challenges the powers that be by daring to become sati is not just a goddess, as her immediate worshippers regard her, but a heroine. She is someone willing to die for her own values, even if they contradict the law of the land. Given an environment in which such acts are punished, she shares some of her heroism with those who flock to adore, implore, and defend her, but she herself is the center of attention. She loses her life for the noble cause, and in fact she dies not for one cause but for several: a woman's right to serve her husband, the defense of Rajput and Rajasthani identity, and the strengthening and glorification of Hindu *dharma*. Her act of self-sacrifice constitutes community among those who share these concerns. That is why it is worthy of such prolonged attention.

The community thus established is, of course, quite different from the one that forms on the other side of the barricades; but there, too, sacrifice constitutes community. For feminists, the existence of a counter-community—aggressive traditionalists like Kalyan Singh Kalvi—helps greatly in the cause, but the lost life of an innocent victim, a sister, is no small impetus. The way to redeem the death is to make it stand as a symbol of the need to abolish widow immolation forever. As Veena Oldenburg says in the last sentence of the essay just concluded,

> If colonial satis founded modern Indian women's consciousness and launched a social reform movement in nineteenth-century India, then Roop Kanwar's "sati" will, I hope, generate the movement that will give our society a genuine respect for women. . . .

Both communities formed in response to what they construe as the vicarious sacrifice of a sati (in utterly different senses) existed in some sense before the death itself. But for both groups, especially in the presence of the opponent, Roop Kanwar's death was a critical catalyst. This process is scarcely new: many scholars—Sigmund Freud, Marcel Mauss, and René Girard, to name but a few—have tried to understand the generative force of sacrifice. Often such scholars have taken archaic events as their subject, but recent work on religious violence points to ways in which human sacrifice still serves the cause of building transcendent community, even today.

I think especially of observations made by Martin Kramer, of the Dayan Center at Tel Aviv University, about the young Shi'a men and women who elected—and were elected—to sacrifice their lives by serving as human vehicles to deliver bombs into the camp of the enemy in Lebanon.[4] Like Roop Kanwar, they tended to be in some special way pure and distinct. These examplars of sacrifice have typically been celibate teenagers who were orphans or otherwise comparatively unanchored to family life. Roop Kanwar's status is in some ways comparable to theirs. She had scarcely left behind virginity and was not yet a mother, so she retained a similar element of marginality in relation to the family she had newly joined. And her sacrifice served posthumously to shore up and even create a larger family, as with the radical Shi'ite communities of Lebanon. The sati solidified the patriarchal lineage of Mal Singh's family by keeping the wife's nourishing powers in attendance on the husband, rather than allowing the wife's body to become a substance alienated from the cultural meaning given to it, as happens in widowhood. Moreover, Roop's continued ministrations to her dead husband freed him from a fate of wandering about as an unfulfilled ghost, hungrily preying on living members of his clan and disrupting the peaceful succession of generations.[5] But as several feminist scholars have shown, the sati of Roop Kanwar also served to solidify larger social units. It brought together Roop's natal and agnate families; her entire village; and members of the Rajput, Bania, and Brahmin castes far beyond Deorala.

A similar thing happened in the opposing community. Roop Kanwar's sati created a situation in which major feminist concerns could more effectively be brought into alignment with those of other groups in modern India: again, a new family was formed. Once it had the chance to coalesce, this alliance made possible the passage of new legislation on sati. It took a martyr to forge these ties. And for feminists and modernists, Roop was also a martyr in another sense: she had been well educated, in some sense initiated into their own community, but her capture by the other camp killed any chance that her education might bring forth fruit. Her ability to function as a modern women was snuffed out by those who thrust sati upon her.

There is no martyr without a body, and much of the force of sati comes from its corporeality. In sati, an idea is wed to flesh. That wedding is ultimately consummated in the moment of immolation, so one might understand it as a form of cooking, metaphorically speaking. Wife and husband are already made one flesh at the time of marriage—from that point on, the woman is said to be the "left side" (*vamangani*) of their shared body—but as in cooking, bringing the concoction to a boil a second time further strengthens it. It seals the fleshly bond between the two persons who die ritually at that moment. The fact that ritual death coincides with physical death for one partner, the wife, adds further strength to the bond.

To speak in this way may seem irreverant, but I hope it is not irrelevant. Jesus's self-sacrifice was sometimes described in similar terms in the pietist hymnody that Bach raised to a level of high art in his passions and cantatas;[6] and in India the symbolism of cooking is far more widespread. Dwellings are demarcated from one another as "cooked" or "raw"—made of brick or of mud; offerings are appropriate to deities in different situations depending on whether they are cooked or not; and marriage is solemnized through numerous offerings by both partners to the Vedic fire and by the circumambulation of it that they make literally tied together as a conjoint entity. Other life processes are described in these terms, too. A fetus is said to be cooked in its mother's womb until ready to emerge; sexual intercourse is heat mutually released; and ascetics transmute gross bodily elements into refined substances by retaining and generating heat internally.

Few women are thought of as ascetics per se. They tend to be expected, instead, to direct their heat-generating powers to benefit others comprehended within the familial boundary forged before the wedding fire. Maternal gestation does this in relation to infants, and a woman's numerous opportunies to fast are thought capable of concentrating her inner heat and directing it outward to her family in general and to her husband in particular. Sati carries this process to its conclusion, releasing feminine actuality in its most basic, potent from— as inner virtue, truth, or reality (*sat*)—for the benefit of a woman's husband.

And not just for his benefit. By submitting to, cultivating, and releasing the *sat* within her in the act of sati, a woman is thought to be able to achieve a new substance, a corporate flesh that she shares with him beyond the boundaries of this life. Many Hindu legists opposed the practice, particularly for Brahmin women, but those who supported it extolled its benefits in remarkable terms. The *Shankha* and *Angiras Smrtis*, which are frequently cited in later writings, say that the sati and her husband will continue in their marriage "for as long as fourteen Indras rule," which is millions of years.[7] As if to confirm this, numerous accounts of satis report that as the woman approaches her death, she is apt to utter two numbers, one referring to the number of times she has become sati for her husband in past lives, and one referring to the number of times she will do so in future lives. This wondrous knowledge of past and future lives—an attribute of advanced yogic adepts—confirms the sense that sati, with its concentrated heat, is capable of forging lasting bonds between parts that otherwise might diverge: a soul from its body; a male body from a female body; an individual person from a social and/or biological whole, the family.

For those who regard it as such, this passage of conjoined male-and-female entity through multiple lives—which is achieved through the most dramatic act of cooking, a sacrifice of oneself—has the undeniable quality of mystery. Here a stable bond replaces the anomie of *sansara*, the repetitive round of life; or to put the matter as Europeans tended to do, love conquers death. To less well-trained eyes, it might seem that the love involved is the woman's and the death her husband's; but according to this view of what happens, the woman's act of self-sacrifice conquers not only her husband's death but her own. By hewing to her marital bond and protecting it against any threat of dissolution, she assures herself of personal transfiguration; she cooks herself into a substance that is death-resistant.

At the same time, she performs this action on behalf of her husband. If she dies clasping him, say the *Shankha* and *Angiras Smrtis*, she purifies him, "[e]ven if the husband be guilty of the murder of a brahmana [i.e., Brahmin] or of a friend or be guilty of ingratitude. . . ."[8] Her self-sacrificing fire has the power to cauterize sin (not only her husband's but her own, as other texts make clear[9]), just as cooking removes impurities in food. In the play on words so closely associated with this event, the inauspicious corpse (*shava*) becomes auspicious (*shiva*) once again.[10] And one aspect of the mystery is that, in relation to herself, her own body, she is at once the cooking agent and the thing cooked. This, presumably, is what the crowds came to see at the immolation of Roop Kanwar: an imponderable mixture that signified the presence of divinity.[11]

They observe other seemingly impossible concatenations as well. One of the most basic binary oppositions in Hindu thought is the distinction between a householder and an ascetic. The man with ground and home, whose state is symbolized by the hearthfire, is held to be incommensurable with the homeless wanderer, whose status is symbolized by the internal fire generated in yogic practice. The latter state is normally denied to a woman, but in the moment of sati one sees its inner force burst forth nonetheless. It happens at the place one would expect—the cremation ground, which is the locus of an ascetic's initiation (he dies to his own past)—yet at the same time it also occurs in the domestic arena. This is the cremation of a married couple.

Paradoxically, an ascetic act, an act of self-sacrifice in the face of death, is required to reconstitute a domestic body that has been torn asunder.[12] This is the corporate body of husband and wife, which is also the basic building block for the larger corporate entity—the family or lineage, which spans generations. Observers of the sati of Roop Kanwar would have expected to witness the onset of that reaggregative process. And when the funeral obsequies were concluded twelve days later, at the *chunari* ceremony, they would have seen its completion. They celebrated what was ideally an act of healing at many levels—a transfiguration, almost in the alchemical sense.

As Dorothy Figueira's essay vividly shows, Europeans were usually ill-equipped to appreciate the terms in which the paradoxes that swirl around Hindu notions of sati were set out. Nonetheless, in some sense, European culture did grasp the paradoxical quality of sati. A fictionalization—indeed, an operatization—of sati may have been required to do the trick, but one way or another the unidimensional sati projected in British colonial legislation was not allowed to survive as the last word on the subject.

Even in the legislative domain, European attitudes toward sati were less clearly defined than Regulation XVII in the Bengal Code of 1829 would suggest. The East India Company, and subsequently the British colonial administration, were at first hesitant to interfere with what they considered to be religious canons held sacred by Hindus. For a time, this meant that British administrators were encouraged to be present at satis occurring in their jurisdictions, to prevent coercion, but were charged not to interfere if there was no sign that force was involved. Additionally, the British attempted to encode into their own principles of operation any restrictions on the practice of sati that were generally accepted in Hindu law. Often the British were not fully aware of the mammoth problems involved in ascertaining just what "Hindu law" was, but in this instance they had an inkling: the Code of Manu, which they took to be the classic "scripture" in this realm, made no mention of sati. Ultimately consultations with pundits persuaded them that the practice of sati was permitted—at a certain point they even judged that it was encouraged[13]—but with certain qualifications: the woman proposing to become a sati must not have small children or be pregnant. The passages to which these pundits referred came principally from the *Shankha*, *Angiras*, and *Brhaspati Smrtis*, usually (and in the case of *Brhaspati*, entirely) mediated through later commentaries and treatises.[14] The same *smrti* passages also forbade the practice to women who were menstruating—a noteworthy caveat, considering Hindu conceptions about the power of sati to purify —but the British evidently regarded this as an area into which secular legislation should not venture, omitting any mention of the subject in their own judgments.[15]

Hindu law on the subject is genuinely complex—much more so than the British redaction would have suggested, if it had not altered so dramatically—and this may once again reflect the sense of mystery that surrounds the idea of sati. The complexity is not only in content but in form, for sati appears at no fixed point in Hindu religious legislation. A certain amount of the discussion relating to it focuses on the caste or class of women (if any) for whom it is appropriate. In particular, legists were concerned that it might be inappropriate to the characteristic *dharma* of the Brahmin caste, although it was more understandable for a *kshatriya* woman—a Rajput, for example—to wish to become a sati. Similarly, legal theorists often seemed reluctant to classify it among the many forms of ritual suicide. Sati was often omitted in such discussions or relegated to its own chapter, rather than being discussed with the rest. There were, however, exceptions: some legists evidently made an effort to relate sati to the limits they wished to place on the practice of ritual suicide in general.

Various regulations emerged. Sometimes, for example, sati was forbidden if a single fire—a single pyre— was not shared by the husband and wife. This caveat was inserted by certain legal commentators as a way to confine an earlier prohibition to a limited range of instances.[16] Other jurists must have found it a welcome means of reducing the number of female suicides, for the literature is deeply suspicious of suicide as a whole.[17] And finally it may have been a way of acknowledging that the ritual force of sati—the transformative power described above in the language of cooking—would have no scope unless a woman actually immolated herself on her husband's pyre.

An overall attitude toward ritual suicide gradually developed, with two basic principles. First, suicide should not be permitted unless the subject's intention was clear and was strictly guided by a desire to obtain the benefits promised for that act by the textual tradition. The effect of this ruling was to guard against suicides driven by emotion pure and simple—a state of mind unable to take careful, discriminating responsibility for its actions.[18] Second, it should be confined to places of pilgrimage that would cancel and reverse the otherwise deleterious karmic consequences of taking one's life. Both intention and religious circumstance, then, were to be taken into account before any act of suicide could be approved.

It is interesting that these principles were rarely, if ever, generalized to the point where they had a significant effect on systematic Hindu attitudes toward sati—although generalization would not have been difficult. In relation to the first caveat about suicide, regulations governing sati certainly do give an element of attention to serious intent, in that the woman is required to make a formal statement of purpose (*sankalpa*) such as would be required in many ritual settings.[19] This would have been especially important with suicide, because one's state of mind at the time of death is thought to have very serious effects on one's destiny—and in this case not only on one's own, but on one's husband's as well. As for the second caveat—the concern that suicides be undertaken at holy places with sufficient intrinsic power to reverse the potentially harmful effects of that act—this element, too, has a certain resonance in the practice of sati. At least among large numbers of its partisans living in modern-day Rajasthan, sati creates its own sacred place. There is plainly a difference between a place like Deorala and cities such as Benares or Allahabad, but Deorala did undeniably become a focus for pilgrimage. The ashes of Roop Kanwar (enhanced, of course, by ongoing rituals and plans for a commemorative temple) made it so.

Given these apparent conformities between the practice of sati and the general contours of Hindu legislation on ritual suicide, it is striking that sati was never really integrated into that body of Hindu legal opinion. To be sure, there are echoes: the stricture against allowing suicide to women who were menstruating, pregnant, or nurturing small children was general, not confined to sati. Yet sati tended not to be discussed alongside other forms of ritual suicide. Neither was it understood as an extreme form of vow (*vrata*), as one might have expected given the way in which sati is conceived in modern Rajasthan. Sati's place in the legal literature is fluid. Most often, perhaps, it was treated under the heading of impurities caused by the death of a relative (*ashaucha*).[20] Yet it remained a special case, something of its own, as if it was not quite capable of systematic treatment or entirely susceptible to regulation. And in some digests it was simply omitted.

Against this background, many of the fundamental perplexities raised by the sati of Roop Kanwar come to seem more understandable, perhaps even appropriate: Should the government attempt to regulate the practice closely? Should legislation about sati be treated as an aspect of criminal law, as the British ultimately ruled, or should it be considered a part of religious law? In the latter realm, the secular government of India professes to take a much more circumscribed role—at least in relation to minority communities, if not in relation to Hindus themselves.

Similarly, this history of legal ambiguity might seem to suggest that the idea of sati impinges in unpredictable—and perhaps unlegislatable —ways upon the practice of sati. If that is true, the sorts of objections raised by both Veena Oldenburg and Ashis Nandy to the edict of 1987 forbidding "the glorification of sati" take on new force. Yet if one looks at things the other way around, one might use the same data to urge that there is no point in outlawing the practice of sati unless one also finds some way to outlaw the concept and worship of sati at the same time.

At the end, then, as at the beginning, we seem forced up against the density of the notion of sati: the difficulty of placing it firmly, once and for all, in a single, indisputable context. That, if anything, seems to be the only theme adequate to invoke in concluding these essays. As a group of authors, we are thoroughly hybrid— half women, half men; some Indians, some Americans, some both; and with a confusing blur of disciplinary attachments. We have neither the univocal confidence to categorize sati as murderous oppression nor the shared optimism to believe that the world has really moved beyond it. Instead we struggle with an old idea that seems constantly to reshape itself in a still growing and often distressing process of reinvented tradition.

Holy violence and holy sexuality are as much a part of the modern, postcolonial world as they were of any previous era, and the maltreatment of women is far from gone. We hope, as a group, that our various and sometimes conflicting views of that unforgiving piece of quartz, sati, will help illumine a shared past that keeps dogging us into the future.

Notes

1. Madhu Kishwar and Ruth Vanita, "The Burning of Roop Kanwar," *Manushi* 42–43 (1987), p. 15. Cf. Sakuntala Narasimhan, *Sati: Widow Burning in India* (New York: Anchor Books, 1992 [orig. 1990]), pp. 151–52.

2. Edward Thompson, *Suttee: A Historical and Philosophical Inquiry into the Hindu Rite of Widow-Burning* (London: Allen & Unwin, 1928), p. 132.

3. *India Today*, October 31, 1987, p. 20.

4. Martin Kramer, "Sacrifice and Fratricide in Shiite Lebanon," in Mark Juergensmeyer, ed., *Violence and the Sacred in the Modern World* (London: Frank Cass, 1992), pp. 30–47.

5. Cf. Paul B. Courtright, "Sacrifice and Regeneration in the Ritual of *Satī*," paper presented to the Thirteenth Annual Conference on South Asia, University of Wisconsin, Madison (1984), pp. 5–7. The *Hārita Smṛti*, one of the texts most

enthusiastic in its endorsement of sati, states that the wife's action purifies not only her husband's family but that of her father and mother as well (Kane, *History* 2:1, p. 631).

6. In "Christ lag in Todesbanden" (BWV 4), for example, the Paschal Lamb is described as being "in heisser Lieb gebraten."

7. P. V. Kane, *History of Dharmaśāstra* 2d ed., 2:1 (Poona: Bhandarkar Oriental Research Institute, 1974), p. 631; text in note 1477.

8. Ibid.

9. E.g., the *Strīdharmapaddhati*, written in the eighteenth century by Tryambakavajvan. See I. Julia Leslie, "Suttee or *Satī*: Victim or Victor?" *Bulletin of the Center for the Study of World Religions, Harvard University* 14:2 (1987/ 1988), pp. 15–16; also Leslie, *The Perfect Wife*, pp. 295–97.

10. Cf. Catherine Weinberger-Thomas, "Cendres d'immortalité: la crémation des veuves en Inde," *Archives de Sciences Sociales des Religions* 67:1 (1989), p. 37.

11. Weinberger-Thomas also depicts the event of sati as a mystery (*mystère*); but according to her reconstruction, the role of sacrificer is played not by the victim herself but by the dead husband, who is represented by his son in the performance of a typical sati (Weinberger-Thomas, "Cendres d'immortalité," pp. 10, 36).

12. In truth, this is not quite a paradox if seen from the point of view of the woman involved, rather than from that of the man—or at least if seen from the woman's point of view as described by men. The *Strīdharmapaddhati* of Tryambakayajvan, for example, makes explicit the analogy between heat-generating ascetic practices (*tapas*), appropriate for men, and the heat generated by a woman's being devoted to her husband (*pativratā*). (See Leslie, "Suttee or *Satī*," p. 18.) A more recent work, the *Satidāha* of Kumudanath Malik, written in Bengali, goes much farther, describing specific ways in which a sati's action is equivalent to the course of discipline expected to be undertaken by a female ascetic (*tapasvinī*). (See Alaka Hejib and Katherine Young, "Sati, Widowhood and Yoga," in Arvind Sharma, *Sati: Historical and Phenomenological Essays* [Delhi: Motilal Banarsidass, 1988], p. 78.)

13. This was, of course, countermanded in the legislation of 1829, which declared that sati "was nowhere enjoined by the religion of the Hindus as an imperative duty; on the contrary . . . ." (Regulation XVII of 1829 in *Bengal Code*, 2d ed., vol. 1 [Calcutta, 1884], p. 267). But Lata Mani has emphasized that in earlier considerations "permission by inference [was] transformed into scriptural recognition and encouragement of *sati*" (Mani, "Contentious Traditions: The Debate on SATI in Colonial India," *Cultural Critique* [fall, 1987], p. 132).

14. For an instance from the *Parliamentary Papers* of 1821, see Mani, "Contentious Traditions," p. 131; on the passages to which reference is made, see Kane, *History* 2:1, p. 631 and note 1477. On the status of these *smṛtis* in relation to the commentarial literature that explores them, see Robert Lingat, *The Classical law of India*, trans. with additions by J. Duncan M. Derrett (Berkeley: University of California Press, 1973 [originally 1967]), pp. 104–22.

15. On menstruation in this context, see Kane, *History* 2:1, pp. 631, 633.

16. See Kane, *History*, 2:1, p. 627.

17. James G. Lochtefeld, "Suicide in the Hindu Tradition: Varieties, Propriety and Practice," master's essay, University of Washington, 1987, p. 1 *et passim*.

18. E.g., Madhavacharya, as discussed in Lochtefeld, "Suicide," p. 21. I can find no justification for Gayatri Spivak's assertion that "the first broad category of sanctioned suicides" is not this, but the provision that "the knowing subject comprehends the insubstantiality or mere phenomenality . . . of its identity" (*tattvajñāna*), although that sort of knowledge might well be expected to contribute to the careful state of mind the texts do require. See Spivak, "Can the Subaltern Speak?: Speculations on Widow Sacrifice," *Wedge* (Winter/Spring, 1985), p. 123.

19. For the typical form of this utterance in the case of sati, see Kane, *History* 2:1, p. 631 n.1477 and p. 634; also Weinberger-Thomas, "Cendres d'immoralité," p. 18; as a general feature in the practice of suicide, see Lochtefeld, "Suicide," p. 37.

20. Cf. Courtright, "Sacrifice and Regeneration," p. 7. James Lochtefeld points out that Kamalakarabhatta treats suicide in general under this rubric ("Suicide in the Hindu Tradition," p. 65).

SELECT GLOSSARY OF
INDIC TERMS

NOTE: Unless otherwise noted, the terms transliterated in parentheses are given as they appear in modern standard Hindi.

abhayamudra (Skt. *abhayamudrā*): The palm-erect hand gesture signifiying "do not fear."

adharma (*adharma*): Irreligion, unrighteousness.

adhikara (*adhikār*, Skt. *adhikāra*): Authority, right.

adhipati (*adhipati*): Authority, superior, overlord.

agarbatti (*agarbattī*): Incense-stick.

agnipariskha (*agniparīkṣā*): Ordeal by fire.

akshata (Skt. *akṣata*): Red powder.

amar suhagin (*amar suhāgin*): One who is eternally blessed, i.e., eternally married.

Angiras Smrti (Skt. *aṅgīras smṛti*): Name of a traditional Hindu legal document.

anumarana (Skt. *anumaraṇa*): "Following [one's husband] in death," a traditional designation for the practice of sati.

arthi (*arthī*): Funeral pyre.

ashastriya (*aśāstrīya*): Unscriptural.

ashaucha (Skt. *aśauca*): Impurities caused by the death of a relative—a category in Hindu ritual law.

avatar (*avatār*, Skt. *avatāra*): Divine "descent," i.e., incarnation.

Bania (*baniā*): Member of one of the castes (*jātī*) that comprise the Hindu merchant or trading classes.

bhadralok (Bgl. *bhadralok*): "Gentlefolk," the urbanized upper middle class in Bengal.

Bhagavad Gita (*bhagavadgītā*): "Song of the Glorious One," a Sanskrit poem (final redaction ca. 1st c. C.E.) forming part of the

187

Mahābhārata, in which Krishna discusses matters of ultimate significance with Arjuna.

bhajan (*bhajan*, Skt. *bhajana*): Religious song.

bharatiya sanskrti (*bhāratīya sāskṛti*, Skt. *bhāratīya saṁskṛti*): Indian culture.

bhat (*bhāṭ*): Caste group who have the traditional occupation of being minstrels and genealogers.

bhibhut (*vibhūti*): Ashes; as a religious symbol, especially associated with asceticism and the worship of Shiva.

bhumia (*bhūmiā*, *bhūmiyā*): Small landholder.

bhut (*bhūt*): Ghost, dangerous spirit.

brahmahatya (*brahmahatyā*): The murder of a Brahmin.

Brahmin (*brāhmaṇ*, Skt. *brāhmaṇa*): Member of the category (*varṇa*) of Hindus especially associated with learning and ritual expertise.

charan (*cāraṇ*): Caste group who traditionally served as eulogizers at royal or semiroyal courts.

charitra (*caritra*): Character, especially good character; narrative.

chhatri (*chatrī*): A stele, stone, or pavilion to honor the memory of a sati.

chita (*citā*): Funeral pyre.

chudakarana (Skt. *cūḍākaraṇa*): The rite of tonsure.

chunari (*chunri, chundri, chundari*) (*cunarī, cū̃daḍī*): Rite solemnizing the death of a sati, which takes place twelve days after the death itself and is so named because of the long piece of cloth (*cunarī, cū̃daḍī*) that is placed on the ashes of the sati in the course of its celebration.

Daksha (*dakṣa*): Father of Sati, who in her view insulted Shiva by failing to invite him to a great sacrifice he was sponsoring.

darbar (*darbār*, Angl. durbar): Royal court.

darshan (*darśan*, Skt. *darśana*): Sight, seeing, vision, especially of a divinity.

dharma: Literally "that which supports," hence moral or sacred order, religion, duty, propriety.

dharmapita (*dharmapitā*): *Dharma*-father, i.e., godfather.

dharmashastra (*dharmaśāstra*): One of a series of didactic texts regarded as providing authoritative guidance in matters of *dharma*.

Durga Puja (*durgā pūjā*): Annual autumn festival in celebration of the great goddess Durga.

gauna (*gaunā*): Ceremony marking the time a bride begins to live with her husband and his extended family—as distinct from the wedding itself.

ghatana (*ghaṭanā*): See *sati ghaṭanā*.

ghi (*ghī*, Angl. ghee): Clarified butter.

goraksha (*gorakṣa*): Cow protection.

Gujar (*gujar, gujjar*): Herdsman caste; sometimes agriculturalists as well.

Hindu Mahasabha (also, All-India Hindu Mahasabha) (*hindū mahāsabhā*) "Great Hindu Assembly," formed in 1913, originally to bring together several regional Hindu assemblies to resist what were seen as special concessions to Muslims by British colonial authorities.

jati (*jātī*): Endogamous caste group.

jauhar (*jauhar, johar*): Women's collective self-immolation in time of war, as practiced on celebrated occasions by Rajput women facing victorious invading armies.

jhankī (*jhãkī*): Tableau.

jhunjhar (Raj. *jhũjhār*): Literally "struggler," a hero who, decapitated in battle, takes revenge by killing many enemies before his body falls to the ground.

jyoti (*jyoti*): Light, luminescence.

jyoti prakat (*jyoti prakaṭ*): Self-manifesting flame.

kaliyuga (*kaliyug*, Skt. *kaliyuga*): The shortest, most deeply degenerated era of world-time; namely, the one in which we now find ourselves.

kama (*kām*, Skt. *kāma*): Passion, desire, lust.

kshatriya (*kṣatriya*): Member of the echelon (*varṇa*) of Hindu society whose traditional occupations are governance, defense, and war-making.

kul (*kul*, Skt. *kula*): clan, lineage.

kuladevi (*kuladevī, kuldevī*): Goddess of a clan or lineage.

Kumarasambhava (Skt. *kumārasaṁbhava*): Epic poem of the late fourth-century Sanskrit author Kalidasa in which "the birth of the young god," i.e., Shiva, and his courtship of Parvati are celebrated.

kusha (Skt. *kuśa*): A kind of grass often prescribed for use in Vedic and Hindu ceremonies.

linga (Skt. *liṅga*): The "emblem" of Shiva, often specifically his erect phallus.

Mahabharata (Skt. *mahābhārata*): The great Hindu epic of internecine warfare, which attained its more or less standard form ca. 400 B.C.E. to 400 C.E.).

mahajan (*mahājan*): Moneylender.

mahasatiyan (Raj. *mahāsatiyã*): Literally, "the great satis," i.e., a cremation ground.

mahayagya (*mahāyajña*): Great yajña. See *yagya*.

Marwari (*māravāḍī*): Member of a group of moneylenders, traders, bankers, and industrialists who have, in the course of several centuries, emigrated from Marwar and contiguous regions of Rajasthan to urban areas throughout the Indian subcontinent.

ma-sati-kal (Tamil *mā satī kal*): Great sati stone.

mata (*mātā*): Mother.

math (*maṭh*, Skt. *maṭha*): Monastery, seat or residence of a Hindu ascetic order.

maya (*māyā*): Illusion, divine magic power.

mehndi (*mẽhadī, mẽhãdī*): Myrtle-leaf paste used to produce a red dye; henna.

mela (*melā*): Festive gathering, fair.

Mina (*mīnā*): In Rajasthan, a herding caste with martial inclinations.

moksha (*mokṣa*): Release from the cycle of birth and rebirth (*saṁsāra*); liberation, salvation.

mundh (*mũḍ, mũḍh*): Memorial, marker stone.

muradi (*murādī*): Granter of boons.

murti (*mūrti*): Image, statue, especially of a deity.

Nai (*naī*): The barber caste.

Narayani Devi (Nārāyaṇī Devī, a.k.a. Nārāyaṇī Satīmātā, Rānī Satīmātā): Seventeenth-century Rajput sati worshipped in the great sati temple at Jhunjhunu.

nari (*nārī*): Woman.

nari dharma (*nārī dharma*): A woman's duty or religion.

navab (*navāb*, Angl. nawab): Muslim ruler or governor of a state or town.

nirvana (Skt. *nirvāṇa*): Liberation from *sansara* (cf. *mokṣa*).

ok (*ok*): Proscription of certain practices or possessions, as pronounced by a *sativrata* shortly before her death.

pagalpan (*pāgalpan*): Craziness, idiocy.

panchayat (*pãcāyat*): Literally, "council of five," therefore a council that governs a municipality or, in a less official way, an endogamous caste or community.

parampara (*paramparā*): Succession, tradition.

Parvati (*pārvatī*): Wife of Shiva, and a subsequent incarnation of Sati.

pati (*pati*): Husband, lord.

patibhakti (*patibhakti*): Devotion to or worship of one's husband.

pativrata (*pativratā*): Woman who is bound by vows she has taken to protect her husband; a woman devoted to her husband.

pativrata dharma (*pativratā dharma*): The duty or religion of being a *pativrata*.

pativratya (*pativrātya*): Devoted service to one's husband.

pith (*pīṭh*): Religious "seat" (literally, "spine") or educational institution.

prachar (*pracār*): Propaganda.

prasad (*prasād*, Skt. *prasāda*): Literally "grace"; food offered to a deity, who samples it (symbolically, some think) and returns it to the devotee as sanctified food.

pratha (*prathā*): See *sati pratha*.

puja (*pūjā*): The standard form of Hindu worship, in which various goods, honors, and services are offered to a deity present in image form.

purana (*purāṇ*, Skt. *purāṇa*): One of a series of texts providing information about matters that are, as the word literally says, "old" and concern primarily the Hindu gods.

Rajput (*rājapūt*): General name for the warrior- or ruling-caste (*kṣatriya*) groups of Rajasthan.

Ramayana (Skt. *rāmāyaṇa*): Epic of the major Hindu hero-divinity Ram (Skt. Rāma), told in many forms and languages.

rani (*rānī*): Queen.

Rani Sati (*rānī satī*): "Queen Sati" of Jhunjhunu. See Narayani Devi.

Rani Satimata (*rānī satīmātā*): "Queen Sati-Mother" of Jhunjunu. See Narayani Devi.

sahagamana (Skt. *sahagamana*): "Going together with [one's husband]," a traditional designation for the practice of sati.

sahagamani (Skt. *sahagamanī*): A sati, i.e., a woman who does *sahagamana*.

sahukar (*sāhūkār*): Moneylender, private banker.

sankalpa (*sākalpa*, Skt. *samkalpa*): Formal statement of purpose announced just prior to or in the course of a ritual.

sansara (*sāsār*, Skt. *samsāra*): Literally "going through, wandering," hence the world understood as the arena where beings pass through many lives and forms.

sanskara (*sāskār*, Skt. *samskāra*): Life-cycle ritual of passage.

sat (*sat*): In general, truth, reality, essence, and therefore essential inner virtue or purity; in specific, the truth or virtue manifested by a woman who becomes a sati.

Sati (*satī*): Literally "one who possesses *sat*"; by extension, depending on one's point of view, (1) a wife who submits to being burned with her recently deceased husband on his pyre so as to join him in death, (2) a widow burned with her husband, or (3) the practice of wife- or widow-burning.

Sati (*satī*): Daughter of Daksha, wife of Shiva, who dies by retreating into an irreversible yogic coma as a protest against an insult directed by her father to her husband.

sati dham (*satī dhām*): Abode of sati.

sati dharma (*satī dharma*): The religion (or dutiful practice) of sati.

sati ghatana (*satī ghaṭanā*): A particular incidence, occurrence, or event of sati, as distinguished from the general practice of sati (*satī prathā*).

satimata (*satīmātā*): "Sati-mother," a woman who has died as a sati and who is subsequently regarded as protecting her kinfolk and devotees in a maternal way.

sati pratha (*satī prathā*): The practice, custom, or "system" of sati.

sati sthal (*satī sthal*, Skt. *satīsthala*): "Place of sati," i.e., sati shrine.

satitva (*satītva*): "Sati-ness," i.e., purity, chastity.

sati vrat (*satī vrat*, Skt. *satīvrata*): A vow to become a sati.

sativrata (*satīvratā*): Woman who takes a vow to become a sati, and thus to join her husband in the afterlife.

sat ka tej (*sat kā tej*): Strength of *sat*.

saubhagya (*saubhāgya*): "Good fortune," auspiciousness—a term used especially for a woman whose husband is alive (cf. *sumaṅgalī*).

shah (*śāh*): Noble, ruler.

shaktapitha (Skt. *śāktapīṭha*): One of a series of locales—usually said to number 108—that owe their power (*śakti*) to the fact that upon them fell various parts of the body of Sati, who was dismembered in range and grief by Shiva after her suicide.

shakti (*śakti*): "Power," a principle in the composition of the cosmos that is understood to be intrinsically female.

Shankaracharya (*śākarācārya*, Skt. *śaṁkarācārya*): One of five Hindu leaders of the *daśanāmī* order of ascetics, all of whom trace their origin to the eminent eighth-century philosopher-theologian Shankara (or Shankaracarya: Shankara, the teacher).

Shankha Smrti (Skt. *śaṁkha smṛti*): Name of a traditional Hindu legal document.

shava (*śav*, Skt. *śava*): Corpse.

Shekhavati, Shekhawati (*śekhāvatī*): Region of northeastern Rajasthan.

Shiva (*śiv*, Skt. *śiva*): One of the great gods of the Hindu pantheon and the archetypal ascetic.

shmashan (*śmaśān*, *śaṁśān*; Skt. *śmaśāna*): Cremation ground.

shraddh (*śrāddh*, Skt. *śrāddha*): Offerings to deceased ancestors, as ordained by the Veda, including especially the set of rituals that culminates on the twelfth day after a person's death.

shrivatsa (*śrīvatsa*): Tuft of hair on Vishnu's chest.

Sonar (*sunār*, *sonār*): Goldsmith, and by extension a low-level artisan caste.

srap, shrap (Raj. *srāp*, MSH *śrāp*, Skt. *śrāpa*): Curse.

stupa (Skt. *stūpa*): Tumulus most familiar in the Buddhist context, where it enshrines relics or books.

suhag (*suhāg*, *saubhāgya*): Marital good fortune. See *saubhagya*.

sumangali (Skt. *sumaṅgalī*): A fortunate woman, i.e., one whose husband is alive.

sumangali bhava (Skt. *sumaṅgalī bhava*): The greeting "may you be fortunate!"

svargalok (*svargalok*, Skt. *svargaloka*): Heaven, in a sense no more clearly defined than the English translation implies.

tapas (*tapas*): The inner heat that ascetics attempt to concentrate and increase.

thakur (*ṭhākur*): Lord, master, landlord.

trishul (*triṣūl*, Skt. *triṣūla*): Trident (weapon or emblem of Shiva and various goddesses).

udni (*oḍhanī*): In certain regions of North India, the upper part of the traditional woman's garb.

vamangani (Skt. *vāmāṅganī*): "One possessing the left-hand part [of a common body]," i.e., a wife in relation to her husband.

vir (*vīr*, *bīr*, Skt. *vīra*): Hero.

virangana (*vīrāganā*): Heroine.

virata (*vīratā*): Manliness, heroism.

vir ras (*vīr ras*, Skt. *vīrarasa*): The heroic sentiment, heroic passion, heroism.

Vishva Hindu Parishad (*viśva hindū pariṣad*): World Hindu Council, an organization founded in 1964 to coordinate the activities of various Hindu groups and work toward consolidating and strengthening Hindu society and values.

vrat (*vrat*, Skt. *vrata*): Vow, especially a vow undertaken by a woman for the welfare of her husband or family, usually involving some form of fasting.

yagya (*yajña*): Sacrifice, in the Vedic mode; in modern times, a broader class of ceremonial and ritual acts so named to designate its continuity with or equivalency to Vedic sacrifice.

yugadharma (*yugadharma*): Style of morality appropriate to one age or era as distinct from another.

yupa (Skt. *yūpa*): Pillar, pole.

zanana (*zanānā*): Women's quarters; thence, women attached to a royal household and typically kept in seclusion.

BIBLIOGRAPHY

Agarwal, Vijay Lakshmi. "Jhunjhunū Melā." In *Kulpalī*. Delhi: Rani Sati Temple, 1984.

Ahmad, Zakiuddin. "Sati in Eighteenth Century Bengal." *Journal of the Asiatic Society of Pakistan* 13:2 (August 1968), pp. 147–64.

Aitken, Bill. "Abomination (Private) Limited." *Statesman*, March 30, 1988.

Ali, S. "A Young Widow Burns in Her Bridal Clothes." *Far Eastern Economic Review* 138 (October 8, 1987), pp. 54–55.

Altekar, A. S. *The Position of Women in Hindu Civilisation*. 2d rev. ed. Delhi: Motilal Banarsidass, 1959.

Amar Vīrāganā Śrī Rānī Satī Jī. Jhunjhunu: Rani Sati Temple, n.d.

Anand, Mulk Raj, ed. *Sati: A Writeup of Raja Ram Mohan Roy About Burning of Widows Alive*. Delhi: B. R. Publishing, 1989.

Appadurai, Arjun. *Worship and Conflict Under Colonial Rule*. Cambridge: Cambridge University Press, 1981.

Badhwar, Inderjit. "A Pagan Sacrifice." *India Today* 12:19 (October 15, 1987), pp. 58–61.

———. "Militant Defiance." *India Today* 12:20 (October 31, 1987), pp. 18–20.

Banwari. "Nar-nārī Sambandh." *Jansattā*, September 29–October 2, 1987.

Barbosa, Duarte. *A Description of the Coasts of East Africa and Malabar*. Translated by Henry E. J. Stanley. New York: Johnson, 1970.

Bayly, C. A. "From Ritual to Ceremony: Death Ritual in Hindu North India." In *Mirrors of Mortality: Studies in the Social History of Death*. Edited by J. Whaley. New York: St. Martin's Press, 1981.

Beer, Michael. *Sämtliche Werke*. Leipzig: E. von Schenk, 1835.

Bentinck, William. "Minute on Sati." *Speeches and Documents on Indian Policy, 1750–1921*. Volume 1. London: Oxford University Press, 1922.

Bloom, Allan. *The Closing of the American Mind*. New York: Simon & Schuster, 1987.

Bracciolini, Poggio and Ludovico de Varthema. *Travelers in Disguise: Narratives of Eastern Travel*. Translated by J. W. Jones. Cambridge, Mass.: Harvard University Press, 1963.

Chandra, Sudhir. "Sati: The *Dharmic* Fallacy." *New Quest* 68 (March–April 1988), pp. 111–14.

Chaudhury, Sushil. "Medieval Indian Society, State and Social Custom: Sati as a Case Study." *Calcutta Historical Journal* 7:1–2 (July 1983–June 1984), pp. 38–60.

Cole, Henry, and A. C. Burnell. *Hobson-Jobson* (rev. ed. by William Crooke). New Delhi: Munshiram Manoharlal, 1979 (orig. 1903).

Coomaraswamy, Ananda K. *The Dance of Shiva: Fourteen Indian Essays.* Bombay: Asia Publishing House, 1948; New York: Noonday Press, 1957; Delhi: Munshiram Manoharlal, 1982.

Courtright, Paul B. *The Goddess and the Dreadful Practice.* New York: Oxford University Press, forthcoming.

———. "Sacrifice and Regeneration in the Ritual of *Satī.*" Paper presented to the Thirteenth Annual Conference on South Asia, University of Wisconsin, Madison, 1984, pp. 5–7.

Crawford, C. "Ram Mohun Roy on Sati and Sexism," *Indian Journal of Social Work* 41:1 (April 1980), pp. 73–90.

Das, Veena, "Strange Response." *Illustrated Weekly of India*, February 8, 1988.

Datta, V. N. *Sati: A Historical, Social, and Philosophical Enquiry into the Hindu Rite of Widow Burning.* New Delhi: Manohar, 1987.

Daruwala, Maja. "Overkill of Sati Bill." *Statesman*, January 21, 1988.

Deshpande, Anjali. "Bill Banning Sati: A Critique." *Mainstream*, December 26, 1987, pp. 4–6.

Deshpande, G. P. "The Riddle of the Sagar Ramayana." *Economic and Political Weekly* 23:43 (October 22, 1988), pp. 2215–16.

Dharmendra ji Maharaj, "Hinduõ kī Divya Satī Paramparā evam Vartamān Sandarbh." Delhi: Rani Sati Temple, n.d.

Dickens, Charles. *The Pickwick Papers.* Oxford: Clarendon, 1986 (orig. 1836–1837).

Dinnerstein, Dorothy. *The Mermaid and the Minotaur.* San Francisco: Harper & Row, 1976.

di Varthema, Ludovico. *The Travels of Ludovico di Varthema.* Translated by J. W. Jones. New York: Burt Franklin, 1963.

Dorville, André Guillaume Dontant. *Histoire des différens peuples du monde, contenant les cérémonies religieuses, l'origine des religions, leurs sectes, leur superstitions, et les moeurs et usages de chaque nation.* 6 volumes. Paris: n.p., 1770.

Dutt, Romesh C. *Pratap Singh: The Last of the Rajputs: A Tale of Rajput Courage and Chivalry.* Allahabad: Kitabistan, 1943.

Eck, Diana L. "The Sacrifice of Dakṣa and the Śākta Pīṭhas." Paper presented to the American Academy of Religion, Atlanta, November 1986.

Embree, Ainslie T. *Charles Grant and British Rule in India.* New York: Columbia University Press, 1962.

———. "Some Aspects of the Indian Administration of Lord William Bentinck, 1828–1835," unpublished M.A. essay, Columbia University, 1955.

Frye, Northrop. *Anatomy of Criticism*. Princeton: Princeton University Press, 1968 (orig. 1957).

Frykenberg, Robert. "Fundamentalism and Revivalism in South Asia." In *Fundamentalism, Revivalists, and Violence in South Asia*, ed. by James Warner Bjorkman. Riverdale, Md.: Riverdale, 1988, pp. 20–26.

Gandhi, Raj S. "Sati as Altruistic Suicide." In *Contributions to Asian Studies*, vol. 10, ed. by K. Ishwaran. Leiden: E. J. Brill, 1977.

Gaur, Meena. *Sati and Social Reforms in India*. Jaipur: Publication Scheme, 1989.

Goethe, J. W. *Sämtliche Werke*. Stuttgart: Vlg. Buchhandlung, 1983 (orig. 1896).

Gogia, Satish. Letter to the editor. *Times of India*, November 5, 1987.

Gold, Ann Grodzins. *Fruitful Journeys: The Ways of Rajasthani Pilgrims*. Berkeley: University of California Press, 1988.

Gupta, Barun D. "Sati Controversy in Calcutta." *Mainstream*, December 19, 1987, pp. 22–23.

Harlan, Lindsey. "Abandoning Shame: Mira Bai's Bad Behavior." Paper presented to the Association for Asian Studies, Washington, D.C., March 1989.

———. *Religion and Rajput Women: The Ethic of Protection in Contemporary Narratives*. Berkeley: University of California Press, 1992.

Harrigan, Patrick D. "Is Tradition Ridiculed by Western Values?" *Statesman*, March 5, 1988.

———. "Tyranny of the Elect?" *Statesman*, November 5, 1987.

Hart, George L. "Sati Just a Form of Human Sacrifice." *Statesman*, March 29, 1988.

Hay, Stephen, ed. *Sources of Indian Tradition*, vol. 2. New York: Columbia University Press, 1988.

Herder, J. G. *Sämtliche Werke*. Ed. by B. Suphan. 33 volumes. Berlin: Weidmannsche Buchhandlung, 1877–1913.

Hodges, William. *Travels in India*. London: the author, 1793.

Inamdar, S., et al. "A Suicide by Self-Immolation—Psychosocial Perspectives." *International Journal of Social Psychiatry* 29 (1983), pp. 130–33.

Iyer, V. R. Krishna. "Sati: Political Paralysis." *Illustrated Weekly of India*, November 8, 1987, pp. 26–27.

Jacobson, Doranne. "The Chaste Wife: Cultural Norm and Individual Experience." In *American Studies in the Anthropology of India*, ed. by Sylvia Vatuk. New Delhi: Manohar, 1987, pp. 95–138.

Jain, Minu. "Sati or Murder?" *Sunday Observer*, January 18, 1988.

Jain, Sharada, Nirja Misra, and Kavita Srivastava. "Deorala Episode: Women's Protest in Rajasthan." *Economic and Political Weekly* 22:45 (November 7, 1987), pp. 1891–94.

Jatia, Kailash. *Shree Rani Satiji is our ancestor. We worship her as our family goddess*. Delhi: Rani Sati Temple, n.d.

Joshi, Prabhash. "Divarālā kī Satī." *Jansattā*, September 18, 1987.

————. "Hamne jo Kahā Hai." *Jansattā*, September 20, 1987.

Kakar, Sudhir. *The Inner World: A Psycho-analytic Study of Childhood and Society in India*. 2d ed. Delhi: Oxford University Press, 1981.

Kamal, K. L. *Party Politics in an Indian State*. Delhi: S. Chand, n.d.

Kane, P. V. *History of Dharmaśāstra*. 2d ed. Volume 2, part 1. Poona: Bhandarkar Oriental Research Institute, 1974.

Kavita, Shobha, Shobita, Kanchan, and Sharada. "Rural Women Speak." *Seminar* 342 (February 1988), pp. 40–44.

Kennedy, R. Hartley. "The Suttee: The Narrative of an Eye-Witness." *Bentley's Miscellany* 13:75 (March 1843), pp. 241–56.

Kishwar, Madhu, and Ruth Vanita. "The Burning of Roop Kanwar." *Manushi* 42–43 (1987), pp. 15–25.

Kramer, Martin. "Sacrifice and Fratricide in Shiite Lebanon," In *Violence and the Sacred in the Modern World*, ed. by Mark Juergensmeyer. London: Frank Cass, 1992, pp. 30–47.

Kramrisch, Stella. *The Presence of Siva*. Princeton: Princeton University Press, 1981.

Kurth-Voigt, Liselotte E. "Existence after Death in Eighteenth Century Literature." *South Atlantic Review* 52:2 (1987), pp. 3–14.

Lawrence, T. E. *Seven Pillars of Wisdom: A Triumph*. Harmondsworth: Penguin Books, 1976 (orig. 1926).

Leitzmann, A. "Quellen zu Schillers und Goethes Balladen." *Kleine Texte für theologische und philologische Vorlesungen und Übungen*. Ed. by Hans Leitzmann. Volume 73 (1911).

Leslie, I. Julia. *The Perfect Wife*. Delhi: Oxford University Press, 1989.

————. "Suttee or *Satī*: Victim or Victor?" *Bulletin of the Center for the Study of World Religions, Harvard University* 14:2 (1988), pp. 5–23.

Lessing, G. E. *Die Erziehung des Menschengeschlechts*. Berlin: C. F. Voss, 1780.

Lingat, Robert. *The Classical Law of India*. Berkeley: University of California Press, 1973.

Lochtefeld, James. "Suicide in the Hindu Tradition: Varieties, Propriety and Practice." Unpublished M.A. essay, University of Washington, 1987.

MacIntyre, Alasdair. *Whose Justice, Whose Rationality?* South Bend, Ind.: University of Notre Dame Press, 1988.

Mahajan, Krishna, "Legal Perspective: Sati Bill Loopholes." *Hindustan Times*, December 22, 1987.

Mainwaring, Mrs. General. *The Suttee, or the Hindoo Converts*, vol. 1. London: A. K. Newman, 1830.

Major, R. H., ed. *India in the Fifteenth Century*. New York: Burt Franklin, 1857.

Majumdar, Ramesh Chandra. *Glimpses of Bengal in the Nineteenth Century*. Calcutta: Firma K. L. Mukhopadhyay, 1960.

Mangalwadi, Vishal. "Making a Carnival of Murder." *Indian Express*, September 15, 1987.

Mani, Lata. "Contentious Traditions: The Debate on SATI in Colonial India." *Cultural Critique* (Fall 1987), pp. 119–56. Reprinted in *Recasting Women:*

Essays in Colonial History, ed. by K. Sangari and S. Vaid. New Delhi: Kali for Women, 1988, pp. 88–126.

———. *Contentious Traditions: The Debate on Sati in Colonial India, 1780–1833*. Berkeley: University of California Press, forthcoming.

———. "Multiple Mediations: Feminist Scholarship in the Age of Multinational Reception." *Feminist Review* 35 (Summer 1990), pp. 24–41.

———. "Production of an Official Discourse on *Sati* in Early Nineteenth Century Bengal." *Economic and Political Weekly* 21:17 (April 26, 1986), pp. 32–40.

Marriott, McKim, and Ronald B. Inden. "Towards an Ethnosociology of South Asian Caste Systems." *The New Wind: Changing Identities in South Asia*. Ed. by Kenneth David. The Hague: Mouton Publishers, 1977, pp. 227–38.

Mathur, Girish. "Sati and Struggle Against 'Alien Elements'." *Link*, October 25, 1987, pp. 7–9.

Mehta, Pradeep S. Letter to the editor, *Times of India*, December 5, 1988.

Menon, Meena, Geeta Seshu, and Sujata Anandan. *Trial by Fire: A Report on Roop Kanwar's Death*. Bombay: Bombay Union of Journalists, 1987.

Menon, Sunil, "Roop Kanwar's Act Was Not Voluntary." *Times of India*, September 25, 1987.

Mishra, Sudhanshu. "Sati: Fortune Behind the Crime." *Link*, September 27, 1987, pp. 4–7.

Mitten, David. "Aspects of Meaning in Greek Burial Customs." Paper presented at the conference, "Representations of Death." Harvard University, November 4, 1988.

Mittra, K. "Suppression of Suttee in the Province of Cuttack." *Bengal Past and Present* 76 (1957), pp. 125–31.

Mojumdar, Modhumita. "A Visit to Deorala 'Peeth'." *Mainstream*, December 26, 1987, pp. 20–22.

Mukhopadhyay, A. "Sati as a Social Institution in Bengal." *Bengal Past and Present* 76 (1957), pp. 99–115.

Nandy, Ashis. *At the Edge of Psychology: Essays in Politics and Culture*. Delhi: Oxford University Press, 1980.

———. "The Human Factor." *Illustrated Weekly of India*, January 17, 1988.

———. *The Intimate Enemy: Loss and Recovery of Self Under Colonialism*. Delhi: Oxford University Press, 1983.

———. "Sati: A Nineteenth Century Tale of Women, Violence and Protest." In *Rammohun Roy and the Process of Modernization in India*, ed. by V. C. Joshi. New Delhi: Vikas, 1975, pp. 168–93. Reprinted in A. Nandy, *At the Edge of Psychology* (Delhi: Oxford University Press, 1980), pp. 1–31.

———. "The Sociology of Sati," *Indian Express*, October 5, 1987.

Narasimhan, Sakuntala. *Sati: Widow Burning in India*. New York: Anchor Books, 1992 (orig. 1990).

Novalis [Friedrich Freiherr von Hardenberg]. *Schriften*. Ed. by Paul Kluckhohn. 4 volumes. Leipzig: Bibliographisches Institut, 1929.

O'Flaherty, Wendy Doniger. *Hindu Myths*. Harmondsworth: Penguin Books, 1980.

Olearius, Adam. *The Voyages and Travels of the Ambassadors.* Translated by John Davies. London: J Starkey and T. Basset, 1669.

Panchal, Chinu. "1,500 Witness 'Sati' Ritual." *Times of India,* October 6, 1986.

Pandey, Raj Bali. *Hindu Saṁskāras: A Socio-Religious Study of the Hindu Sacraments.* Varanasi: Motilal Banarsidass, 1969.

Parekh, B. C. "Between Holy Text and Moral Void." *New Statesman,* March 24, 1989, pp. 29–33.

Pathak, Rahul. "Confess to Murder, Cops Tell Family." *Indian Express,* January 13, 1988.

Peggs, James. *India's Cries to British Humanity,* 3d ed. London: Simpkin and Marshall, 1832.

Pires, Tomé. *The Suma Oriental.* Liechtenstein: Kraus, 1967.

Qanungo, K. L. *Studies in Rajput History.* Delhi: S. Chand. 1969.

Raya, Binaya Bhushana. *Socioeconomic Impact of Sati in Bengal and the Role of Raja Rammohun Roy.* Calcutta: Naya Prokash, 1987.

Richman, Paula, ed. *Many Rāmāyaṇas: The Diversity of a Narrative Tradition in South Asia.* Berkeley: University of California Press, 1991.

Ridding, C. M. *The Kadambari of Bana.* London: Royal Asiatic Society, 1896.

Rogerius, Abraham. *Le Théâtre de l'idolatrie ou la porte ouverte.* Translated by Thomas La Grue. Amsterdam: J. Schipper, 1670.

———. *Offene Thür zu dem verborgenen Heydentum,* Nürnberg: J. Schipper, 1663.

Roy, Rammohun. "Second Conference Between an Advocate for and an Opponent of the Practice of Burning Widows Alive." In *The English Works of Rammohun Roy,* ed. by Kalidas Nag and Debyajyoti Burman. Calcutta: Sadharan Brahmosamaj, 1945–1948, Part 3.

Rudolph, Susanne, and Lloyd Rudolph. *Essays on Rajputana: Reflections on History, Culture, and Administration.* Delhi: Concept, 1984.

Sahay, S. "Perspective on Sati." *Telegraph,* January 26, 1988.

Sangari, Kumkum. "Perpetuating the Myth." *Seminar* 342 (1988), pp. 24–30.

Sangari, Kumkum, and Sudesh Vaid. "Sati in Modern India: A Report." *Economic and Political Weekly* 16:31 (August 1, 1981), pp. 1284–88.

———. "The Politics of Widow Immolation." *Imprint* (October 1987), pp. 27–31.

Sarkar, Latika, and Radha Kumar. "Flaws in New Sati Bill." *Times of India,* December 15, 1987.

Saxsena, R. K. *Social Reform: Infanticide and Sati.* Delhi: Trimurti, 1975.

Schiller, J. C. F. von. *Sämtliche Werke.* Stuttgart: Cotta, 1822–26.

Schopenhauer, Arthur. *The World as Will and Representation.* Translated by E. F. Payne. 2 volumes. New York: Dover, 1969.

Seed, G. "The Abolition of Suttee in Bengal." *History* (October 1955), pp. 286–99.

Sharma, Arvind. "Suttee: A Study in Western Reactions." *Journal of Indian History* 54:3 (1976). Reprinted in Sharma, *Sati: Historical and Phenomenological Essays* (Delhi: Motilal Banarsidass, 1988), pp. 1–13.

Sharma, Arvind, with Ajit Ray, Alaka Hejib, and Katherine K. Young. *Sati: Historical and Phenomenological Essays.* Delhi: Motilal Banarsidass, 1988.

Sharma, Raman Kant. *Śrī Nārāyaṇī Carit Mānas.* Bombay: Śrī Rānī Satī Jī Maṇḍal, n.d.

Shweder. Richard. *Thinking Through Cultures: Expeditions in Cultural Psychology.* Cambridge: Harvard University Press, 1991.

Singh, Deol. *Land Reforms in Rajasthan: A Report of a Survey.* New Delhi: Government of India, 1964.

Sinha, Saroj, ed. *Women and Violence.* Delhi: Vikas, 1989.

Sircar, D. C. *The Śākta Pīṭhas.* Delhi: Motilal Banarsidass, 1973.

Skinner, Thomas, "The Suttee." In *The Oxford Book of Travel Verse,* ed. by Kevin Crossley-Holland. Oxford: Oxford University Press, 1986, pp. 299–302.

Sleeman, William Henry. *Rambles and Recollections of an Indian Official.* Oxford: Oxford University Press, 1915 (orig. 1844).

Sonnerat, Pierre. *Voyage aux Indes orientales et la Chine.* 2 volumes. Paris: n.p., 1782 [*Reise nach Ostindien und China.* Frankfurt: A. G. Schneider, 1784].

Sontheimer, Günther-Dietz. "The Religion of the Dhangar Nomads." In *The Experience of Hinduism,* ed. by Eleanor Zelliot and Maxine Berntsen. Albany: SUNY Press, 1988, pp. 109–30.

Spivak, Gayatri Chakarvorty. "Can the Subaltern Speak?: Speculations on Widow-Sacrifice." *Wedge* (Winter/Spring 1985), pp. 120–30. Reprinted in *Marxism and the Interpretation of Culture,* ed. by Cary Nelson and Lawrence Grossberg. Urbana: University of Illinois Press, 1988, pp. 271–313.

Śrī Rānī Satī Carit Mānas: Prāmāṇit Jīvan Caritra Evam Stutiã. Jhunjhunu: Rani Sati Temple, n.d.

Srivastava, Sanjeev. "Deorala Revisited." *Illustrated Weekly of India,* May 22, 1988.

Srivastava, "Doctor Elusive about Deorala Incident." *Times of India,* June 4, 1988.

Stein, Dorothy. "Women to Burn: Suttee as a Normative Institution." *Signs: Journal of Women in Culture and Society* 4:2 (1978), pp. 253–73.

Stutchbury, Elizabeth. "Blood, Fire and Meditation: Human Sacrifice and Widow Burning in Nineteenth Century India." In *Women in India and Nepal,* ed. by Michael Allen and S. N. Mukherjee. Canberra: Australian National University Monographs on South Asia, number 8.

Sunder Rajan, Rajeswari. "The Subject of Sati: Pain and Death in the Contemporary Discourse on Sati." *Yale Journal of Criticism* 3:2 (1990), pp. 1–23.

Tagore, Abanindranath. *Rājkāhinī.* Calcutta: Signet Press, 1956.

Tagore, Rabindranath. *Racanābalī.* Calcutta: Viśvabhāratī, 1987.

Taknet, D. K. *Industrial Entrepreneurship of Shekhawati Marwaris.* Jaipur: the author, 1986.

Thakur, Upendra. *The History of Suicide in India: An Introduction.* Delhi: Munshi Ram Manohar Lal, 1963.

Thapar, Romila. "In History." *Seminar* 342 (1988), pp. 14–19.

The Commission of Sati (Prevention) Act, 1987 [Act No. 3 of 1988] with Short Notes. Lucknow: Eastern Book Co., n.d.

Thompson, Edward. *Suttee: A Historical and Philosophical Inquiry into the Hindu Rite of Widow-Burning.* London: Allen & Unwin, 1928.

Timberg, Thomas. *The Marwaris: From Traders to Industrialists*. Delhi: Vikas, 1978.

Toulmin, Stephen. *Cosmopolis: The Hidden Agenda of Modernity*. New York: Free Press, 1990.

Turner, R. L. *A Comparative Dictionary of Indo-Aryan Languages*. London: Oxford University Press, 1966.

Twining, Thomas. "The Hindoo Widow." In *Travellers' India*, ed. by H. K. Kaul. Delhi: Oxford University Press, 1979, pp. 92–96.

Vaid, Sudesh. "Politics of Widow Immolation." *Seminar* 342 (1988), pp. 20–23.

——— and Kumkum Sangari. "Institutions, Beliefs, Ideologies: Widow Immolation in Contemporary Rajasthan," *Economic and Political Weekly* 26:17 (April 27, 1991), pp. WS-2–18.

van den Bosch, Lourens P. "A Burning Question: Sati and Sati Temples as the Focus of Political Interest." *Numen* 37:2 (1990), pp. 174–94.

Vir, [Mahatma] Ram Chander, *Satī Paramparā, Jvalant Jyoti Śikhayā*. Virat Nagar, Rajasthan: Pãc Khand Pīṭh, 1986.

Virmani, Shabnam. "The Spirit of Sati Lives on." *Times of India*, September 12, 1987.

Wacziarg, Francis and Aman Nath. *Rajasthan: The Walls of Shekhawati*. Delhi: Vikas, 1982.

Wagner, R. *Gesammelte Schriften und Dichtung*. Edited by W. Golther. 10 volumes. Berlin: Deutsches Verlagshaus Bong, 1913.

Walker, Benjamin. *Hindu World*. 2 volumes. New York: Praeger, 1968.

Weinberger-Thomas, Catherine. "Cendres d'Immortalité: La Crémation des Veuves en Inde," *Archives de Sciences Sociales des Religions* 67:1 (1989), pp. 9–51.

Woodruff, Philip. *The Men Who Ruled India*, vol. 1. New York: Schocken, 1964 (orig. 1954).

NOTES ON THE CONTRIBUTORS

Karen McCarthy Brown is professor of the Sociology and Anthropology of Religion in the Graduate and Theological Schools at Drew University. Since 1973, she has carried out research on Haitian culture and traditional religion, both in Haiti and in the Haitian immigrant community in Brooklyn. Her written work includes numerous articles on women and on Vodou, as well as the book, *Mama Lola: A Vodou Priestess in Brooklyn* (University of California Press, 1991).

Paul B. Courtright is Professor and Chairman of the Department of Religion at Emory University. He is the author of *Ganesa: Lord of Obstacles, Lord of Beginnings* (Oxford University Press, 1985) and *The Goddess and the Dreadful Practice* (Oxford University Press, forthcoming). He is currently engaged in research on the early period of British colonialism and its relations with the Hindu tradition.

Vidya Dehejia is Associate Professor in the Department of Art History and Archaeology at Columbia University. Her recent publications include *Yogini Cult and Temples: A Tantric Tradition* (National Museum, New Delhi, 1986), *Slaves of the Lord: The Path of Tamil Saints* (Munshiram Manoharlal, 1988), *Art of the Imperial Cholas* (Columbia University Press, 1990), and *Antal and Her Path of Love: Poems of a Woman Saint from South India* (SUNY Press, 1990).

Ainslie T. Embree is Professor of History Emeritus at Columbia University, where he was formerly Director of the Southern Asian Institute, Chairman of the Department of History, and Associate Dean of the School of International and Public Affairs. His recent publications include *Imagining India: Essays on Indian History* (Oxford University Press, 1989) and *Utopias in Conflict: Religion and Nationalism in India* (University of California Press, 1990).

Dorothy M. Figueira is Assistant Professor of Comparative Literature at the University of Illinois at Urbana–Champaign. She is the author of *Translating the Orient* (SUNY Press, 1991) and various articles dealing with the representation of India in French and German letters.

Lindsey Harlan is Professor of Religious Studies at Connecticut College. She is the author of *Religion and Rajput Women: The Ethic of Protection in Contemporary Narratives* (University of California Press: 1992) and has edited with Paul Courtright *From the Margins of Hindu Marriage: New Essays on Gender, Religion, and Culture* (Oxford University Press, 1994). She is currently writing a book on hero veneration.

John Stratton Hawley is Director of the Southern Asian Institute at Columbia University and is Professor and Chair in the Department of Religion at Barnard College. His published works include several books on the devotional literature of Krishna, a co-edited study of Indian goddesses (*The Divine Consort*, Beacon Press, 1986), and an introductory survey of the major poet-saints of North India (*Songs of the Saints of India*, with Mark Juergensmeyer, Oxford University Press, 1988). His edited volume *Fundamentalism and Gender* has just appeared from Oxford University Press.

Robin Jared Lewis is Associate Dean and Director of the International Affairs Program at the School of International and Public Affairs of Columbia University. He served as Executive Editor of *The Encyclopedia of Asian History* (Scribner's, 1989) and is the author of *E. M. Forster's Passages to India* (Columbia University Press, 1977), as well as various articles on modern Indian history, literature, and society.

Ashis Nandy is one of India's foremost social theorists. A psychologist by training, he writes prolifically on matters ranging from the colonial legacy in India to contemporary Hindu religion, modernism, and the culture of science. His books include *At the Edge of Psychology* (1980), *The Intimate Enemy* (1983), *Traditions, Tyranny and Utopias* (1987), and an edited volume, *Science, Hegemony and Violence* (1990), all published by Oxford University Press, and *The Tao of Cricket* (Viking/Penguin, 1989). He is Fellow and Director of the Centre for the Study of Developing Societies and Chairman of the Committee for Cultural Choices and Global Futures.

Veena Talwar Oldenburg, Associate Professor of History at Baruch College of the City University of New York, has interests in British colonial history and women's history. She is author of *The Making of Colonial Lucknow, 1856–1877* (Princeton University Press, 1984) and is currently working on another book, entitled *Dowry Murders?: Reinvestigating a Cultural Whodunit.*

INDEX